The Greek Article

Linguistic Biblical Studies

Series Editor

Stanley E. Porter

Professor of New Testament at McMaster Divinity College
Hamilton, Ontario

VOLUME 9

This series, Linguistic Biblical Studies, is dedicated to the development and promotion of linguistically informed study of the Bible in its original languages. Biblical studies has greatly benefited from modern theoretical and applied linguistics, but stands poised to benefit from further integration of the two fields of study. Most linguistics has studied contemporary languages, and attempts to apply linguistic methods to study of ancient languages requires systematic re-assessment of their approaches. This series is designed to address such challenges, by providing a venue for linguistically based analysis of the languages of the Bible. As a result, monograph-length studies and collections of essays in the major areas of linguistics, such as syntax, semantics, pragmatics, discourse analysis and text linguistics, corpus linguistics, cognitive linguistics, comparative linguistics, and the like, will be encouraged, and any theoretical linguistic approach will be considered, both formal and functional. Primary consideration is given to the Greek of the New and Old Testaments and of other relevant ancient authors, but studies in Hebrew, Coptic, and other related languages will be entertained as appropriate.

The titles published in this series are listed at brill.com/lbs

The Greek Article

A Functional Grammar of ὁ-items in the Greek
New Testament with Special Emphasis on the
Greek Article

By

Ronald D. Peters

BRILL

LEIDEN • BOSTON
2014

Library of Congress Cataloging-in-Publication Data

Peters, Ronald D.
  The Greek article : a functional grammar of o-items in the Greek New Testament with special emphasis on the Greek article / by Ronald D. Peters.
    pages cm. — (Linguistic Biblical studies, ISSN 1877-7554 ; volume 9)
  Includes bibliographical references and index.
  ISBN 978-90-04-25722-1 (hardback : acid-free paper) — ISBN 978-90-04-26231-7 (e-book) 1. Greek language, Biblical—Article. 2. Greek language, Biblical—Grammar. 3. Bible. New Testament. Greek. I. Title.
  PA844.P48 2014
  487'.4—dc23

                                                                    2013040381

This publication has been typeset in the multilingual "Brill" typeface. With over 5,100 characters covering Latin, IPA, Greek, and Cyrillic, this typeface is especially suitable for use in the humanities. For more information, please see www.brill.com/brill-typeface.

ISSN 1877-7554
ISBN 978-90-04-25722-1 (hardback)
ISBN 978-90-04-26231-7 (e-book)

MIX
Paper from
responsible sources
FSC
www.fsc.org   FSC® C109576

Printed by Printforce, the Netherlands

For Suzanne

CONTENTS

INTRODUCTION

To date, the first and only comprehensive grammar of the Greek article was Thomas Fanshaw Middleton's *The Doctrine of the Greek Article*, published in 1828. Nearly two centuries later, it is plain to see that our understanding of the article's function has advanced significantly. At its most fundamental level, modern grammarians have been forced to concede, contrary to their predecessors, that the Greek article does not operate in a manner that is analogous to the English definite article. Definiteness and indefiniteness are not established in Greek by the presence or absence of the article. Despite this recognition, grammatical treatments of the Greek article continue to operate on analogy with the English definite article. Though they qualify their explanations by stating that the two articles function differently, they proceed by beginning with the translation equivalent *the*, then explain the Greek article's function as either conformity to or deviation from this norm. Since Middleton, no author has taken up the task of producing a comprehensive grammar of the Greek article based exclusively on descriptions derived from observations of its usage in Koine Greek.

One might question the necessity of expending so much labour upon what may be perceived as a relatively insignificant element of language. Indeed, what is at stake? To that question I would respond, a great deal. While scholarship has made great strides in recognizing what the Greek article does not do, there has yet to be a definitive attempt to address what it does do. Additionally, the methodologies employed are demonstrably inadequate. As a result, there are ramifications that impact important matters involving both translation and exegesis, both of which affect Christian theology and practice. To this day, scholars continue to appeal to the presence or absence of the article as definitive regarding matters of translation and theology. This may be illustrated in a recent article in *The Bible Translator*. In this article, Clint Tibbs addresses the question of when the phrases ἅγιον πνεῦμα, τὸ ἅγιον πνεῦμα and τὸ πνεῦμα τὸ ἅγιον should be translated "the Holy Spirit," "holy spirit," or "a holy spirit." Going back to Athanasius of Alexandria, the answer to this question was determined in no small part by the presence or absence of the article.[1] As he attempts to

---

[1] Tibbs, "The Holy Spirit," 153. This is the first of two articles Tibbs has published in *The Bible Translator* on this topic. The thesis he presents is continued in his second article,

resolve the issue, the author himself bases his argument on articular and anarthrous constructions. However, though he acknowledges the importance of the *presence* (or absence) of the article, at no point does he actually address the *function* of the article in these constructions and how its presence (and absence) may affect the meaning of the words involved. Perhaps he believes that the article's function is obvious, a grammatical given that needs no explanation. He may believe that its presence alone is all that matters, that there is nothing else significant beyond this basic fact. Whatever his motive, the absence of any discussion of the article's function is noteworthy. I would argue that the author's conclusions would have been significantly improved had he addressed how the article influences the meaning and discourse function of the elements in question.

Another reason for revisiting the grammar of the Greek article has to do with the current state of the grammatical treatment of the article in general. Historically, grammarians equated the function of the Greek article with the English definite article as a one-to-one correspondence. The view was reinforced by arguments that associated the Greek article with the historical demonstrative pronoun. Whether implicitly or explicitly, the reasoning proceeded from a simple and straightforward premise: just as the English definite article is a reduced form of the demonstrative pronoun, so too the Greek article is descended from the demonstrative pronoun. Thus, both articles are analogous in function. Recent scholarship has been forced to acknowledge that any view that maintains such a one-to-one correspondence is unsustainable. There are simply too many instances of the Greek article that show no correspondence to the English definite article. Despite this recognition, analogy with the English definite article continues to be the primary method of grammatical explanation. It will be argued below that a methodology that assumes a close association between the function of the English definite article and the Greek article is fundamentally inadequate for the purpose of generating a grammatical description of the later. In addition, the assertion that the Greek article has retained demonstrative force, particularly into the Hellenistic era, is something that is assumed rather than proved. On strictly morphological grounds, it is arguable that the article is more closely akin to the relative pronoun than the demonstrative pronoun. While this is occasionally

---

"ΠΝΕΥΜΑ as "Spirit World" in Translation in the New Testament." For other discussions of this topic, see also Steve Swartz, "The Holy Spirit: Person and Power. The Greek Article and *Pneuma*;" Stephen H. Levinsohn, "Anarthrous References to the Holy Spirit: Another Factor."

acknowledged, it is rarely explored as a means of providing a comprehensive description of the article's function. Just as association with the English definite article must be challenged (indeed it has, to a degree, and been found wanting) so too must be the diachronic association with the demonstrative pronoun. As the survey of grammatical treatments of the article below will demonstrate, these unchallenged assumptions have resulted in descriptions of the article's function that are characterized by "detached and unconnected rules,"[2] rules that are all too often internally inconsistent if not contradictory. By challenging these long held assumptions, as well as employing a synchronic analysis that examines the Greek article's grammatical and discourse function in the corpus of the New Testament, it will be demonstrated that, by the Koine era, both the form and function of the Greek article were more closely associated with the relative pronoun and that both had all but severed any functional association with the demonstrative pronoun. The continued association of the Greek article with the historical demonstrative pronoun and the English definite article not only leads to incorrect descriptions of its function, but also distracts the researcher from more productive paths of investigation and ultimately more accurate descriptions of the article's function.

The purpose of the following investigation is to revisit the grammar of the Greek article with the objective of producing an updated description of its function. It will operate within a theoretical framework that views the article as a reduced form of the relative pronoun, and that both parts of speech share certain defining functional characteristics that demonstrate and justify this co-classification. The results of this investigation will be used to formulate a comprehensive description of the article's function that will account for its usage in a manner that is consistent, coherent, and comprehensive. This description will, in turn, be used to generate an updated functional grammar of the article. The information outlined in this grammar will serve as a tool of translation and interpretation, which scholars like the one cited above, may use to inform their work, resulting in more nuanced understanding and greater accuracy in expression. To this end, we will begin with a historical survey of the grammatical treatment of the Greek article, beginning with the writings of the ancient Greeks and culminating with the most recent work at the end of the twentieth and beginning of the twenty-first centuries. Next, it will be demonstrated that the article functions as a reduced form of the relative pronoun. This

---

[2] Middleton, *Doctrine*, vi.

will be accomplished by means of an examination of how structures that incorporate these two elements perform the same or similar functions. We will observe that both parts of speech are used by the speaker or writer to indicate that information is being provided that the recipient is to use for the purpose of identification. In this manner, the Greek article orients the identification of the referent to the speaker or writer. This stands in contrast to the English definite article and demonstratives, which indicate that the recipient possesses the information necessary for identification or direct the recipient to the information respectively. In addition, we will explore the discourse function of the article. This will be accomplished by asking why the speaker or writer chooses to employ or not employ the article. Such a choice is a meaningful decision that affects the characterization of the head term. This characterization performs a function at the discourse level. Historically, grammars have attempted to explain how the article modifies the head term, but have not addressed questions regarding how the characterization functions within the discourse. This neglect, coupled with inaccurate grammatical description, explains much of the inconsistency in previous grammars. By addressing both the disourse function and the grammatical function of the article, we will be able to gather data that will produce a multidimensional picture of the Greek article. Finally, we will formulate a description of the article's function based on this examination, which will be then applied to the article's usage with various individual parts of speech and group structures.

Simply stated, the Greek article indicates that the speaker is providing the information necessary for identifying the referent to the recipient. As stated above, it orients the identifying information to the speaker, who provides this information to the recipient. By employing the article, the speaker characterizes the head term (that is, the part of speech modified by the article) as *concrete*, as belonging to experience of an actual thing or instance. In such instances, the speaker indicates that the information grammaticallized by the head term is the identifying characteristic of the referent.

CHAPTER ONE

HISTORICAL OVERVIEW

1. The Article in Ancient Greek Writings

a. *Ancient Greek Grammarians*

The Greek article appears as far back as Homer. Discussion of its function dates back to the Classical era. The classic writers placed it under the category ἄρθρον (*arthron*), which is generally translated *joint*. Typically, ἄρθρον was used in a physiological sense with reference to joints such as in the neck, hip, arms or legs.[1] This idea of *joint* was extended to grammar where ἄρθρον referred to a joining word, especially the article.[2] This designation provides initial insight into the article's function as it was understood by native speakers of the language. Rather than operating as a simple modifier with a relationship to its head term only, the Greek article appears to have also been used to indicate a relationship between the head term and another word or part of speech. It was the *joint* that connected the two.

A modern English speaker might be inclined to interpret *joint* or *joining word* as a conjunction. In Greek, a grammatical *joint* was functionally distinct from a conjunction, which was placed under the category σύνδεσμος, *binding word*. Dionysius of Halicarnassus credits the Stoics with making the distinction between σύνδεσμοι and ἄρθρα:[3]

ἡ σύνθεσις ἔστι μέν, ὥσπερ καὶ αὐτὸ δηλοῖ τοὔνομα, ποιά τις θέσις παρ᾽ ἄλληλα τῶν τοῦ λόγου μορίων, ἃ δὴ καὶ στοιχεῖα τινες λέξεως καλοῦσιν. ταῦτα δὲ Θεοδέκτης μὲν καὶ Ἀριστοτέλης καὶ οἱ κατ᾽ ἐκείνους φιλοσογήσαντες τοὺς χρόνους ἄχρι τριῶν προήγαγον, ὀνόματα καὶ ῥήματα καὶ συνδέσμους πρῶτα μέρη τῆς λέξεως ποιοῦντες. οἱ δὲ μετὰ τούτους γενόμενοι, καὶ μάλιστα οἱ τῆς Στωικῆς αἱρέσεως ἡγεμόνες, ἕως τεττάρων προὔβιβασαν, χωρίσαντες ἀπὸ τῶν συνδέσμων τὰ ἄρθρα.[4]

---

[1] LSJ, 239. The following is a selection of examples the lexicon provides as examples of ἄρθρον as *joint*: "κρᾶτα καὶ ἄρθρα the head and *joints of the neck*, Id. *Ph.* 1208 (lyr., codd.); esp. *the socket of the ankle-joint*, ὁ ἀστράγαλος ἐξεχώρησε ἐκ τῶν ἄ. Hdt. 3.129. 2. generally, of *limbs*, etc., esp. in pl., ἄ. ποδοῖν the ankles, Id. *OT* 718, cf. 1032; of the legs, βραδύπουν ἥλυσιν ἄρθρων προτιθεῖσα E. *Hec.* 67 (lyr.); ἄ. τῶν κύκων eyes, S. *OT.* 1270; ἄ. στόματος the mouth, E. *Cyc.* 625."

[2] LSJ, 139: "II. Gramm., *connecting word*, Id. *P.* 1457ᵃ6; esp. of the *article*, Id. *Rh. Al.* 1435ᵃ35, Chrysipp. *Stoic.* 2.45, D.H. *Th.* 37, al."

[3] DeJonge, *Between Grammar and Rhetoric*, 172.

[4] Dionysius of Halicarnassus, *On Literary Composition*, 2.

Composition is, as the very name indicates, a certain arrangement of the parts of speech, or elements of diction, as some call them. These were reckoned as three only by Theodectes and Aristotle and the philosophers of those times, who regarded nouns, verbs and connectives as the primary parts of speech. Their successors, particularly the leaders of the Stoic school, raised the number to four, separating the articles from the connectives.[5]

This is certainly true in the case of the Stoic Philosopher Chrysippus, who, in two separate lists of the parts of discourse, separately and distinctly refers to *conjunctions* and *the article*, though the lists are not in complete agreement:[6]

τοῦ δὲ λόγου ἐστὶ μέρη πέντε, ὥς φησι Διογένης—καὶ Χρύσιππος· ὄνομα, προσηγορία, ῥῆμα, σύνδεσμος, ἄρθρα.[7]

There are five parts of speech, as Diogenes... and Chrysippus say: noun, proper noun, verb, conjunction, article.

κατὰ δὲ τὸν αὐτὸν λόγον καὶ τὰ τῆς φωνῆς στοιχεῖα γεννᾶν πρῶτον μὲν τὰς συλλαβάς, εἶτα ἐξ αὐτῶν γεννᾶσθαι τό τε ὄνομα καὶ τὸ ῥῆμα καὶ τὴν πρόθεσιν ἄρθρον τε καὶ σύνδεσμον.[8]

According to the same work also the elements of speech producing first syllables, then from them comes the noun and the verb and the preposition, article and conjunction.

Upon closer examination, it appears that Dionysius was mistaken about the number of parts of speech identified by Aristotle. In *Poetics*, Aristotle records a list of the parts of speech that is significantly longer than Dionysius gives him credit:

Τῆς δὲ λέξεως ἁπάσης τάδ' ἐστὶ τὰ μέρη, στοιχεῖον συλλαβὴ σύνδεσμος ὄνομα ῥῆμα ἄρθρον πτῶσις λόγος.[9]

Here are the parts of all speech: letter, syllable, conjunction, noun, verb, joint-word (article), case, statement.

Contrary to Dionysius's assertion, Artistotle's list is made up of eight parts of speech, not three:[10] στοιχεῖον (letter), συλλαβή (syllable), σύνδεσμος (conjunction), ὄνομα (noun), ῥῆμα (verb), ἄρθρον (joint-word/article), πτῶσις

---

[5] Roberts, *Dionysius of Halicarnassus*, 71.

[6] Gould, *The Philosophy of Chrysippus*, 69.

[7] Chrysippus, *On Dialectic*, 147.

[8] Chrysippus, *On Dialectic*, 148.

[9] Aristotle, *Poetics*, 20.

[10] See also Roberts, *Dionysius of Halicarnassus*, 71, who also makes this observation in his footnotes. DeJonge suggests that Dionysius's statement is possibly a reference to

(case), λόγος (statement). Clearly, the Stoics were not the first to distinguish between σύνδεσμοι and ἄρθρα. As with Dionysius and Chrysippus, the categories of *conjunction* and *article* are listed separately, and Aristotle defines each individually. Of both he says that they are φωνὴ ἄσημος ἢ οὔτε κωλύει οὔτε ποιεῖ φωνὴν μίαν σημαντικὴν ἐκ πλειόων φωνῶν, *a non-significant sound which neither prevents nor produces a significant sound from many sounds.*[11] By non-significant, Aristotle appears to mean that words that fall into the categories of *conjunction* and *article* are unlike words such as nouns (ὀνόματα) and verbs (ῥήματα), which have referents, i.e. they *signify* something like a thing, idea, or action. While ὀνόματα and ῥήματα may be classified as content words, σύνδεσμοι and ἄρθρα are procedural or functional words that "are used in discourse to connect together and indicate the relations of the content words."[12] When he says they neither prevent nor produce significant sounds from many sounds, he likely means that such words are more than letters (στοιχεῖον) or syllables (συλλαβή), the basic building blocks of words. Neither are they the kind of word that can be added to an existing word to create a new meaning or alter it semantically, such as a prepositional prefix. However, the philosopher notes differences in usage and function. Conjunctions (σύνδεσμοι) are:

πεφυκυῖα συντίθεσθαι καὶ ἐπὶ τῶν ἄκρων καὶ ἐπὶ τοῦ μέσου, ἣν μὴ ἁρμόττει ἐν ἀρχῇ λόγου τιθέναι καθ' αὑτήν, οἷον μέν δή τοί δέ.[13]

placed on their own [lit. "rogue"] at the ends and in the middle, though not placed by itself at the beginning, of a statement.

He cites words such as μέν, δή, τοί and δέ as examples of σύνδεσμοι. In contrast, an ἄρθρον is:

φωνὴ ἄσημος ἢ λόγου ἀρχὴν ἢ τέλος ἢ διορισμὸν δηλοῖ.[14]

a non-significant sound which shows the beginning, end or division of a statement.

The most puzzling element of his definition is the words he cites as examples of ἄρθρα, τὸ ἀμφί καὶ τὸ περὶ καὶ τὰ ἄλλα.[15] The statement itself is

---

Aristotle's Rhetoric, Between Grammar and Rhetoric, 172. In any event, Dionysius is clearly mistaken.

[11] Aristotle, *Poetics*, 20.
[12] Porter & O'Donnell, "Conjunctions," 6.
[13] Aristotle, *Poetics*, 20.
[14] Aristotle, *Poetics*, 20.
[15] Aristotle, *Poetics*, 20.

difficult to understand. There are three possible interpretations. The first
option assumes that Aristotle is citing the two prepositions as examples
of an ἄρθρον, along with "others" (τὰ ἄλλα), i.e. others of that sort.[16] This
interpretation is compromised for two reasons: there is a textual variant
for ἀμφί, which in some texts is the verb φημί, and prepositions do not
conform to the standard definition of ἄρθρον. The second option does not
take the prepositions as examples of an ἄρθρον, but rather as substantives.
Both prepositions have similar meanings, even to the point of περί replacing ἀμφί in later Greek.[17] Thus, it is possible that Aristotle does not mean
that prepositions themselves are ἄρθρα, but that the kind of word that is on
"both sides" (τὸ ἀμφί), the kind of word that is "round about" or "around"
(τὸ περί) and others of this sort (τὰ ἄλλα) are examples of ἄρθρα. This possible interpretation is reinforced by the fact that these words are articular, which is in contrast to the examples of σύνδεσμοι, previously listed.
Unfortunately, this leaves the reader to interpret what exactly a "both
sides" or "round about" word is. The third option is that Aristotle does
not intend the reader to focus on the prepositions themselves, but the
articles instead. Thus, one should read τὸ ἀμφί καὶ τὸ περὶ καὶ τὰ ἄλλα, *THE*
ἀμφί, THE περί, and others [or perhaps THE others]. If the textual variant
is read as φήμι, this interpretation becomes stronger. In this reading, the
verb and preposition(s) are incidental. Instead, the emphasis is upon
the articles themselves. The weaknesses of the first option have been
demonstrated, thus it is the least likely interpretation of Aristotle's statement. The second and third options both have the benefit of consistency
with the standard definition of ἄρθρον. If the second option is adopted,
then the interpretation remains ambiguous and difficult to understand.
One might draw a connection between the notion of "*both sides*" or "*round*
about" type words with what Aristotle previously said about an ἄρθρον
showing "the beginning, end or division of a statement." The third option
enjoys the advantage of being simple and straight forward in meaning.
However, if the philosopher meant to emphasize the articles themselves,
he would have chosen head terms that were more common. The solution
would appear to be found in the other two statements Aristotle makes

---

[16] Earlier in the chapter, Aristotle employs the article to identify individual letters
and syllables: τὸ Σ καὶ τὸ Ρ, *the S and the R;* τὸ Γ καὶ τὸ Δ, *the G and the D;* τὸ ΓΡ ἄνευ τοῦ Α
συλλαβὴ καὶ μετὰ τοῦ Α, οἷον τὸ ΓΡΑ, *GR without A is a syllable as well as with A, likewise GRA,*
Poetics, 20.
[17] LSJ, 89.

regarding an ἄρθρον. In both instances, the philosopher is concerned with two characteristics of such words: their meaning and their position in a statement. This suggests that the second option is best, that *both sides* and *round about* refer to the position an ἄρθρον may occupy in a statement. Based on this interpretation, Aristotle is stating that an ἄρθρον may occupy any position in a statement: at the front, at the end, or any place in between. This positional freedom distinguishes it from other lexical items, such as postpositive conjunctions, which have fixed limitations regarding their positions.

For our current purpose, though Aristotle's treatment of ἄρθρον provides little information, what he does say is nevertheless helpful. The categorical distinction between σύνδεσμοι (*binding words* or conjunctions) and ἄρθρα (*joint words* or articles) is instructive. The functions of *binding* and *joining* performed by elements of these categories suggest *cohesion*.[18] The argument that will be made below is that the article and relative pronoun are categorically related based on shared morphology and function. By the New Testament period, both had been almost completely severed from any functional connection to the historical demonstrative pronoun. One of the functions of the relative pronoun is "to bring clauses into relation to each other."[19] If, for the Greeks, the article was connected to the relative pronoun in any way, this would explain Aristotle's remarks concerning its *joining* (that is, *cohesive*) function.

Cohesion is not the only possible function of the article. In his work, *The Art of Rhetoric*, Aristotle provides instructions which differentiate lofty style from style that is concise. To achieve the lofty style, "each word should have its own article, as in τῆς γυναικὸς τῆς ἡμετέρας [of {*art.*} woman {*art.*} our]." By contrast, to be concise, he says, "use the reverse, τῆς ἡμετέρας γυναικός [of {*art.*} our woman]."[20] In addition to its grammatical function, the article served an aesthetic role that influenced the reader or listener's

---

[18] In language, cohesion is what defines a text as text: "The word TEXT is used in linguistics to refer to any passage, spoken or written, of whatever length, that does form a unified whole," Halliday & Hasan, *Cohesion in English*, 1. *Cohesion* is that quality or element(s) of the text that gives it unity: "It refers to relations of meaning that exist within the text, and that define it as text," Halliday & Hasan, *Cohesion in English*, 4. Jeffrey T. Reed has written extensively on the topic of cohesion and New Testament studies from the perspective of Hallidayan Systemic Functional Linguistics: "Cohesive Ties in 1 Timothy;" *A Discourse Analysis of Philippians*; "The Cohesiveness of Discourse," in *Discourse Analysis and the New Testament: Approaches and Results*.

[19] Porter, *Idioms*, 132.

[20] Aristotle, *The Art of Rhetoric*, 3.6.

perception, and perhaps reception, of what was said. Thus, the article also performed a function that altered the register of the discourse in which it was employed. *Register* "is a functional variety of language—the patterns of instantiation of the overall system associated with a given type of context (a situation type)."[21] It refers to variations in discourse based on factors such as audience, subject material, occasion, and media, to name a few. These variations may be realized by lexical choices, conformity to recognized grammatical patterns, and syntax. Thus, a person's "style" will vary based on whether he or she is writing an email to a friend or a cover letter to accompany a job application. Lexical choices will vary greatly based on subject material. If one is writing or speaking about a football game, terminology associated with that game will play a greater role in the discourse. Certain situations or audiences may influence the degree of formality employed, or use of technical language that might otherwise seem inappropriate or out of place. Based on this, a single individual may be capable of employing a wide variety of registers. As we will see, the article is an element that may be employed in a variety of ways to alter the register of discourse.

b. *Conclusion*

The treatment of the article by ancient writers is difficult to interpret. Categorically, the article was labeled an ἄρθρον, a *joint word*, which suggests a possible cohesive function. Unfortunately, the writers do not explain what they mean by this, or how it was accomplished. Nevertheless, it appears to indicate cohesion. The level at which this cohesion was realized may have been perceived differently than in the modern linguistic sense.

The article may also be used to produce various, sometimes complex, syntactical constructions. Understanding the nature of these constructions will prove valuable in discourse analysis. Such variations are indicative of choices on the part of the speaker or writer, which provide material to analyze the register of the discourse.

---

[21] Halliday, *Functional Grammar*, 27. For an overview of the theory of register, see Helen Leckie-Tarry, *Language & Context: A Functional Linguistic Theory of Register*; Douglas Biber and Susan Conrad, *Register, Genre, and Style*. For discussion of *register* in the context of New Testament Greek, see J.T. Reed, *A Discourse Analysis of Philippians*, 53–57.

2. The Influence of German Scholarship

a. *German Grammatical Categorization*

For centuries, German scholarship has played a highly influential role in shaping the subfields within biblical and theological studies. This is no less true regarding New Testament Greek studies. Well into the late nineteenth and early twentieth centuries, New Testament Greek scholars were heavily, if not solely, dependent upon grammars written in German.[22] Early English language Greek grammars were translations of German originals.[23] Thus, the categories used by the writers were based on comparisons and contrasts between Greek and German. This categorization was subsequently carried over into the English translations. Later authors, though writing in English, had learned Greek from these German based grammars.[24] As a result, they perpetuated the German categorizations.

The association of the Greek article with the demonstrative pronoun in English language Greek grammars may, in fact, be the result of German influence and the particulars of that language. In German, the definite article, demonstrative pronoun, and relative pronoun share a common form, *der, die, das*. While in Koine Greek these categories are grammaticalized

---

[22] Important works include: Kühner and Blass, *Grammatik der Briechischen Sprache.* 2 vols; Schwyzer, *Griechische Grammatik,* 2 vols.

[23] Examples include: Buttman, *A Grammar of the New Testament Greek,* translated by J.H. Thayer; George Benedict Winer and Gottlieb Lünemann; *A Grammar of the Idiom of the New Testament,* 7th ed., edited by J.H. Thayer, translated by Edward Masson; Blass and Debrunner, *A Greek Grammar of the New Testament and Other Early Christian Literature,* translated by R.W. Funk. Though not a grammar, one cannot omit the highly influential Adolf Deissmann, *Light from the Ancient Near East,* originally translated from the German in 1927 by Lionel R.M. Strachan.

[24] Robertson admits such dependency: "But I wish to record my conviction that my own work, such as it is, would have been impossible but for the painstaking and scientific investigation of the Germans at every turn," *Grammar,* ix. Note as well that the first several pages of Robertson's first chapter focus exclusively on the work of German scholarship. In the first edition of J.H. Moulton's *Prolegomena,* the title page included a statement of dependence upon his father W.F. Moulton's translation of G.B. Winer's *Grammatik des neutestamentlichen Sprachidioms.* In the preface to the second edition, the younger Moulton noted that this statement of dependence had been removed "Since the present volume is entirely new, and does not in any way follow the lines of its great predecessor," *Prolegomena,* vii. Like Robertson, Moulton acknowledges his debt to the Germans: "Next to the Cambridge influences are those which come from teachers and friends whom I have never seen, and especially those great German scholars whose labours, too little assisted by those of other countries, have established the Science of Language on the firm basis it occupies to-day," *Prolegomena,* xi.

by discrete forms, when translated into German each is represented by
a single form. Thus, German grammars place these words in a common
category. For example, Kühner and Blass write, *Das einfachste Demonstrativ ist der sog. Artikel ὁ ἡ τό, der, die, das.*[25] The relative pronoun is also
lumped into this category, though not necessarily distinguished from the
article in meaning or function.

> In der griechischen Sprache mischen sich einigermassen die Formen für das
> Demonstrativ und Relativ, wie auch im Deutschen der die das beide Funktio-
> nen übernimmt; kommen doch auch im Gebrauche das ἄρθρον προτακτικόν,
> d. i. der Artikel ὁ, und das ἄ. ὑποτακτικόν, d. i. das Rel. ὅς, ausserordentlich
> nahe aneinander heran: Doch hat gerade die attische und gemeine Sprache
> das alte Relativum gesondert bewahrt: ὅς ἥ ὅ = sanskr. jas ja jad, und erst in
> den Dialekten zeigt sich die Mischung.[26]

In their second volume on the Greek language, Kühner and Blass continue
in this explanation of the origins and function of the article.

> Unter sämtlichen Demonstrativpronomen hat das Pronomen ὁ ἡ τό die
> grösste syntaktische Wichtigkeit, teils wegen der Mannigfaltigkeit seiner
> Bedeutung, indem es nicht allein als Demonstrativpronomen, sondern auch
> als Relativpronomen und als Artikel gebraucht wurde, teils weil wir die all-
> mähliche Entwickelung des Artikels aus diesem Demonstrativpronomen
> geschichtlich genau verfolgen können.[27]

Thus also Schwyzer, *Das ererbte allgemeine Demonstrativ ὁ ἡ τό (besser ὅ ἥ
τό)...*[28] This lack of discrete forms in German presented German grammarians with a unique challenge when addressing the grammar of the
Greek article. Since it was often translated by *der, die, das*, it was naturally

---

[25] Kühner and Blass, *Grammatik der Griechischen Sprache Teil 1*, 603: "The simplest
demonstrative is the so-called article ὁ ἡ τό, *the*."

[26] Kühner and Blass, *Grammatik der Griechischen Sprache Teil 1*, 608: "In the Greek
language, the forms of the demonstrative and relative are somewhat blended, just as in
German der, die, das take both functions. However, it also appears in usage as the ἄρθρον
προτακτικόν [prefixed article], i.e. the article ὁ, and the ἄ. ὑποτακτικόν [placed after article],
i.e. the relative ὅς, being exceptionally near to each other. But the attic and common language have demonstrated that the old relative is separate: ὅς ἥ ὅ = Sanskrit jas ja jad, and
only the dialects demonstrate the mixture."

[27] Kühner and Blass, *Grammatik der Griechischen Sprache Teil 2*, 575: "Under all the
demonstrative pronouns, the pronoun ὁ ἡ τό has the greatest syntactical importance, partly
because of its multiple meanings, while used not only as a demonstrative pronoun, but
also as a relative pronoun and as an article, partly because we are able to track precisely
the gradual development of the articles from this historical demonstrative pronoun."

[28] Schwyzer, *Griechische Grammatik*, 207: "The inherited general demonstrative ὁ ἡ τό
(better ὅ ἥ τό)."

placed under the category *Demonstrativa und Verwandtes*.[29] Since the three grammatical categories are realized in a single form, one is left with the impression that categorization is inherent in the original Greek. Certainly this appears to be the perspective of the German grammarians.

> Dem griechischen deomonstrativpronomen ὁ ἡ τό entspricht in Form und Bedeutung das gotische *sa, sô, thata*, Gen. *This, thizôs, this* u. s. w.), der, die, das. Auch dieses Pronomen hat wie das griecheische die dreifache Bedeutung.[30]

By assigning a tri-fold meaning to the article, German grammarians leave the reader with the impression that the function of the article also conforms to this tri-fold meaning.[31]

b. *Conclusion*

German grammarians analyzed the Greek article's function diachronically. They operated from the assumption that the article was in origin a demonstrative and carried this function forward into the classical and Koine periods. Though they acknowledged that its demonstrative force had been diminished, this diachronic approach led them to conclude that this force continued to be felt. This perspective influenced their understanding of its function.

Their diachronic approach also led them to conclude that the Greek article bore a strong resemblance to a part of speech in their own language: *der, die, das*, which could function as a demonstrative pronoun, relative pronoun, or definite article. This led to the further conclusion that the Greek article also performed a "tri-fold" function.

In the following sections, we will observe that English language Greek grammars, working under the influence of German grammars, perpetuate the Germans' categorization of the Greek article, as evidenced by their near universal association of the Greek article with the demonstrative pronoun.

---

[29] Schwyzer, *Griechische Grammatik*, 207: "Demonstratives and Related Forms."

[30] Kühner and Blass, *Grammatik der Griechischen Sprache*, 575: "The Greek demonstrative pronouns ὁ ἡ τό correspond in form and meaning to the gothic sa, sô, thata, Gen. This, thizôs, this u. s. w., der, die, das. Also, these pronouns have, like the Greek, the tri-fold meaning."

[31] As further evidence of the influence of the German grammarians on English speaking Greek grammarians, note Robertson, writing about the form ὁ, ἡ, τό: "This form, like *der* in German and *this* in English, was used either as demonstrative, article, or relative. See Kühner-Gerth, I, p. 575." *Grammar*, 694.

3. The Article in Classical Greek Grammars

Though the study of biblical Greek has become a field in its own right, in the early days it was a subset of the broader field of Greek language studies, which was dominated by a study of the classics. Those who engaged in the study of the Greek New Testament, and who went on to write grammars, were often educated in classical or Attic Greek.[32] It is necessary, therefore, to engage in a brief survey of select, representative classical Greek grammars in order to illustrate the influence of this broader field on the study of Biblical Greek.

a. *W.E. Jelf,* A Grammar of the Greek Language *(1851)*

Classical grammarians are nearly universal in agreement that, in origin, the article was a demonstrative. This is the assertion of W.E. Jelf, whose Grammar was based chiefly on the German work of Raphael Kühner. In his second volume he writes,

> Of all the adjectival attributives the article ὁ, ἡ, τό, is the most important; to understand its nature we must trace it back to its original demonstrative force.
>   It had originally—1st, a demonstrative—2nd, a relative force.[33]

Regarding this demonstrative function, he continues,

> In Homer it is used as pointing out some object as known or spoken of, and directing the mind of the reader to it: there are however in Homer some instances of an approach to the Attic use of it, though Homer probably never used it quite as the simple article.[34]

Jelf states that the demonstrative ὁ, ἡ, τό also functions as the relative ὅς, ἥ, ὅ, which also passed to the Ionic and Doric writers. However, he asserts that the Attic comic and prose writers did not admit this relative force.[35] Eventually, Jelf continues, the article lost its demonstrative force.

---

[32] So writes Moulton, "Till four years ago, my own teaching work scarcely touched the Greek Testament, classics and comparative philology claiming the major part of my time," *Prolegomena*, ix. Robertson also notes the important contribution of the broader field of Greek language studies to the understanding of Biblical Greek, *Grammar*, 12–24. Middleton's *The Doctrine of the Greek Article* cites heavily from classical Greek primary sources as well as classical Grammars.

[33] Jelf, *Greek Grammar Vol. 2*, 106.
[34] Jelf, *Greek Grammar Vol. 2*, 106.
[35] Jelf, *Greek Grammar Vol. 2*, 109.

The article ὁ, ἡ, τό lost so much of its demonstrative force, that at last it was used merely to represent the notion expressed by the substantive as viewed by the speaker as an individual, one of a class, and distinct from all the members of that class; this usage of the article properly belongs to the æra of Attic prose.[36]

In this last statement, Jelf reveals a perspective on the article that will continue as the dominant view, that the article is used with lexical items that are substantives. In this view, the article does not modify or alter the word, but merely reinforces or makes explicit its substantival state.

b. *A.N. Jannaris*, An Historical Greek Grammar: Chiefly of the Attic Dialect *(1897)*

In his *Historical Grammar*, A.N. Jannaris writes,

> Originally the article ὁ, ἡ, τό was a demonstrative pronoun, as is shown by the Homeric poems, where it is almost exclusively so used. On the other hand, its articular force and use appear fully established in all subsequent dialects without exception. Nevertheless, its final development becomes apparent only in [Attic] *prose*.[37]

He later writes of its relationship to the demonstrative, "ὁ, ἡ, τό, had assumed the office of the article even in pre-classical antiquity."[38] According to William Goodwin's *Grammar* (originally published in 1892), "In Homer the article appears generally as a demonstrative or personal pronoun; sometimes (in the form beginning with *t*) as a relative."[39] Of later Greek he writes, "In Attic Greek the article generally corresponds to our article *the;* as ὁ ἀνήρ, *the man*."[40] He continues, "In Attic prose the article retains its original demonstrative force chiefly in the expression ὁ μέν ... ὁ δέ, *the one ... the other*."[41]

c. *H.W. Smyth*, Greek Grammar, *Revised by Gordon Messing (1956)*

A half-century later, this view remains unchanged. In Gordon Messing's revision of Smyth's grammar (first published in 1920), we read, "In Homer ὁ, ἡ, τό is usually a demonstrative pronoun and is used substantively or

---

[36] Jelf, *Greek Grammar Vol. 2*, 109.
[37] Jannaris, *Historical Grammar*, 317.
[38] Jannaris, *Historical Grammar*, 351.
[39] Goodwin, *A Greek Grammar*, 204–5.
[40] Goodwin, *A Greek Grammar*, 206.
[41] Goodwin, *A Greek Grammar*, 212.

adjectively; it also serves as the personal pronoun of the third person... The demonstrative ὁ, ἡ, τό is used as a relative pronoun in Homer only when the antecedent is definite."[42] Regarding the article's origin, he writes, "The definite article is a weakened demonstrative pronoun."[43] Regarding the article in Attic, "The demonstrative force of ὁ, ἡ, τό survives chiefly in connection with particles (μέν, δέ, γέ τοί; and with καί preceding ὁ)."[44] As to function, Smyth writes, "The article ὁ, ἡ, τό marks objects as definite and known."[45] Additionally, "The article has the power to make substantival any word or words to which it is prefixed."[46]

d. *The Article in the New Millennium*

At the beginning of the twenty-first century, the situation regarding the grammar of the article has seen little change. For example, in Luschnig's *Introduction to Ancient Greek*, we read, "Corresponding to the English definite article, *the*, is ὁ, ἡ, τό in Greek."[47] The author goes on to say, "In general, the definite article corresponds to English *the*, but is used in some instances where English would omit it."[48]

Stephanie Bakker notes that the grammar of the Greek article has continued unchanged. As the title of her book makes clear, her interest is in the noun phrase, "This book is about the noun phrase (NP) in ancient Greek. Its aim is to provide a functional analysis of the factors that determine the structure of the NP, viz. the ordering and articulation of its constituents."[49] However, one of the primary constituents of the noun phrase is the article. Bakker provides a summary of her observations regarding its treatment in grammatical texts, a summary that is both insightful and quite correct.

> For a description of the use and function of the Greek article we have to rely on the standard grammars. The overall structure of the descriptions of the article in these grammars, which date back to the beginning of the

---

[42] Smyth, *Greek Grammar*, 284–5.
[43] Smyth, *Greek Grammar*, 94. Also 284, "The article ὁ, ἡ, τό, was originally a demonstrative pronoun and as such supplied the place of the personal pronoun of the third person. By gradual weakening it became the definite article. It also served as a relative pronoun. (Cf. Germ. *der*, demonstrative article and relative; French *le* from *ille*.)."
[44] Smyth, *Greek Grammar*, 285.
[45] Smyth, *Greek Grammar*, 286.
[46] Smyth, *Greek Grammar*, 292.
[47] Luschnig, *Introduction to Ancient Greek*, 30.
[48] Luschnig, *Introduction to Ancient Greek*, 30.
[49] Bakker, *The Noun Phrase*, 1.

last century, is highly similar. After the general observation that the article marks a particular or general noun as definite and known, they continue to describe the use of the article by using various categories, such as the article with proper names, the article with predicate nouns, the article with abstract nouns, the article in prepositional phrases, etc.[50]

Bakker's summary of the treatment of the article is consistent with my own observations. As we will see in the next chapter, this approach is not limited to grammarians of classical Greek, but is employed by many biblical Greek grammarians as well.

Bakker goes on to cite what she sees as the shortcomings in treatment of the article in traditional grammars. First, they are unnecessarily complicated.

> Instead of trying to define a basic meaning for the article on the basis of which its use in the various categories can (at least largely) be explained, most of the grammars state only briefly that the article marks an object or person as a particular individual... as distinct... or as known/present to the mind... Subsequently, they give a lengthy presentation of circumstances for each category in which an NP does or does not receive an article, even if this can be explained on the basis of the definitions of the use of the article they formulated earlier.[51]

Second, "The grammars present manifold rules for the use of the article, but do not supply a hierarchy for the application of these rules. In this way, there will be numerous instances where various rules are in conflict with each other."[52] In the end,

> The studies present a lengthy enumeration of the use of the article in all kind of circumstances, instead of formulating a definition of the function of the article, by means of which its use in the various circumstances can be explained.[53]

Bakker's observations and her conclusion regarding the current state of research on the Greek article are quite correct.

In order to address this, Bakker dedicates an entire chapter to the function of the article. After reviewing the treatment of the article in classical grammars, she addresses recent work on the Greek article, focusing specifically on the writings of David Sansone and Albert Rijksbaron on

---

[50] Bakker, *The Noun Phrase*, 146–47.
[51] Bakker, *The Noun Phrase*, 147.
[52] Bakker, *The Noun Phrase*, 147.
[53] Bakker, *The Noun Phrase*, 148.

the topic.[54] Next, she reviews research on the nature of definiteness in English. Though the general methodology she employs in addressing the noun phrase is not based in cognitive linguistics, her description of the article's function appears to proceed from this framework. She concludes that, "a definite article is appropriate if the speaker presents the referent in question as unequivocally relatable to an available cognitive structure[55] that is relevant in the given discourse."[56] Bakker then proceeds to present her own explanation of the Greek article's function, examining whether it functions like the English definite article as marking the referent of the noun phrase as identifiable.[57] In contrast to Sansone and Rijksbaron, she states, "My data seems to indicate that the general function of the article in Greek is to mark the discourse referent as identifiable."[58] By this she means that, when the article is present, "the discourse referent can be unequivocally related to an available cognitive structure."[59] She later qualifies this: "It should be stated explicitly that the definiteness of an NP is not sensitive to the (non-) specificity of the NP. The definite [sic] article marks the referent as identifiable, irrespective of the fact whether the speaker has or has not a particular referent in mind."[60] Thus, "identifiability is the general function of the article we were looking for."[61] In her corpus (the writings of Herodotus), she finds that only around six percent of the referential noun phrases do not conform to her general rule.[62] Thus she supplements with five further refinements to the rule. Bakker concludes her treatment of the use of the article with the following summary,

---

[54] David Sansone, "Towards a new doctrine of the article in Greek;" Albert Rijksbaron, *Over bepaalde personen.* According to Bakker, "Both studies assume a relation between the presence of the article and a pragmatic marking of the referent." She states that Sansone interprets the article as a "topicality marker," while for Rijksbaron, when used before proper names, "it underlines the special position of the character in question in a passage that is of special importance for the development of the story," *The Noun Phrase*, 149–150.

[55] Bakker defines *cognitive structure* as, "my theory-unspecified term to refer to frames, scripts and schemata, i.e. data structures representing generic concepts stored in memory. These data structures are hierarchical networks of the various elements that are generally related to some object or (sequence) of event(s)." *The Noun Phrase*, 296.

[56] Bakker, *The Noun Phrase*, 162.
[57] Bakker, *The Noun Phrase*, 162.
[58] Bakker, *The Noun Phrase*, 162.
[59] Bakker, *The Noun Phrase*, 162–3.
[60] Bakker, *The Noun Phrase*, 170.
[61] Bakker, *The Noun Phrase*, 171.
[62] Bakker, *The Noun Phrase*, 172.

Although recent research seemed to hint in another direction, the use of the article in Ancient Greek is, in general, comparable to its use in modern European languages. That means that an Ancient Greek [noun phrase], like its modern European counterparts, is definite if the referent is present as identifiable, viz. as unequivocally relatable to the knowledge of the addressee(s).[63]

Bakker's description may be further refined to produce a more accurate description. First, the notion of the article marking *definiteness*, qualified as it is, must be abandoned. Other linguistic features make this determination.[64] Even in light of refined definitions, descriptions of the article's function will be better served through the use of improved terminology. Second, comparison with other Indo-European languages, though helpful for the purpose of illustration, also tends to create a false sense of continuity in function across the languages. The development of the Greek article followed a different course, and ultimately arrived at a different destination, than, for example, German *der/die/das*. While it is not entirely incorrect to suggest that the function of the Greek article is "comparable" to the article in modern European languages, the degree to which they are comparable has been overestimated. This is not to say that comparisons cannot be made. Rather, to say they are comparable has, historically, assumed greater similarity than actually exists. Use of this term must be heavily qualified to avoid such misconception. Third, Bakker's use of the term *identifiability* draws near to the theory of the article's function that will be argued below. At its root is the notion of *identity*, which is what I believe lies at the heart of the function of the Greek article. Rather than indicating or producing *identifiability*, the function of the article is to *generate or produce identity*. Fourth, Bakker employs a cognitive framework for her treatment of the article's function. The treatment below will employ a functional approach.

e. *Conclusion*

Bakker's summary of the current state of research regarding the article in classical Greek is insightful and accurate. While it is hardly a neglected

---

[63] Bakker, *The Noun Phrase*, 211.

[64] "Although the basic rules for the use of the article in Ancient Greek are analogous to those in other languages marking definiteness, there are some notable differences. First of all, Ancient Greek considers the marking of definiteness in NPs with a demonstrative or possessive more important than other European languages." Bakker, *The Noun Phrase*, 212.

field, clearly there is much left to do. Most notably, a functional approach
to the article has yet to be attempted. Such an approach will provide a
fresh and distinctive view, which will yield valuable insights and will significantly advance our understanding of its usage in the New Testament
specifically and Koine Greek in general.

4. THE ARTICLE IN INTERMEDIATE AND ADVANCED BIBLICAL GREEK GRAMMARS

In this section we will examine the treatment of the Greek article in intermediate and advanced biblical Greek grammars. It will be clear that the
overwhelming tendency has been to associate the article with the demonstrative pronoun with regard to origin (history and development), classification, and function. The choice of grammars was based on several
criteria. First, our goal is to trace the development, or lack of development, of the grammar related to the article. Therefore, texts have been
chosen based on date of publication in order to serve as representatives
of the corresponding period in time. Second, many were also chosen
because of their significant influence on Greek language study. Works by
authors such as Moulton and Robertson are widely regarded classics in
the field. More recent works, such as those by Wallace and Porter, have
become standards and are widely used. Third, certain authors were chosen because they reflect a unique insight or contribution, or provide a
unique presentation.

a. *George B. Winer*, A Grammar of the Idiom of the New Testament *(1822)*

Winer's grammar could have been addressed earlier in the chapter on the
influence of classical German scholarship. Though available in English
translation, it clearly reflects the German perspective. It is placed here
because of its early use by English speaking Greek scholars. It serves as a
bridge between German language grammars and grammars produced by
English speakers.

Winer's grammar was first published in German in 1822 and passed
through six editions, each based solely on his work. The seventh edition
was expanded by Dr. Gottlieb Lünemann in 1866. This seventh edition
was translated into English by J.H. Thayer in 1868, with the revised fourth
edition of Thayer's translation appearing in 1874. At this point in time,
English speaking New Testament scholars had few options for Greek

grammars originally published in their own language. Thus, they were dependent upon translations of German language grammars such as this one. As a result, German grammatical categories and notions of function were adopted by English speaking scholars.

As one might expect, in English translation, Winer is consistent with German scholarship in general in associating the article with the demonstrative pronoun via diachronic analysis, "The article ὁ, ἡ, τό was originally a demonstrative pronoun and is regularly employed as such in epic poetry."[65] Conversely, he states that the article functioned as demonstrative in prose only in certain constructions, such as ὁ μὲν … ὁ δέ.[66]

Winer states unequivocally that the function of the article is to make the head term definite, "When ὁ, ἡ, τό is employed as strictly an Article before a noun, it marks the object as one definitely conceived."[67] He acknowledges that the article was sometimes used as a relative in Ionic and Doric, as well as in Byzantine, but questions whether this usage is present in the New Testament.[68] He also states that the Greek language also possessed an indefinite article, realized by τις, or a weakened form of εἷς.[69]

Consistent with the time, his presentation indicates the understanding that certain parts of speech are substantives by their very nature, irrespective of the presence or absence of the article.[70] As will be seen, this view will prevail well into the twentieth century and will exert considerable influence on how the article's function is understood.

Winer argues that, under certain circumstances, the article is absolutely necessary, "[I]t is utterly impossible that the Article should be omitted where it is decidedly necessary, or employed where it is not demanded."[71] However, he continues, "On the other hand, the Article may sometimes, with equal (objective) correctness, be either employed or omitted." Thus, he leads the reader to conclude that, in such circumstances, the article's absence or presence has no effect upon the head term; it is merely a stylistic choice on the part of the writer or speaker. This view will also continue well into the twentieth century and be reflected in many grammars, implicitly or explicitly.

---

[65] Winer, *Grammar of New Testament Greek*, 104.
[66] Winer, *Grammar of New Testament Greek*, 104.
[67] Winer, *Grammar of New Testament Greek*, 105.
[68] Winer, *Grammar of New Testament Greek*, 107.
[69] Winer, *Grammar of New Testament Greek*, 117.
[70] Winer, *Grammar of New Testament Greek*, 108, 114.
[71] Winer, *Grammar of New Testament Greek*, 115.

b. *Alexander Buttmann*, A Grammar of New Testament Greek *(1895)*

In contrast to Winer, Buttmann does not argue for the presence of both an indefinite and definite article in Greek. Though he agrees that εἷς and τις perform the kind of indefinite function attributed to them by Winer, he does not categorize them as an indefinite article.[72] Regarding the article, he is in agreement with Winer, whom he cites. Interestingly, Buttmann concedes defeat in the task of producing a comprehensive description of its function. He is quoted here at length:

> In reference to the definite article the rules and the regulations given in the grammars hold good,—so far as in a subject so delicate as this we can talk of rules. For in the endeavor to lay down fixed laws respecting the use of the article, many a learned and laborious inquiry has already come to naught; and the intention ought at length to be abandoned of forcing the use or the omission of the article under precise regulations, which find the proof of their nullity and uselessness in the throng of exceptions which it is necessary to subjoin straightway to almost every rule laid down.[73]

The reason for this frustration arises not only from misconceptions about the article itself, but also in the presuppositions regarding the head terms it modifies, particularly nouns. The first is the prevailing notion that the article indicates definiteness on the part of the head term. Certainly such an assumption will quickly lead to frustration as the exegete is confronted by instances that do not conform to this notion. For German writers such as Buttmann and Winer, this no doubt arose from associating the Greek article too closely with German *der, die, das.* English grammarians will encounter the same difficulty as they closely associate the function of the Greek article with English *the.* Second is the prevailing diachronic association of the article with the demonstrative pronoun, which only serves to reinforce the first assumption. Thirdly, by proceeding from the position that a lexical item is a substantive apart from the presence of the article, the grammarian has handicapped himself with inaccurate data, leading to frustrated results. Buttmann articulates what is left unsaid by other Greek grammarians, which provides further insight into their methodology. Since they do not observe that the article has a significant effect on "substantives" (by which they usually mean nouns), they can only attempt to provide general explanations as to what circumstances one might expect to see the article employed. Yet by their own admission these can hardly

---

[72] Buttmann, *Grammar of New Testament Greek*, 85.
[73] Buttmann, *Grammar of New Testament Greek*, 85.

be seen as rules and must be accepted as mere guidelines, subject to the whims of the individual speaker or writer. In the end, the article's role is syntactical, lacking any functional relationship to the head term.

c. *J.H. Moulton, A Grammar of New Testament Greek. I. Prolegomena (1906). J.H. Moulton and W.F. Howard, A Grammar of New Testament Greek. II. Accidence and Word Formation (1929)*

In his *Prolegomena*, Moulton provides only a brief treatment of the article, "We pass on to the Article, on which there is not much to say, since in all essentials its use is in agreement with Attic."[74] He simply observes that the New Testament's usage of the article is "remarkably 'correct' when compared to the papyri."[75]

Regarding the classification of the article, Moulton's position echoes that of Winer. He observes no relationship between the article and the relative pronoun outside of Ionic and Doric, and the papyri: "[The New Testament] shows no trace of the use of the article as a relative, which is found in classical Greek outside Attic, in papyri from the first [century?], and to some extent in MGr."[76] Moulton observes that in the papyri one encounters evidence that the article functions as a demonstrative.[77] He briefly touches on the use of the article with proper names, noting that "scholarship has not yet solved completely the problem."[78]

In volume 2, *Accidence and Word Formation*, Moulton and Howard provide further insight into their classification of the article, "The forms of the Article should strictly be presented among the other Pronouns, to which it belongs by historical syntax."[79] However, they do not elaborate upon which pronoun(s) to which it was historically related. With regard to its function, they write, "the Article has detached itself for special functions answering generally to those of our own *the*."[80] In this we observe the continued general approach of explaining the article's function by means of general analogy with the English definite article. The authors clearly believe that the two are analogous.

---

[74] Moulton, *Prolegomena*, 80–81.
[75] Moulton, *Prolegomena*, 81.
[76] Moulton, *Prolegomena*, 81. See also Moulton and Howard, *Accidence and Word Formation*, "The forms of the Article should strictly be presented among the other Pronouns, to which it belongs by historical syntax" (117).
[77] Moulton, *Prolegomena*, 81.
[78] Moulton, *Prolegomena*, 83.
[79] Moulton and Howard, *Accidence and Word Formation*, 117.
[80] Moulton and Howard, *Accidence and Word Formation*, 117.

Moulton and Howard's treatment of the article is too brief to draw much by way of conclusions. However, we may observe a general consistency with the grammarians of the time regarding its origin and function. The article is essentially demonstrative and conforms to English *the*. They provide the reader with a few examples of its use. However, it is clearly not their intention to engage in a comprehensive treatment of the article's function in these volumes.

d. *A.T. Robertson*, A Grammar of the Greek New Testament *(1914)*

For his categorization of the Greek article, Robertson takes his cue from Kühner and Blass, quoting them directly: "Ο, ἡ, τό. This was the simplest demonstrative."[81] Robertson continues to follow the lead of the German grammarians[82] by stating that the Greek article "like *der* in German and *this* in English, was used either as demonstrative, article, or relative."[83] However, he quickly qualifies this by stating: "One is not to trace actual historical connection between ὁ and *der*."[84] Here his dependence upon German language Greek grammars is clearly evident. He also acknowledges a historical association with the relative pronoun, "The use of the *t* forms of ὁ, ἡ, τό as relative is very old in Greek."[85] Robertson cites numerous examples of its use as such.[86]

Like his predecessors and contemporaries, Robertson employs a diachronic approach. He affirms the historical and categorical relationship between the article and the demonstrative. Though he categorizes the article as a demonstrative, Robertson makes it clear that it does not function as such: "The article, unlike the demonstrative, does not point out the object as far or near. It is not deictic."[87] However, he clearly associates the article with some sort of deictic function: "The article is associated with gesture and aids in pointing out like an index finger. It is a pointer."[88]

---

[81] Robertson, *Grammar*, 693. See also 755, "The Greek article is the same form as the demonstrative ὁ, ἡ, τό."

[82] Robertson cites as an example Kühner and Gerth, *Ausführliche Grammatik der griechischen Sprache* Τ1, 575.

[83] Robertson, *Grammar*, 694. See also 711, and 755, "Indeed the German *der* is used as demonstrative, article, and relative."

[84] Robertson, *Grammar*, 694. He directs the reader to Brugmann, *Griechische Grammatik*, 559.

[85] Robertson, *Grammar*, 734.

[86] Robertson, *Grammar*, 734–35. The examples he cites are primarily outside the New Testament. Those found in the New Testament are mostly debatable, though he does not rule out the possibility that the article is being used as a relative.

[87] Robertson, *Grammar*, 755.

[88] Robertson, *Grammar*, 756.

Robertson acknowledges a historical connection to the relative pronoun, as well as the article's usage as relative. He even observes, "The article with the participle is very common as the equivalent of a relative clause."[89] However, this connection does not inform his grammar, which is based solely on the article's connection with the demonstrative pronoun.

He states clearly that definiteness is a quality associated with the article. It "is therefore τὸ ὁριστικὸν ἄρθρον, the definite article."[90] As a result, "Whenever the Greek article occurs, the object is certainly definite. When it is not used, the object may or may not be."[91] He does not suggest that this is the primary function of the article: "The Greek article is not the only means of making words definite."[92] In fact, though he considers it "very convenient and useful," the article "is not essential to language."[93] Thus, Robertson reveals a perspective on the article observed earlier in Winer: the article does not modify the head term but reflects a quality already inherent, which results in the view that the article is useful but not necessary.

To his credit, Robertson's treatment is quite exhaustive; he dedicates an entire chapter to it as well as additional treatment under the pronoun heading. Like the ancients, he categorizes it as τὸ ἄρθρον.[94] His methodology is essentially the same of the Classical Greek grammarians. Rather than develop an overarching theory that describes the article's usage, he enumerates a lengthy and diverse series of categories which seek to provide a comprehensive presentation of the article's multitudinous usages. These categories are, for the most part, based on the article's use with individual parts of speech: substantives, proper names, adjectives, etc. He also categorizes its usage based on usage according to case and position. This methodology, the physical length in pages, and plethora of categories, create a sense of exhaustiveness. However, it does not translate into a succinct, comprehensive theory of usage. Instead, the reader is left with the impression that there are a dizzying variety of functions that must be identified on a case by case basis and are determined by the article's syntactical relations, not an overarching function it inherently possesses. Thus, both his methodology and results leave much room for scrutiny and improvement.

---

[89] Robertson, *Grammar*, 764.
[90] Robertson, *Grammar*, 756.
[91] Robertson, *Grammar*, 756.
[92] Robertson, *Grammar*, 756.
[93] Robertson, *Grammar*, 756.
[94] Robertson, *Grammar*, 754.

e. *H.E. Dana & J.R. Mantey*, A Manual Grammar of the Greek
New Testament *(1927)*

Dana and Mantey begin their treatment of the article by stating, "Nothing is more indigenous to the Greek language than its use of the article."[95] This is an important observation and should caution the reader against too easily employing one for one comparison with the English definite article. Rather, the Greek article must be understood "indigenously," without the imposition of foreign notions and categories. They write about the Greek article with exuberance: "It is also true that we are entering one of the most fascinating fields of linguistic research, for, without a doubt, 'the development of the Greek article is one of the most interesting things in human speech.'"[96]

Regarding the article's origin and development they write:

> The article was originally derived from the demonstrative pronoun ὁ, ἡ, τό, and is clearly akin to the relative pronoun ὅς, ἥ, ὅ. It always retained some of the demonstrative force. This fact is evidenced by its frequent use in the papyri purely as a demonstrative pronoun (e.g., *P. Elph.* 1.15). Robertson says, "Hence ὁ is originally a demonstrative that was gradually weakened to the article or heightened to the relative."[97]

Dana and Mantey's volume, first published in 1927, draws upon earlier work of A.T. Robertson: *A Short Grammar of the Greek New Testament* (1908), and *A Grammar of the Greek New Testament* (1914). In the quotation above, they separate themselves from previous writers. While many (if not most) grammarians emphasize the demonstrative force of the article, the authors seem to take greater notice of its relationship to the relative pronoun. Their citation of Robertson's *Short Grammar* is instructive and insightful. By assigning greater credence to the relationship between the article and the relative pronoun, they separate themselves from their predecessors.

Despite this insight, Dana and Mantey understand the function of the article identically with their contemporaries: "The function of the article is to point out an object or to draw attention to it."[98] Specifically, they cite Robertson's statement that, when the article is present, "the object

---

[95] Dana & Mantey, *Manual Grammar*, 135.
[96] Dana & Mantey, *Manual Grammar*, 136. Citing Robertston, *Grammar*, 754.
[97] Dana & Mantey, *Manual Grammar*, 136. Citing Robertson, *Short Grammar*, 68.
[98] Dana & Mantey, *Manual Grammar*, 137.

is certainly definite."[99] They perpetuate the view that the article does not modify the head term, but instead simply draws attention to it, performing a deictic function. Their view of the article's function is structural, rather than a part of speech that impacts the meaning of the head term: "In harmony with its basal significance there are certain constructions in which the article is normally used."[100] Thus, while the authors reflect an advanced perspective into the Greek article's close relationship with the relative pronoun (drawn from Robertson), regarding its function they are in agreement with contemporary grammars.

f. C.F.D. Moule, Idiom Book of New Testament Greek (1953)

Moule demonstrates the same attachment to the English definite article as his predecessors, "Βασιλεύς, a *king*, but ὁ Βασιλεύς, the (*particular*) *king* (*in question*)."[101] At the same time he demonstrates a unique insight into its usage:

> [The article] also offers (when used before a participle or adjective) a neat way of expressing what would otherwise have to be expressed by a relative clause: instead of ὃς ἔρχεται one may say ὁ ἐρχόμενος; for ὃ περισσεύει one may say τὸ περισσεῦον. In Acts xiii. 9 we have Σαῦλος δέ, ὁ καὶ Παῦλος, where *who is also Paul* is expressed by the article conjoined with the name, without even a participle like ὤν or λεγόμενος. As an illustration of how the article with participle can be interchanged with a relative clause, take Rom. ii. 21–3 ὁ οὖν διδάσκων ἕτερον... ὁ κηρύσσων... ὁ λέγων... ὁ βδελυσσόμενος, followed by the relative clause ὃς ἐν νόμῳ καυχᾶσαι (which is clearly an exact parallel to the preceding clauses); or Matt. vii. 24, 26 πᾶς οὖν ὅστις ἀκούσει... πᾶς ὁ ἀκούων.[102]

On this point Moule expresses an understanding of the article's function that draws near to that which will be argued below. Though he does not categorize the article along with the relative pronoun, it is this recognition that the article is often used to produce structures that function as a relative clause that strongly suggests that the article and relative pronoun may be jointly classified.

Moule does not engage in a systematic, comprehensive treatment of the article; his presentation is relatively brief. He merely provides the reader

---

99 Dana & Mantey, *Manual Grammar*, 137. Citing Robertson, *Grammar*, 756.
100 Dana & Mantey, *Manual Grammar*, 141.
101 Moule, *Idiom Book*, 106.
102 Moule, *Idiom Book*, 106.

with some examples of the article's use that illustrate his understanding of the article's function.

g. *Friedrich Blass & Albert Debrunner,* A Greek Grammar of the New Testament and other Early Christian Literature *(1961),* Translated by R.W. Funk

The first edition of Blass's grammar was published in German in 1896. At the printing of the fourth edition in 1913, it received a thorough "linguistic revision" by Albert Debrunner, focusing primarily on "the sections on phonology and accidence."[103] Debrunner further revised the seventh edition in 1943, at which time he altered the format and added new manuscript material.[104] Robert Funk provided English speaking Greek grammarians with a translation of this classic work, which was published in 1961. The chapter on the article is introduced with a brief history of its origin in both form and use:

> The original use of ὁ ἡ τό as a demonstrative pronoun is retained in classical usage in certain fixed phrases; the forms of the old relative pronoun ὅς ἥ ὅ replace it occasionally in classical and more frequently in Hellenistic times. The origin of this confusion was, on the one hand, the old sigmatic alternative form of ὁ: ὅς which in Greek had become identical with the relative form; and, on the other, the Epic and dialectal use of ὁ ἡ τό as a relative pronoun (cf. The article *der* in German which serves as article, relative and demonstrative; in English *that* is both demonstrative and relative and is related to the article).[105]

This treatment of the article represents, on the one hand, a fuller treatment of the article and its relationship to the demonstrative and relative pronouns, while on the other hand illustrates the difficulty in classifying it (is it demonstrative or relative?). In both form and function, Blass and Debrunner recognize the relationship of the article to the relative pronoun. In classification, however, they place it in the category of demonstrative.

Blass and Debrunner continue the same methodology as their predecessors. Their grammar lacks an overarching theory that describes the function of the article. Instead, they present the reader with a succession of categories that illustrate its diversity of usage. As with Robertson and

---

[103] Blass and Debrunner, *Greek Grammar,* ix.
[104] Blass and Debrunner, *Greek Grammar,* xi.
[105] Blass and Debrunner, *Greek Grammar,* 131.

the classical grammarians, this leaves the reader with the perception that the article lacks a functional relationship to the parts of speech to which it is affixed, modifying them in some way.

h. *N. Turner*, A Grammar of New Testament Greek. III. Syntax *(1963)*.
IV Style (1976)

In the third volume of the grammar begun by J.H. Moulton, Nigel Turner follows the standard diachronic approach of tracing the origin of the article to the demonstrative pronoun, "In the beginning the def. art. grew out of the old demonstrative pronoun in Homer: *this one, he.*"[106] However, he is emphatic that, in the New Testament, it never functions as a relative pronoun and only rarely as a demonstrative.[107]

Syntactically, Turner addresses the article's use under several categories. He begins volume three with the observation that adjectives and attributive adverbs with the article may serve as substitutes for nouns in subject, object, and predicate.[108] Next he addresses the *substantival article*, of which he writes, "[it] has always preserved its demonstrative force."[109] The phrases in the Greek manuscripts τὸ καὶ τό, τὰ καὶ τά are translated *this and that.*[110] Thus, in use "it separates some from others, individualizing something as this and not that."[111] Similarly, the *adjectival article* "particularizes an individual member of a group or class."[112] In all this, Turner does not appear to be concerned with the *effect* the article has upon the head term or part of speech it modifies. Rather, he is concerned only with its presence, which is the identifying mark of certain syntactical patterns. Its use is not based on a functional relationship to the head term, but is determined by idiomatic constructions that will ordinarily demand its presence or absence.[113] These constructions are arranged into a wide variety of classifications or categories. Turner also believes that the

---

[106] Turner, *Syntax*, 36.

[107] Turner, *Syntax*, 36, 165. The only exceptions he cites are when it is used with μέν and δέ, and in the poetic quotations in Acts 17:28.

[108] Turner, *Syntax*, 13–16.

[109] Turner, *Syntax*, 36.

[110] Turner, *Syntax*, 36.

[111] Turner, *Syntax*, 36.

[112] Turner, *Syntax*, 165.

[113] See, for example, his assessment of 1 Peter 3:19, 20: "The omission of the article is not good Greek at 3[19.20] when the participle follows a definite antecedent. There are times when no good reason is evident for the omission." Turner, *Style*, 129.

presence or absence of the article may be the result of influence from the Hebrew language:

> Perhaps the omission of the definite article on occasions when normal Greek requires it betrays the habit of thinking in terms of the construct state...However, sometimes Hebrew idiom will influence the Greek writers toward a needless insertion of the article, reflecting the emphatic state in which a noun is made more definite in order to denote a special person or object.[114]

What is lacking is a single, overarching theory of the article's function that may account for its presence or absence in each category. Though he does not say so explicitly, Turner's treatment seems to reflect the same despair expressed by Buttman: while one may be able to formulate rules governing the use of the article, he or she must expect that those rules will not be universally or uniformly followed.[115] Indeed, regarding the use of the article in the book of Revelation he writes: "The use is as arbitrary as in all Biblical Greek literature."[116] This leads Turner to conclude that speakers and writers enjoyed freedom with regard to the use or non-use of the article,

> Considering the total use of the article, it is true that the higher the type of Greek above ordinary speech the less prolific is the use of the article, so that whereas Atticistic style keeps fairly close to the norm established by Attic prose popular speech uses the article freely.[117]

If such freedom did indeed exist, then one will rightly conclude that the article was not a necessity of speech, that by its nature it had no effect upon the parts of speech it modified. However, if it can be demonstrated that there is a functional relationship between the article and the head term, then this notion of free use is called into question.

One observation Turner makes is worth special consideration, as it relates to the central premise of the thesis that will be presented below. With regard to abstract nouns he writes,

> They tend to be anarthrous if there is greater emphasis on the abstract quality, but no vital difference was felt in class. Greek; the passage is too easy from articular to anarthrous...omission of the art. tends to emphasize the

---

[114] Turner, *Style*, 33. See also 153.

[115] See, for example, Turner's remarks regarding The Individual Article with Common Nouns, "the art. is often omitted where we expect it by the rules." Turner, *Syntax*, 173.

[116] Turner, *Style*, 153.

[117] Turner, *Syntax*, 36.

inherent qualities of abstract nouns while the art. makes them more concrete, unified and individual...The difficulty therefore is to account for the
presence of the art., just as with concrete nouns the problem is rather to
account for its absence.[118]

Turner's language suggests he may have sensed something that he was
unable to quantify. As with others, this was likely due to the assumptions that he brought to his analysis. It will be argued below that it is not
merely the use of the article with abstract or concrete nouns that must be
accounted for. Rather, its inherent "substantivizing" function determines
its presence and absence and is what makes a part of speech concrete or
abstract respectively, particularly when that part of speech is a noun.

From this survey of Turner's treatment of the Greek article, we conclude that he categorized the Greek article as a demonstrative. Though he
acknowledges a historical association with the relative pronoun, this does
not inform his grammar. His understanding of the function of the article
is based on kinship with the demonstrative, resulting in perceived parallel
with English *the*. He provides the reader with a handful of examples that
are illustrative, in his estimation, of the article's function, without engaging in a methodologically rigorous or exhaustive treatment. The presence
or absence of the article is a matter of syntax, rather than functioning
as an item that modifies the head term. Ultimately, its employment is
arbitrary.

i. *Maximilian Zerwick*, Biblical Greek Illustrated by Examples *(1963)*

Zerwick begins his treatment of the article by stating, "The function of
the article is to point out (it was in origin a demonstrative), to determine, to set apart from others, to identify as *this* or *these* and not simply
'such'."[119] It is his last statement, that the article functions, "to identify
as *this* or *these* and not simply 'such'," that approaches the description
of the article's function that will be presented below, though it requires
correction. The identification of the article with *this* or *these* reflects a
continuation of the influence of the sense of the demonstrative, and thus
definiteness. However, by recognizing that its absence reflects the sense of
such, Zerwick reflects an understanding that will also be developed below.
He later expands this point:

---

[118] Turner, *Syntax*, 176–77.
[119] Zerwick, *Biblical Greek*, 53.

> The *omission* of the article shows that the speaker regards the person or
> thing not so much as this or that person or thing, but rather as *such* a person
> or thing, i.e. regards not the individual but rather its nature or quality.[120]

Though close, this statement may be nuanced in such a way to more accurately reflect the article's function. In this manner, by more accurately
describing a word's sense apart from the article, we will also more accurately understand the change to its sense when the article is present.

Like those before him, Zerwick does not articulate a clear methodology
by which he arrives at his conclusions. He briefly provides the reader with
a statement regarding the role of the article and then provides several
pages worth of examples of its various uses. In this he follows the pattern
of previous grammars, though in abridged form. His grammar does not
reflect any advancement in the methodology of the study of the article or
a description of its function.

j. *Robert Funk*, A Beginning-Intermediate Grammar of Hellenistic Greek (*1973*)

In his *Personal Word* at the beginning of the first volume of his grammar,
Funk draws attention to the importance of modern linguistics to the study
of language, stating that "a revolution had taken place in the study and
learning of language."[121] Accordingly, he attempts to utilize the insights of
linguistics in his treatment of the language. Most notably, he categorizes
his work as a "descriptive grammar."[122]

Despite this commitment to modern linguistics, Funk's grammar shows
no advancement in an understanding of the function of the article. In fact,
it is simply a repetition of what has come before.

> The Greek article was originally a demonstrative pronoun (it was so used in
> Homer). It was subsequently weakened to the status of article, then serving
> merely as a pointer. Cf. the article *der* in German, which serves as article,
> relative, and demonstrative pronoun; in English *that* is both demonstrative
> and relative and is related to the article. In Greek the article is definite.
> Greek does not, strictly speaking, have an indefinite article (corresponding
> to *a, an* in English).
>
> For the most part, the article functions in Greek as it does in English.
> A number of the idiomatic uses of the article in Greek can be learned by
> observation, and will occasion no difficulty.[123]

---

[120] Zerwick, *Biblical Greek*, 55.
[121] Funk, *Beginning-Intermediate Grammar Vol. 1*, xxvi.
[122] Funk, *Beginning-Intermediate Grammar Vol. 1*, 14.
[123] Funk, *Beginning-Intermediate Grammar Vol. 1*, 79, see also 197.

Categorically, the article is placed under "Determiners" and functions accordingly in that its head term is determined to be *individualized, generic*, or *par excellence*.[124] Funk echoes the perception of previous writers that the article is essentially a demonstrative, that it indicates definiteness, and functions in a manner parallel to German *der* and English *the*.

Despite any lack of progress in his presentation of the article's classification, Funk's linguistic sensitivities are an advancement reflected in his treatment of the article's function above the level of word group (foreshadowing the work of discourse analysis). He argues that the article is used to signal structure.[125] While this signaling function is mostly seen in the word group, Funk argues that the article also indicates "changes in the speaker in a dialogue or shifts in subject matter," which he attributes to its demonstrative function.[126] The influence of modern linguistics hints at a shift in methodology regarding the study of the Greek language as a whole, if not the article specifically. Viewing the article in terms of structure, however, illustrates that Funk understands the article's function to be a matter of syntax, rather than having an impact on the meaning of the head term.

k. *J.A. Brooks & C.L. Winbery*, Syntax of New Testament Greek *(1979)*

The view of the Greek article as the *definite* article persisted well into the late 20th century, as evidenced by Brooks and Winbery's *Syntax of New Testament Greek*:

> The basic function of the Greek article is to point out, to draw attention to, to identify, to make definite, to define, to limit. Generally, though not always, substantives with the article are definite or generic, while those without the article are indefinite or qualitative. It would probably be an accurate summary statement to say that the presence of the article emphasizes identity, the absence of the article quality.[127]

Thus, we see retention of the notion of *definiteness* attached to the article. However, Brooks and Winbery do advance a notion that is consistent with what will be later argued, that the article emphasizes *identity*, while its absence emphasizes *quality*.

---

[124] Funk, *Beginning-Intermediate Grammar Vol. 2*, 555.
[125] Funk, *Beginning-Intermediate Grammar Vol. 1*, 85–86.
[126] Funk, *Beginning-Intermediate Grammar Vol. 1*, 86.
[127] Brooks and Winbery, *Syntax*, 73.

the articular "qualitative" and the anarthrous "categorical."[133] This reality challenges the notion of determining definiteness based on the presence or absence of the article. Such determinations "must be made on the basis of the wider context."[134]

As a whole, Porter's grammar is influenced by and employs the principles of modern linguistics, including his treatment of the article. He is rightly critical of grammarians who seek to explain its usage based on a historic relationship with the demonstrative pronoun.[135] It is beyond the scope of his book to engage in an exhaustive treatment of the article, thus he offers the reader several examples that are illustrative of distinctive uses. The use of linguistics, combined with a synchronic approach to the study of the Greek language, reflects a significant advancement in the field.

m. *Daniel B. Wallace*, Greek Grammar: Beyond the Basics *(1996)*

On the one hand, Wallace's grammar includes certain elements that reflect advancement in the understanding of the Greek article. On the other, he maintains much of the old.

With regard to the origin of the Greek article, Wallace writes:

> The article was originally derived from the demonstrative pronoun. That is, its original force was to *point out* something. It has largely kept the force of drawing attention to something.[136]

Thus he maintains the traditional view of the article's origin as a demonstrative, as well as its basic *pointing* function. Conversely, Wallace recognizes the non-definite nature of the article:

> The function of the article is *not* primarily to make something definite that would otherwise be indefinite. It does *not* primarily "definitize."... No one questions that the article is used frequently to definitize, but whether this captures the essential idea is another matter.[137]

After making a clear assertion of what the Greek article is not, or does not do, Wallace writes regarding what the article does do: "At bottom, the article intrinsically has the ability to *conceptualize*... [It] is able to turn

---

[133] Porter, *Idioms*, 104. His scheme is an adaptation from Carson, *Exegetical Fallacies*, 82–84.

[134] Porter, *Idioms*, 104.

[135] Porter, *Idioms*, 106.

[136] Wallace, *Greek Grammar*, 208.

[137] Wallace, *Greek Grammar*, 209.

just about any part of speech into a noun, and therefore, a concept."[138] He goes on to say, "In terms of basic force, the article conceptualizes. In terms of predominant *function*, it *identifies*. That is to say, it is used predominantly to stress the identity of an individual or class or quality."[139] Wallace's use of the term *conceptualize* is questionable due to its ambiguity. At some level, any part of speech is a concept. They may be conceptualized as an abstraction or something concrete. The terms *concept* and *noun* are presented as synonyms, which is also questionable. In addition, by an overwhelming margin, the majority of occurrences of the article in the New Testament have nouns as a head term. If the article turns its head term into a noun, one is still left to question what it does with nouns. Wallace's definition of the article's force ends up applying to a small minority of occurrences and is ultimately not very useful. As noted in earlier grammars, his association of the article's function with *identity* draws near the mark, but requires further development.

Wallace allows that the article functions as a relative pronoun, but believes that when translated this way, it is a matter of accommodation to English:

> To say that the article is functioning like a relative pronoun is only an *English* way of looking at the matter. Thus it is not truly the semantic force of the article ... We translate it as a relative pronoun because this is less cumbersome than something like "our Father, the [one] in heaven."[140]

The question that drives the following treatment of the article grows from this type of assertion. Why does Wallace not allow for the possibility that this usage provides insight into the Greek article's function? In part, the answer lies in his methodology, which favors traditional grammar over modern linguistic theory, with the result that many of his conclusions are based on translation equivalency.[141] The fact that the translation he provides is cumbersome does not mean that this is not how Greek speakers used the article. What is perceived as cumbersome to one who speaks English may be perfectly natural to one who speaks Greek. Wallace, like many others, interprets the Greek usage of the article by employing English as the baseline for comparison. What Wallace rejects will in

---

[138] Wallace, *Greek Grammar*, 209.
[139] Wallace, *Greek Grammar*, 209–10.
[140] Wallace, *Greek Grammar*, 214.
[141] Though Wallace asserts, "I use linguistics," it is not at all evident that his methodology is driven by modern linguistic theory, Wallace, *Greek Grammar*, xviii.

fact be used in the following grammar as the defining characteristic of the article's function.

While his grammar reflects advances in the grammar of the article, Wallace's treatment suffers from several weaknesses, many of which stem from a single systemic source: they are based on English language categories. First, a more accurate grammar of the article requires better terminology. As noted, to say that the article is able to turn virtually any part of speech into a noun is true in a sense, but ultimately unsatisfactory, since one of its most frequent uses is with nouns. Wallace is closer to the heart of the article's function when he says that it *identifies*, though this also needs modification. Second, though exhaustive, Wallace's plethora of categories of use is based on *dynamic* equivalence, rather than true correspondence. While it's true that the various uses of the article will result in an even wider diversity of translations, it is methodologically inappropriate to use these multi-various translations as the basis for categorization. Categories of usage should grow organically from the language itself. Third, many of his categories rest on analogy with the English definite article, despite Wallace's admitted recognition that the two articles are not functionally equivalent. Categories such as his *Monadic ("One of a Kind" or "Unique" Article)*,[142] or *Well Known ("Celebrity" or "Familiar" Article)*,[143] assume a one-for-one functional correspondence with the English definite article. In English, when the definite article is so employed, it is typically accompanied by change of inflection: italics in writing (*the* article) or rising vocal pitch in speaking. Additionally, these categories only work in English because of the inherent *definiteness* of the article. Since definiteness in Greek is established by more than the presence of the article (even if it is a component of the process), categories requiring definiteness should not rest on the presence of the article alone. Fourth, Wallace's emphasis on categories represents a continuation of his predecessors' methodology, taking their proliferation *ad infinitum*, if not *ad absurdum*. The lack of an overarching theory means that there is nothing that governs, informs, and most importantly limits, this multiplication of categories. Instead of alleviating the weaknesses of his predecessors, he exacerbates them. Wallace's grammar represents progression in the understanding of the article. However, it suffers from weaknesses based on problems of methodology.

---

[142] Wallace, *Greek Grammar*, 223.
[143] Wallace, *Greek Grammar*, 225.

n. *Conclusion*

The most notable advancement in the grammar of the article is the rejection of the concept of definiteness. The article is not definite, nor does it reflect definiteness on the part of items it modifies. However, there is still a strong tendency to explain the article's function by means of analogy with the English definite article. On the one hand, this is understandable. Between the two articles in English, the definite article bears the strongest resemblance to the Greek article. On the other hand, even though it is recognized that too close an association is problematic, the Greek article is still defined in terms of correspondence to, or deviation from, the English definite article. As seen in Wallace, categories of usage are too often based on dynamic equivalence. In the end, definiteness is denied in principle, but reinforced in practice.

At a broad level of categorization, the article continues to be associated with the old demonstrative. This association is uneven throughout the grammars: some emphasize this more, others less. However, this continues to inform the function of the article, as seen in Wallace's emphasis on its pointing force. Though there is, at times, recognition that the article is related to the relative pronoun, this recognition does not inform its grammar. A synchronic study of the article will reveal that the historical association with the demonstrative has played too large a role, while association with the relative pronoun has been either neglected or given minimal relevance.

Most importantly, there continues to be a need for a single, overarching theory that accounts for the article's function. The reason this remains elusive is due in large part to a sense of exasperation regarding the article's function with nouns. As stated above, it will be argued that this is the result of a misunderstanding of the nature of Greek nouns in general. Historically, it has been assumed that nouns in particular are substantive by their nature. I wish to ask the following question: "If the article turns any part of speech into a substantive, how does this inform our understanding of its function with nouns?" A logical conclusion is that it performs the same function with nouns. This leads to the further conclusion that, apart from the article, nouns are not substantive. If this is true, it reveals that the historical problem of the article lies in inaccurate assumptions and terminology regarding not only the article itself but also the parts of speech it modifies. Carrying this substantivizing function over to nouns enables us to formulate a single, overarching theory of use. In addition, it will demonstrate that the basic use of the article is far from arbitrary. It is

not a matter of mere personal whimsy or idiomatic syntactical constructions. Rather, it is a necessary part of speech with clearly defined rules
that result in fairly uniform usage.[144] Speakers and writers of Greek knew,
at least intuitively, when to use it and why.

5. The Article in Beginning Biblical Greek Grammars

The importance of a quality beginning Greek grammar cannot be over-
stated. In an ideal world, students of the language would continue their
education by means of a thorough study of intermediate and advanced
grammars. Their exegesis of the original text would be informed primarily
by what they learned from this study. In practice, it is too often the case
that the knowledge acquired in beginning Greek is the primary grammar
that informs the interpreter. When questions of grammar arise, it is the
beginning Greek textbook, that tried and true friend from college, which
is first consulted.[145] This reality, as much as anything, explains much of
the misinformation that persists regarding the function of the article, as
is demonstrated below.

a. *J.H. Moulton*, An Introduction to the Study of New Testament Greek *(1895)*

The origin of the Greek article is explained by Moulton thus, "As in English, the definite article (ὁ, ἡ, τό,) was once a demonstrative pronoun."[146]
By citing parallel origin, and by implication parallel lines of development,
it is only natural for a scholar to conclude that the Greek article and the
English definite article will consequently function in a parallel manner. So
Moulton, "[T]he article answers to our *the*; and in all cases which do not
come under the rules following, the student must be careful to translate
it by *the*, omitting *the* in English as far as possible where the Greek does

---

[144] I say "fairly uniform" since no one living now or in the first century uses perfect
grammar at all times. When dealing with language, one must make allowances for grammatical slips in speech and writing. "Fairly uniform" means that the theory I will advance
accounts for usage in the overwhelming majority of occurrences, if not all.

[145] This is not merely my own observation: "Students tend to retain their first-year
grammar as the 'bible' that guides all of their further study." Porter et al., *Fundamentals of
New Testament Greek*, x.

[146] Moulton, *Introduction*, 157.

not show it."[147] In this we see the author reflecting the same perspective as his predecessors.

With regard to the article's function, Moulton's primary observation is that it can turn various parts of speech, such as adjectives, adverbs, or even a collection of words, into a noun.[148] By this he communicates what is universally accepted. However, this leaves the student or grammarian with one last difficulty: if the article converts various parts of speech into a noun, what does it convert nouns into? It is this very question that will be addressed in the grammar proposed below.

b. *J. Gresham Machen*, New Testament Greek for Beginners *(1928)*

Machen's treatment of the Greek article is very brief. However, it is illustrative of the prevailing perspective at the time his grammar was written.

> The use of the article in Greek corresponds roughly to the use of the definite article in English. Thus λόγος mean *a word; ὁ λόγος* mean *the word;* λόγοι means *words;* οἱ λόγοι means *the words.* The differences between the Greek and English use of the article must be learned by observation, as they occur. For the present, the presence or absence of the Greek article should always be carefully indicated in the English translation.[149]

By paralleling the Greek article with the English definite article, even if roughly so, Machen creates a perception that the two are indeed, in essence, of like kind. Differences are perceived as variations from this norm. Though he does not elaborate further, the student who learns Greek from this textbook comes away believing that concepts such as definiteness and indefiniteness are determined by the presence and absence of the Greek article, respectively.

Machen's treatment of the article is very brief. He simply provides the student with the paradigm, discusses the matter of agreement between the article and the word it modifies, and devotes a single paragraph to its function (cited in its entirety above). Thus, we are left with no insight into the methodology he employs for arriving at his conclusions or his rationale. As an introductory primer to the language, a brief treatment is to be expected. However, it also illustrates how inaccurate grammar can lay a foundation of misinformation that is difficult to overturn, especially when an argument or theory becomes a structure built on that foundation.

---

[147] Moulton, *Introduction*, 158.
[148] Moulton, *Introduction*, 157–58.
[149] Machen, *New Testament Greek*, 35.

c. *Ray Summers*, Essentials of New Testament Greek *(1950)*

The treatment of the article in Summers' grammar is also very brief. While he informs the student that Greek lacks an indefinite article, he states conversely that it does have a definite article, thus "ὁ ἄνθρωπος means 'the man.' "[150] He then goes on to instruct the reader, "Do not insert an English 'the' in the translation unless the Greek article appears; do not insert a Greek 'ὁ' unless the English 'the' appears."[151] Consciously or unconsciously, Summers has laid a foundation that will be difficult for his students to overturn.

While the pragmatics of Summers' presentation leave the reader with an inaccurate understanding of the article, his short treatment of its function closely approximates the argument that will be made below, "The Greek article is used to point out particular *identity* . . . The anarthrous construction is used to indicate quality or characteristics."[152] Though on the right track, this definition requires some modification and expansion. The problem with the author's presentation lies in the lack of reinforcement of this understanding. By encouraging a one-for-one procedure, translating the Greek article by the English definite article, the student is trained to think in terms of a one-for-one correspondence in function as well.

d. *J.W. Wenham*, The Elements of New Testament Greek *(1965)*

First published in 1965, Wenham's book is based on H.P.V. Nunn's work.[153] Since then it has been through multiple reprints, a reprint with corrections in 1999, and several more reprints, testifying to its popularity and influence. He first informs the reader that,

---

[150] Summers, *Essentials*, 16.
[151] Summers, *Essentials*, 16.
[152] Summers, *Essentials*, 16.
[153] H.P.V. Nunn, *Key to the Elements of New Testament Greek*. In his preface, Wenham acknowledges that the publishers allowed him "if necessary, to write a new book, leaning heavily on Nunn," with the result that, "As work on the book progressed, so the possibilities of improvement seemed to multiply. The result in the end has been literally thousands of changes, many very small but many quite considerable." *The Elements of New Testament Greek*, vi. The nature of these changes was the simplification of the third-declension, conditional sentences, and -μι verbs, as well as the omission of virtually all accents, *Elements*, vii. Other changes involved replacing the uncommon words of the original with more common ones, as well as general rearrangement of the material, *Elements*, viii–ix. No mention is made of any alterations of material pertaining to the treatment of the article.

There is no indefinite article in Greek. When, therefore, a word like λογος
stands alone, it usually means 'a word'. But it can mean simply 'word'. The
right translation is nearly always obvious from the context.[154]

Implicit in Wenham's statement is a belief that the nature or meaning
of a particular lexical item is self-evident and that the translator or exegete may rely on his or her instincts to correctly draw a conclusion. One
would hope that the flaw in this mentality would be just as self-evident.
It places interpretation solely in the realm of the subjective inclinations
of the interpreter, offering no objective means by which an interpretation may be measured or tested. If English speakers could read the Greek
New Testament with such ease of intuition, there would be no need for
advanced grammars to explain how the two languages accomplish the
same communicative tasks in such different ways. Nor would beginning
Greek students suffer the cognitive dissonance so often felt when learning
Greek, especially when confronted with the article. Translators do indeed
need a comprehensive theory of the article's function in order to guide
and test both translation and interpretation. Surprisingly, though Wenhem provides the reader with the full paradigm of the Greek article, he
offers no significant explanation of its function.

e. *Huber L. Drumwright*, An Introduction to New Testament Greek *(1980)*

Drumwright provides the student with virtually no insight into the article's function. Regarding anarthrous constructions he writes, "The student may translate an indefinite article if the context in Greek and the
English idiom combine to suggest the appropriateness of such."[155] One
is left to ask what contextual features the reader should look for in order
to make this determination. Nor is the reader provided insight into the
kinds of English idioms that might combine the enigmatic Greek contextual features in order to derive the correct translation. Like Wenhem, he
apparently thinks this is self-evident. An argument has already been made
against this perception above.

The author is equally unhelpful regarding articular constructions. The
closest he comes to a functional explanation is in the implication underlying his statement regarding grammatical concord, "The definite article
'the' in Greek must agree in number, gender, and case with the noun it

---

154 Wenham, *Elements*, 30.
155 Drumwright, *Introduction*, 28.

modifies."[156] The reader must imply from this statement that the appropriate translation of the Greek article is simply "the."

f. *William D. Mounce*, Basics of Biblical Greek, 3rd ed. *(2009)*

The first edition of Mounce's grammar was published in 1993. Now in its third edition, it has become one of the most popular textbooks for professors teaching beginning New Testament Greek (at least this is the claim made on the back cover). As a result, many, if not the majority, of current and future generations of students will have had their understanding of the Greek article shaped primarily, if not exclusively, by this textbook.

Mounce introduces the Greek article as the "definite article" but quickly provides the following qualification, "There is no indefinite article ... For this reason you can refer to the Greek article simply as the 'article.' "[157] This simple, seemingly innocuous, statement represents a progression in the understanding of the article. Mounce's treatment works from the modern recognition that the presence of the article does not indicate definiteness. Thus, the label "definite article" is inaccurate and deceptive.

Regarding translation, he encourages students to employ English "the."[158] However, he quickly qualifies this recommendation, informing the reader that Greek speakers "do not use the article the same way we do," which requires the student to be "a little flexible."[159] By addressing this in his grammar, Mounce brings this reality to the student's attention, which is commendable. Unfortunately, he does not provide a more helpful alternative gloss that might be employed in instances where *the* is inadequate or confusing.

Further into his grammar, Mounce expands the reader's understanding of the article.

> The article in Greek is much more than just the word "the." It is a "weak demonstrative," which means it can perform as a demonstrative ("that"), a relative ("who"), or even a personal pronoun ("he," "one"), depending on the needs of the context. You will usually have to add a word into your translation to help, such as "who" or "which." Let the context determine which is appropriate.

---

[156] Drumwright, *Introduction*, 28.
[157] Mounce, *Basics of Biblical Greek*, 35.
[158] Mounce, *Basics of Biblical Greek*, 37.
[159] Mounce, *Basics of Biblical Greek*, 37.

What appears to be driving Mounce's methodology, and that of other recent grammars as well, is an approach that is based on translation equivalency. The student is led to believe that, because we have to represent a certain part of speech in Greek by a certain part of speech in English, we can read the semantics and function of the English representative back into the original Greek. While we may, indeed, represent the article by a variety of English lexical items, this does not demonstrate functional correspondence. The grammar of the Greek is based on English analogy, rather than observations and conclusions that are based on the native linguistic environment. While this may simplify the student's ability to produce a comfortable English translation, it does not empower him or her to understand Greek.

In the final chapter of his grammar, Mounce provides the student with what is meant to be a more detailed description of the article's function. Ultimately, though presented as "functions," his presentation is a succession of diverse "usages" that lack a single, overarching theory that provides unity, and necessary limitation, to the diversity.

In the final analysis, it can be positively said that Mounce's grammar reflects advancements in our understanding of the Greek article, while negatively leaving much room for improvement.

g. *S.E. Porter, J.T. Reed, and M.B. O'Donnell*, Fundamentals of New Testament Greek *(2010)*

This most recent addition to the plethora of beginning Greek grammars brings with it a fundamental shift in pedagogical philosophy with regard to beginning Greek grammar, as well as in theory as the authors bring a more linguistically based approach than classically oriented grammars. The authors have altogether abandoned the appellation "definite" and refer to the Greek article as "the Article," recognizing that "It is misleading to refer to the Greek article as the *definite* article."[160] Having said this, though, they retain the language of definiteness, stating that the article does indeed sometimes mark definiteness.[161] If we recognize, as the authors do, that definiteness in Greek is not a function of the article, then persistence in usage of the terminology merely perpetuates inaccuracy.

---

[160] Porter et al., *Fundamentals*, 30.
[161] Porter et al., *Fundamentals*, 30.

The authors briefly address the substantivizing function of the article, particularly in regard to adjectives[162] and participles.[163]

h. *Conclusion*

A few observations may be made about the treatment of the article in beginning Greek grammars. First, it must be admitted that beginning grammars are just that, they are designed to provide an introduction and to lay a foundation. No element of grammar will be treated exhaustively. However, it must be equally recognized that a poor or faulty foundation will result in an unstable structure. The presentation of the article in a beginning grammar will of necessity be incomplete. However, if in its attempt to simplify it sets the student off plumb from the very beginning (to continue the foundation metaphor), then it has let the student down. For some authors, this may be the result of assigning the article value that is in direct proportion to size (being arguably the smallest lexical item in the language). As James writes in his epistle, small things can have a big impact (Jas 3:1–12).

Second, on a more positive note, one can observe progress in more recent grammars regarding the function of the article. Much of what was taken for granted in previous grammars, such as one-for-one correspondence with *the*, as well as absolute notions of definiteness, have been either heavily qualified or abandoned. However, in the absence of any recent comprehensive treatment of the article, authors do not have any positive new material to incorporate into their grammars. They can communicate to the student how it does not work, but are left to use outdated categories and descriptions to communicate how it does function.

Third, there remains a strong current associating the article with the category of *demonstrative*. As long as this persists, grammarians will continue to describe its function within this theoretical framework. A more accurate broad category must be proposed in which the article more naturally belongs.

Fourth, students are either given too few options with regard to gloss (simply *the*), or too many (*the, he, that, who, etc.*) without any kind of overarching, unifying definition. Again, beginning grammars are not the place for exhaustive treatments. However, it is both possible and necessary to

---

162 Porter et al., *Fundamentals*, 31.
163 Porter et al., *Fundamentals*, 108–9.

provide students with a simple definition of the article's function that is accurate and lays a solid foundation for future engagement.[164]

6. Monographs on the Greek Article

a. *Thomas Fanshaw Middleton*, The Doctrine of the Greek Article *(1828)*

To date, Middleton's book is the sole attempt at a comprehensive grammar of the Greek article. In spite of this, his work has been largely ignored. First published in 1828, *The Doctrine of the Greek Article* predates by over half a century English language Greek grammars that went on to become standards within the guild, yet these grammars either completely ignore Middleton or at best mention him in passing without actually interacting with him. In 1948, it was determined that a new edition of the book would be published. Hugh James Rose took up the task of superintending this new edition, "Having long felt the highest veneration for Bishop Middleton's character and abilities."[165] He notes in his "Preliminary Observations" that, "inquiry into the Greek Article is a work to which sufficient justice has not been done in this country. I have been surprised to find how many men to whom I am accustomed to look with the highest respect, have not even read the volume."[166] As we close in on the bicentennial of its initial publication, Rose's words appear to be just as true now as they were when first penned. Seeking an explanation for this neglect, he suggests,

> One reason probably is, that as it does not consist of detached and unconnected rules, but is, in point of fact, a very refined and ingenious theory, professing, at least, to account for all the usages of the Article on one principle, it cannot be examined in parts, but must be considered as a whole.[167]

Perhaps this observation is correct. It is possible that scholars have viewed the size of Middleton's work as disproportionate to the subject of

---

[164] As one who has taught Greek for many years, I have struggled with the dilemma of, on the one hand, wanting to avoid associating the Greek article with English *the*, while on the other hand recognizing that English provides no other realistic option for a simple gloss. Having experienced this for myself, I have a degree of grace for textbooks that oversimplify. However, I have found that my students have benefited from my encouragement to not think of the article as simply "the," but rather "the one who/that which." By employing this understanding from the very beginning, a good deal of the cognitive dissonance has been avoided.

[165] Middleton, *Doctrine*, v.

[166] Middleton, *Doctrine*, v.

[167] Middleton, *Doctrine*, vi.

inquiry. It is also possible that scholars simply were not persuaded by his arguments.[168]

Rose notes that the standard treatment of the article consists of "detached and unconnected rules." If this was true in the middle of the nineteenth century, it is no less true today. A survey of standard grammars published over the last century, right up to the most recent, reflect this same approach. Middleton's single most valuable contribution is his attempt "to account for all the usages of the Article on one principle."

Middleton begins his *Doctrine* with a brief survey of ancient writers and their comments on the article. First, he tackles Aristotle's remarks on the article in *Poetics* 20.[169] Though he was more than adequately equipped to translate classical Greek, his attempts to make sense of the philosopher's remarks were ultimately frustrated: "Whatever be the true interpretation of this passage, I despair of discovering in it any thing to my present purpose,"[170] a conclusion, he notes, which was not his alone.[171] He next cites the second century writer Apollonius Dyscolus. Though he did not define the article, Middleton finds his remarks on it instructive:

> I do not perceive that he has any where defined the Article, and consequently he has no theory; though he has many facts, for the most part corroborating the theory, which I suspect to be the true one. He makes Articles and Pronouns to be different things, yet he allows a relation between them, and says that if the Article lose [sic] its Substantive, it then becomes a pronoun.[172]

While virtually all Greek grammars recognize this point, its importance for understanding the function of the article cannot be understated. In English, the definite article has developed to the point that it has completely lost its ability to function as a pronoun.[173] The Greek article had not advanced this far and still retained some of its force as a pronoun. The open question, however, remains: what kind of pronoun? The overwhelming consensus of Greek grammarians is that it is a demonstrative that occasionally functions as a relative. Middleton (as well as the treatment below) argues the reverse.

---

[168] The editor certainly suggests this possibility (see vi–vii).

[169] See the discussion above in 1.1, 8–11.

[170] Middleton, *Doctrine*, 3.

[171] Middleton, *Doctrine*, 2.

[172] Middleton, *Doctrine*, 3.

[173] While the definite article is a reduced form of *that*, it cannot function as a head term while the pronoun can, Halliday and Matthiesen, *Functional Grammar*, 315.

Another important point may be taken from Middleton's observation. He states that Dyscolus "has not theory; though he has many facts." Middleton's assessment of Dyscolus may be applied to the vast majority of modern grammars as well, as observed above. Though they have gathered together a plethora of facts regarding the article, they have not brought those facts together into a single, comprehensive theory.

Chapter two, *Article Defined*, is Middleton's grammar proper. His very first statement sets him apart from virtually all who follow: "The Greek Prepositive Article is the Pronoun Relative Ὁ, so employed that its relation is supposed to be more or less obscure."[174] He later cites Apollonius as confirmation of this categorization, who states that, "the *Article with a Noun* is equivalent to the Pronoun Relative."[175] Thus from the very beginning he distinguishes himself from other grammarians by categorizing the article as a relative, rather than demonstrative, pronoun.

Like his successors, Middleton recognizes the earliest extant examples of the use of the article are found in Homer. He therefore engages in a detailed examination of the poet's usage. Middleton takes exception with writers who argue that, in Homer, the article functions differently than later Greek, being akin to αὐτός and ἐκεῖνος, and not the full-fledged article of the Attic and Koine periods. Though he does not deny that the article functions as a pronoun in Homer, he cites numerous examples to demonstrate usage as the article as well.[176] He summarizes his conclusions regarding Homer's usage thus: "Homer's Article, it is admitted, is a Pronoun: but so is the Article universally; and Homer's usage of the Article, as the reader must be convinced, from the instances adduced, has nothing in it peculiar, but accords strictly, so far as it goes, with the practice of succeeding ages."[177]

Middleton moves on to consider examples from Plutarch and Eustathius. The latter is of great interest. On the authority of *Reizius de Prosodia Graeca*, Middleton writes, "It asserts only, that 'when the Articles throw away their Nouns, and thus become Pronouns, they are pronounced with a greater vehemence of tone."[178] This observation, if correct, is important for understanding the category under which the article falls and its relationship to other parts of speech. This "greater vehemence of tone" is one of the key

---

[174] Middleton, *Doctrine*, 6.
[175] Middleton, *Doctrine*, 22.
[176] Middleton, *Doctrine*, 7–11.
[177] Middleton, *Doctrine*, 11.
[178] Middleton, *Doctrine*, 12.

distinctions between the article and relative pronoun (though clearly not the only difference), which are otherwise very similar in morphology and phonology.[179] This lends strength to the argument that the two should be broadly categorized together. Middleton concludes by writing:

> The Article ὁ and the Pronoun ὁ are then, essentially the same thing, differing only in having or not having an Adjunct: and the Pronoun in both these ways is repeatedly employed by Homer. Hence it appears that the opinion of the Stoics... was not incorrect: ὁ is always a Pronoun, though it usually retains that name only when it is a *defined Article*, i.e. when the object of its relation is so plainly marked that no mistake can arise, and when, consequently, no Adjunct is requisite; they called it an *undefined Article*, when such addition became necessary to the perspicuity of its meaning.[180]

Middleton explores the possibility that the relative ὅς may have occasionally functioned as an article. Citing a passage from Theodore Gaza, he writes, "it was affirmed that there are two Articles, the Prepositive ὁ and the Subjunctive ὅς; though according to that Grammarian, the Prepositive only, strictly speaking, deserves the appellation."[181] After examining potential examples from Xenophon and Homer, Middleton concludes that ὁ "should come to be considered as the only legitimate Article; the pronoun ὅς not having connection with any Noun, except, that to which it was *subjoined*."[182]

Middleton addresses the problem of *definiteness* and how it relates to the presence of the article. He again cites Apollonius who asserted that, "the Article is applied not only to *defined* persons, but also to that, which in its nature is most *undefined*."[183] The cognitive dissonance this observation produces is not lost on Middleton:

---

[179] Admittedly, "vehemence of tone" cannot be quantified in an absolute sense. One must have direct access to instances of spoken language, such as recordings of actual conversations, to make such a determination. With regard to the Greek of the New Testament, the only available indication of tonal variation (the exact nature of which is debatable, though not likely *vehemence*) is in the form of accent marks. This difference is most notable in the distinction between the masculine singular of the article, ὁ, and the relative pronoun ὅς, as well as the feminine singular of the article, ἡ, and the relative pronoun, ἥ.

[180] Middleton, *Doctrine*, 13–14.

[181] Middleton, *Doctrine*, 19. Note that Middleton is not using "subjunctive" in the sense of a verbal mood form, but rather in the sense of "subjoined," which stands in contrast to "prepositive."

[182] Middleton, *Doctrine*, 19–20. Regarding *subjoined*, Middleton offers no elaboration. One can only theorize that by *subjoined* he means the use of the relative pronoun to indicate a relationship between a noun and a relative clause.

[183] Middleton, *Doctrine*, 22.

> Now these instances and this admission of the great Grammarian are alone sufficient to excite a surmise, that the reference of the Article is very different from that which is commonly supposed; for surely nothing can be more improbable, than that anything, in its nature one and the same, should be subservient to purposes diametrically opposite. Either the Article marking *definiteness* must be essentially different from that used to signify *indefiniteness* (which, however is not pretended,) or else its reference must be of such a nature, as, properly understood, to combine and unite in one form these contradictory appearances.[184]

He provisionally disagrees with the grammarians who wish to make the article a mere *Definitive*, stating, "In objecting to this doctrine, I do not deny that the Greeks, whenever they wish to speak of anything *definitely*, do employ the article: and this end could not by other means be attained more fully."[185] He continues, "Still, however, the Article is not in its nature a Definitive...it answers to the purpose of a Definitive merely κατὰ συμβεβηκός."[186] Middleton's use of κατὰ συμβεβηκός leaves the reader to interpret his meaning. Though literally "according to occurrence," the use of "merely" suggests Middleton may have meant something akin to "based on happenstance." On the one hand, he may be saying that the simple fact that the Greek article follows a syntactical pattern similar to the English definite article, in that they often occupy the same position in respect to their head term, does not mean that they perform the same *definitive* function. On the other hand, he may be saying that it is merely on the basis of context, as it happens or occurs.[187] Thus, we observe that Middleton was a man ahead of his time in questioning the notion of definiteness with regard to the article, yet was himself unable to dispense with the notion completely.

Though ahead of his time in defining what the Greek article is not, as well as his categorization of the article with the relative pronoun, Middleton's single principle by which every occurrence may be accounted is elusive. For this reason, later grammarians may perhaps be forgiven for their lack of engagement with his work. At no point does he offer the reader a simple, clear, concise definition of the article's function. Interestingly, though, he writes that the article is "the symbol of that which is

---

184 Middleton, *Doctrine*, 22.
185 Middleton, *Doctrine*, 24.
186 Middleton, *Doctrine*, 24.
187 Thanks to Dr. Porter for suggesting this interpretation of Middleton's statement.

uppermost in the speaker's mind."[188] This leads him to provide the closest thing we find to a definition, though he does not state this explicitly:

> On the whole, it appears that the Article may be used either when, conjointly with its Predicate, it recalls some former idea, or when it is intended to serve as the subject of a hypothesis. All the various uses of the Article will come under one of these two divisions.[189]

Based on this, we may conclude that Middleton, like so many others, understood the article's function in terms of structure or syntax. It was a marker of some inherent property of the head term or the writer/speaker's use of the head term, rather than exerting influence on the head term's meaning by modifying it in some way. However, his statement that the article "recalls some former idea" suggests a pronominal function as well, perhaps akin to that of the relative pronoun (though he does not here state this explicitly).

His belief that he had produced a single, defining principle of the article's function meant that Middleton did not share the despair found in so many grammarians that followed him. Regarding individual usage he wrote: "Is it, then, to be concluded, that the Article may generally be used at pleasure? This is the very hypothesis which I would combat."[190] The use or non-use of the article was not a matter of personal preference or idiom. With regard to his hypothesis, he wrote:

> I am next to show that, if it be admitted, it is capable (if I may use the expression) of solving the principal *phænomena*: in other words, that it will account for the most remarkable peculiarities in the usage of the Article, and that what my to some appear to be *arbitrary custom*, is in truth, supposing the principles laid down to be sufficiently established, a natural, if not a necessary consequence.[191]

The use of the Greek article, in his opinion, was not arbitrary. It was determined by principles that the speakers of the language intuitively recognized and to which they adhered.

---

[188] Middleton, *Doctrine*, 25. Middleton's assertion on this point will be confirmed below. See chapters 6 and 9.3.

[189] Middleton, *Doctrine*, 25.

[190] Middleton, *Doctrine*, 134.

[191] Middleton, *Doctrine*, 31.

b. *Conclusion*

As already noted, this survey illustrates the many ways in which Middleton diverged from those who would follow him. Regarding notions such as definiteness, he anticipated shifts that would take another two hundred years to become main-stream. Regarding Middleton's categorization of the article as a relative pronoun, though a relationship between the two parts of speech is at times admitted, this relationship did not supersede the view that the article is more closely related to the old demonstrative pronoun. Nor did it inform views of the article's function in any significant way. Despite these unique contributions, Middleton paralleled his successors in one important way: his theory of the article's function operated from the view that its role was one of syntax or structure. It did not enter into a meaningful relationship with its head term, whereby the head term's meaning was influenced or changed by the presence of the article. Rather, the article served as a marker. In function, "the Article itself is in strictness always *anticipative*."[192]

Nearly two centuries have passed since Middleton first published his work. In that time, no comprehensive treatment of the Greek article has been produced. Nor have many of the unique perspectives offered by Middleton been seriously engaged.

7. Specialized Studies on the Greek Article

Over the years, a number of specialized studies have been produced addressing issues that, among other things, factor into our understanding of the Greek article to a greater or lesser degree. The list of such topics is too long to enumerate. The following is a survey of specialized studies in which the Greek article plays a central role. They have been chosen based on their impact on Greek grammar, the longevity of their influence, and their relevance to this present work.

a. *Colwell's Construction*

In 1933, E.C. Colwell published what was to become a highly influential article in the *Journal of Biblical Literature*. "A Definite Rule for the Use of the Article in the Greek New Testament" was his attempt to formulate a

---

[192] Middleton, *Doctrine*, 23.

rule that explained under what circumstance the predicate nominatives of linking verbs would include the article. Simply stated, he concluded that, "A definite predicate nominative has the article when it follows the verb; it does not have the article when it precedes the verb."[193] Colwell's rule eventually gained widespread acceptance, with the result that it come to be known simply as "Colwell's Rule" or "Colwell's Construction."[194] According to Colwell, it was the study of John 1:49; 5:27; and 9:5 that ultimately suggested his rule.[195] In particular, he cites John 1:49: σὺ εἶ ὁ υἱὸς τοῦ θεοῦ· σὺ βασιλεὺς εἶ τοῦ Ἰσραήλ. He notes that in the first clause, the predicate nominative ὁ υἱός has the article, while in the second clause the predicate nominative βασιλεύς does not.[196] Colwell reasons, "It seems probable that the article is used with 'Son of God' because it follows the verb, and is not used with 'King of Israel' because it precedes the verb."[197] Working from this premise, he concludes that, when a linking verb is involved, definite predicate nominatives that follow the verb will have the article, while those that precede it will not.

Colwell's rule, and the methodology by which he arrived at it, reveal certain assumptions that are relevant to this present work. The first has to do with the notion of definiteness. Regarding the passage under consideration, he simply states that,

> When the passage is scrutinized, it appears at once that the variable quantum is not definiteness but word-order. "King of Israel" in this context is as definite as "Son of God."[198]

As Porter observes, "this still begs the question of what a definite noun is."[199] Colwell assumes definiteness without actually establishing it. As we saw in the survey of grammars above, Colwell was not alone in this assumption. Though not stated explicitly, grammarians operate from instinct, rather than employing objective principles for determining definiteness. In fact, it is hardly clear at all from the context that "King of Israel" is as definite as "Son of God" in this context. Colwell's rule only stands as long as the assumption can be proved true. Below, it will be argued that his assumption is not true, that βασιλεύς in this context is not definite, though it is

---

[193] Colwell, "A Definite Rule," 13.
[194] See for example Wallace, *Greek Grammar*, 256.
[195] Colwell, "A Definite Rule," 12–13.
[196] Colwell, "A Definite Rule," 13.
[197] Colwell, "A Definite Rule," 13.
[198] Colwell, "A Definite Rule," 13.
[199] Porter, *Idioms*, 109.

neither indefinite. Yet it is the assumption of definiteness that underpins Colwell's interpretation of his data, of which he writes:

> They show that a predicate nominative which precedes the verb cannot be translated as an indefinite or a "qualitative" noun sole because of the absence of the article; if the context suggests that the predicate is definite, it should be translated as a definite noun in spite of the absence of the article.[200]

Again we must question what contextual features are present that indicate definiteness. In the absence of clearly defined criteria, the conclusion is highly subjective. It is arguable that βασιλεύς in this context is in fact qualitative, though perhaps not in the manner Colwell understood the term. This reveals another related issue, that of terminology, which leads to the further problem of question framing. For Colwell, the only two possible options for the character of the head term are definite or indefinite. If indefinite, then it may be qualitative. As a result of the limitations established by the terminology, only certain options will be available and the questions will be framed based on these options. By employing new terminology, while at the same time breaking the shackles of prevailing assumptions, it is possible to reframe the questions and draw new conclusions. For example, it is possible to argue that βασιλεύς is indeed qualitative. Jesus is not the king of Israel in the definite sense: he does not have political authority, he does not command Israel's army, he does not sit in the seat of the judges. Thus, at this stage, he is king in a more qualitative sense rather than definite sense. However, the term qualitative is less than satisfactory. If we employ more accurate terminology and allow for the possibility that βασιλεύς is not definite, we will be able to reframe the questions and create the opportunity to formulate a more satisfying description of usage. In the description of the article's function below, it will be argued that anarthrous nouns, such as βασιλεύς in this instance, are in fact *abstract*, which is indicated by the absence of the article, whereas ὁ υἱός is *concrete*, and is made so be the presence of the article. Thus, Nathanael's declaration may be properly translated, "You are the Son of God; you are king of Israel." A full explanation of what is meant by the terms *abstract* and *concrete* will be provided below.[201]

A further issue with Colwell's methodology is revealed in the same quotation cited above: "the variable quantum is not definiteness but word-order." We have observed that, to an overwhelming degree, traditional

---

[200]　Colwell, "A Definite Rule," 20.
[201]　See below 9.1, 227.

attempts to formulate rules for the use of the article have been based on syntax. Colwell certainly employs this approach. Since he assumes that the head term is definite and definiteness is not an operation of the article, Colwell cannot observe a definite relationship between the article and the head term. The only observable pattern is one of syntax. Had he allowed for the possibility that the head term might not be definite, it is at least possible that he may have looked for some relationship between the article and head term. However, he was a man of his time. The prevailing notions of definiteness were too deeply embedded for him or others to entertain such a possibility. As stated above, the description below will argue that the relationship between the article and head term is not merely one of syntax, but of modification. The meaning of the head term is directly related to the presence or absence of the article. The article also performs a role in syntax, but this is at a level above that of its relationship to the head term as a modifier.

b. *The Granville Sharp Rule*

Published in 1798, the full title of Sharp's book, in which he articulates his highly influential rule, is *Remarks on the Uses of the Definitive Article in the Greek Text of the New Testament, Containing Many New Proofs of the Divinity of Christ, from passages which are wrongly translated in the Common English Version.* As the title indicates, Sharp believes that the article bore special significance with regard to both translation and exegesis. Central to his concern is the divinity of Christ and how the Greek writers of the New Testament reflect this belief through their use of the article. In his own words, Sharp's rule states that,

> When two personal nouns of the same case are connected by the copulative kai, if the former has the definitive article, and the latter has not, they both relate to the same person.[202]

Sharp then proceeds to cite numerous examples that confirm his basic rule. For our purposes, the rule serves to illustrate Sharp's adherence to the general perspective of his era, that the Greek article is the "definitive article." The rule indicates that Sharp's interest in the article is limited to its syntactical role rather than its functional relationship to the head term. His subsequent rules and qualifications regarding them are also limited to matters of syntax.

---

[202] Sharp, *Remarks*, 3.

The prevailing view that nouns may be defined as substantives by their very nature is also reflected in Sharp's presentation. In reference to John 20:28, he writes: "If the two nouns (viz. ὁ Κυριος and ὁ Θεος [sic]) were the leading nominative substantives of a sentence."[203] Throughout his presentation of the numerous examples he cites in support of his rule, as well his interpretation the exegetical significance of these passages, Sharp's interest is strictly focused on syntax. At no point does he indicate that he believes that the article's relationship to the head term as a modifier in any way affects the meaning of the head term.

Daniel Wallace made Sharp's rule the central focus of his doctoral dissertation, which later became the basis of his book, *Granville Sharp's Canon and Its Kin: Semantics and Significance.*[204] Like Sharp, Wallace's exegetical concerns are "in relation to syntax."[205] Thus, he is primarily concerned with the article's role as a marker of syntax. He provides only a brief definition of the article's function, consistent with his *Greek Grammar: Beyond the Basics.* Wallace writes: "the article has the ability to conceptualize, for its principle function is not determinative but notional."[206] He continues:

> To be sure, the Greek article does serve a determining function quite often. But a hierarchy of usage would suggest that determination has a tertiary role: after conceptualization (e.g., as in anaphora) comes determination.[207]

What Wallace means by the terms "conceptualize" and "notional" is unclear. For example, he later writes:

> With reference to TSKS construction, conceptualization is of foremost importance. That is to say, the primary thrust of the article in TSKS is to bring together two substantives into a conceptual unity.[208]

Without defining the term *conceptual*, Wallace seems to indicate that his general approach to the article apart from its role in Sharp's canon is based like so many others on syntax alone. In fact, his use of TSKS, which means "article-substantive-καί-substantive"[209] leaves the reader question-

---

[203] Sharp, *Remarks*, 29.

[204] For a critique of Wallace's treatment of the Granville Sharp Rule, see Stanley E. Porter, Review of *Granville Sharp's Canon and Its Kin: Semantics and Significance.*

[205] Wallace, *Sharp's Canon*, 19.

[206] Wallace, *Sharp's Canon*, 89.

[207] Wallace, *Sharp's Canon*, 89.

[208] Wallace, *Sharp's Canon*, 90. The acronym TSKS stands for article-substantive-καί-substantive, Wallace, *Sharp's Canon*, xx.

[209] Wallace, *Sharp's Canon*, 5. See also 90, footnote 5.

ing whether the "substantives" in question are substantive by nature or made so by the presence of the article.

Finally, Wallace claims that the body of his work on TSKS constructions is comprised of three parts: "historical, linguistic, exegetical."[210] While the historical and exegetical elements of his work are quite extensive, one wonders about the claim of being *linguistic*. Wallace makes clear to the reader that he has no formal training in linguistics and holds no allegiance "to any particular linguistic theory."[211] As a result, one of his three parts is severely limited, as he himself states. This limitation is due to what Wallace identifies as "the imperfect state of linguistics—a discipline that is still in a state of flux."[212] In addition, "because of such shifting currents, the approach taken in the work will not be tied to any one school."[213] Though he acknowledges that, "the various competing schools of linguistics find a significant amount of common ground,"[214] he does not articulate what this common ground is or how it informs his work. In fact, the only direct appeal he makes to modern linguistics is his use of a diachronic rather than synchronic approach, which he attributes to the work of Saussure.[215] Otherwise, though he makes frequent reference to linguistic evidence or modern linguistics, he fails to appeal to specific theories or evidence. There are moments when his presentation suggests some influence from the field of linguistics, such as distinguishing between sense and referent, as well as denotative and connotative meaning.[216] However, he cites only a secondary source: Cotterell and Turner's *Linguistics and Biblical Interpretation*, so this is only a guess.[217]

In the end, the Granville Sharp rule or canon, like most of the other rules we have observed, is limited to matters of syntax. He and his followers, like Wallace, focus exclusively on the article's role in grammatical constructions, showing little to no interest in questions related to its relationship to the head term as a modifier.

---

[210] Wallace, *Sharp's Canon*, 23.
[211] Wallace, *Sharp's Canon*, 19.
[212] Wallace, *Sharp's Canon*, 18.
[213] Wallace, *Sharp's Canon*, 18.
[214] Wallace, *Sharp's Canon*, 18.
[215] Wallace, *Sharp's Canon*, 13.
[216] Wallace, *Sharp's Canon*, 103.
[217] One is left with the impression that Wallace is more interested in the rhetorical power of appealing to linguistics than he is in actually engaging linguistics.

c. *Robert Funk*, The Syntax of the Greek Article: Its Importance
for Critical Pauline Problems *(1953)*

After Middleton, the only major monograph on the Greek article is
Robert Funk's unpublished 1953 doctoral dissertation. His objective was
not a comprehensive treatment of the article, like that of Middleton or
the present work. His concern was with syntax, in particular what he perceived to be a distinctively Pauline syntactical style with regard to the
usage of the article, rather than the grammar of the article in general.
However, his presentation illustrates the state of the grammatical understanding of the article in the mid-twentieth century. Additionally, syntax
is an element of the article's functionality and will be addressed below.

With regard to the present study, the significance of Funk's dissertation
has to do with his belief that the use of the article is a matter of personal
style, that it is idiomatic:

> [The] constant, and sometimes automatic, repetition of this part of speech
> tends to make it more idiomatic, more revealing of an author's tempera-
> ment and disposition; in this respect it corresponds closely to the particles,
> though, of course, exceeding them in frequency.[218]

He later writes,

> In the NT, as elsewhere then, the article is not used without purpose, but
> at the same time it often depends on a fineness, an individualistic idiom, a
> particular nuance for its motive.[219]

This assertion is foundational and indispensable to Funk's thesis. If the
use of the article is flexible enough to be subject to the whims or personal
preferences of individual speakers or writers, then it is indeed possible
to associate certain patterns or frequencies of occurrence with certain
individuals. Funk's assertion is true in one sense, but requires significant
modification and qualification. A distinction must be made between
the use of the article as the modifier of a head term and the use of the
article in other syntactical constructions. The choice of whether or not
to use the article to modify a head term is different than the choice, for
example, to employ the so-called first or second attributive position, in
which the article plays a key role. Also, at times the article and the head
term are used to bracket additional modifiers, including instances in

---

[218] Funk, "Syntax," 3.
[219] Funk, "Syntax," 7.

which the modifiers that typically follow the head term are moved in front of it. Individuals may indeed be more adept at employing these kinds of syntactical constructions. They may even have individual preferences. However, these variables may also be motivated by factors associated with the discourse rather than individual style, which will be discussed below. Suffice it to say, specific variations in syntactical style may be associated with certain individuals. However, there is much more involved that must be taken into consideration. This is an entirely different matter than the question of whether or not to employ the article as a modifier.

Funk makes another observation about the article that must be addressed:

> Another characteristic of the article is that it is a luxury of the language, though never without meaning. The article is not needed to make a substantive definite; yet when the article is employed it assures definiteness and often adds a nuance not available to authors working under other grammatical systems.[220]

The underlying grammatical assumption represented in this statement is one of the chief points that must be challenged. Like his predecessors and contemporaries, Funk maintains that the article indicates definiteness. However, he makes a further statement that must also be addressed. He writes, "The article is not needed to make a substantive definite..."[221] Funk reinforces this notion in the title of his second chapter, "The Article with Substantives."[222]

These two assertions allow Funk to draw the following conclusion:

> Frequency, plus the fact that proper use of the article adds much finesse and delicacy to the style of any author, leads naturally to wide variation in usage, not only from generation to generation, but from author to author. Here is a tool, then by mean of which individual creativeness and artistic genius can find its expression; only one among many, to be sure, but an important one.[223]

---

[220] Funk, "Syntax," 3.

[221] In contrast to Funk, I will argue that individual lexical items or larger units of discourse are not "substantive" apart from modification by the article. Rather, it is the function of the article to characterize these elements as substantive, or "concrete." Thus, the article is not a "luxury of the language," by the Koine era, it is a necessity. See below, 6.1–3, 179–87; 9.1, 226–29.

[222] Funk, "Syntax," 31.

[223] Funk, "Syntax," 3–4.

This assertion is not entirely false, but the statement must be heavily qualified. Syntax may reveal personal style, even as he says "creativeness and artistic genius," but frequency does not. Frequency is relevant in this manner only if the article truly is a "luxury of the language." However, if certain semantic realities require the presence of the article, while others demand it be left off, then frequency is no longer determined by individual style, but is rather a function of the discourse.

Regarding the origin and function of the article, Funk is consistent with his contemporaries. He maintains that in origin it was a demonstrative and "often exhibits obvious affinities with its original function."[224] Definiteness is still associated with its function, but in a qualified manner. The article places stress on "individuality rather than definiteness...it defines by pointing out individual identity."[225] He continues:

> While the article makes a substantive definite, that is not to say that when the article is absent the substantive may not be definite. Many substantives in the NT are definite though anarthrous. In each case the context must decide.[226]

Methodologically, this makes the interpretation of articular and anarthrous constructions just as subjective as the supposed usage of the article. Translators and exegetes have no theory of grammatical or syntactical usage to adjudicate between differing positions.

Funk makes one observation that remains partly true to this day. He observes at the time of the writing of his dissertation that, "There are not many good Koine Greek grammars; among the best ones, there are even fewer that have anything like adequate treatment of the article."[227] Since the time of his writing, many good Koine Greek grammars have been produced. However, as he notes, there remains a lack of anything like adequate treatment of the article.

d. *Denny Burk*, Articular Infinitives in the Greek of the New Testament: On the Exegetical Benefit of Grammatical Precision *(2006)*

Burk's treatment of the article with infinitives provides further evidence of how the traditional approach to the article impacts both grammar and exegesis, and why this approach must be challenged. Like his predecessors,

---

[224] Funk, "Syntax," 31.
[225] Funk, "Syntax," 32.
[226] Funk, "Syntax," 32–33.
[227] Funk, "Syntax," 4.

he focuses on syntax rather than semantics to explain the article's function. In his introduction, he writes:

> While I maintain that the article is employed primarily as a *function* marker, other grammarians have proposed different answers. Generally speaking, New Testament scholars have attributed more semantic value to the articular infinitive than is warranted. These scholars go beyond what I maintain to be a strict structural significance for the article. However there are those who have at times underestimated the significance of the article. These interpreters fall short of seeing the article's value as a *function* marker.[228]

He later writes:

> This book proceeds from the assumption that when it can be demonstrated that the article is syntactically required, one should not look for any further semantic significance of the article ... While the use of the article with nouns in general is motivated by both semantic and syntactic considerations, the use of the article with infinitives in particular is motivated by syntactic considerations only.[229]

The reason Burk arrives at this conclusion is because he operates from the view that the Greek article is classified as a determiner.[230] He cites D.A. Black's list of characteristics of determiners:

> Black observes that determiners are grammatical elements (1) that co-occur with nominals; (2) that agree in case, gender, and number with a head noun; (3) that can be used interchangeably with one another; and (4) that are non-recursive modifiers, that is, that cannot be used in combination.[231]

Based on the characteristics of determiners he cites, this classification may be questioned. First, he notes that, "Syntactically, the main characteristic of a determiner is that it co-occurs with nouns (or noun phrases)."[232] This is certainly true in English. Historically, grammarians have observed that the Greek article co-occurs with nouns and noun phrases and concluded that it, too, is a determiner. In fact, this conclusion is based on a merely superficial assessment. Such a conclusion assumes, but does not prove, that the grammatical relationship is one of determination. Second, agreement in case, number, and gender indicates that the item in question functions as a modifier, but does not of itself indicate that the nature

---

[228] Burk, *Articular Infinitives*, 5.
[229] Burk, *Articular Infinitives*, 45.
[230] Burk, *Articular Infinitives*, 28.
[231] Burk, *Articular Infinitives*, 33.
[232] Burk, *Articular Infinitives*, 30.

of the modification is that of determination. Third, interchaneability is also assumed, not proved. Before one argues that the Greek article may be used interchangeably with other elements, such as demonstrative pronouns, it must be proved that these elements are grammatically related and are actually performing the same function. Once again, historically, this has been assumed, not proved. As noted above, the continued production of disconnected and contradictory descriptions of the article's function should suggest that it does not function like determiners. Finally, with regard to recursiveness, both Burk and Black acknowledge that the article violates this rule. It is, in fact, used in combination with Greek determiners. Based on this, Burk concludes that "the syntax of the article is distinguished from the demonstratives."[233] It is noteworthy that there is no suggestion that the evidence is interpreted as indicating that the article is not a determiner, or that such an interpretion is even entertained. The thesis of the present work is that this is indeed the correct interpretation.

e. *The Use of the Article with Proper Names*

Wallace has articulated the difficulty associated with the use of the Greek article with proper names as well as anyone:

> The difficulty with the article with proper names is twofold: (1) English usage does not correspond to it, and (2) we still cannot achieve "explanatory adequacy" with reference to the use of the use of the article with proper names—that is, we are unable to articulate clear and consistent principles as to why the article is used in a given instance.[234]

Nevertheless, attempts have been made to come up with some explanation of its usage in this regard. In the January, 1971 volume of *New Testament Studies*, Gordon Fee published an article titled "The Use of the Definite Article with Personal Names in the Gospel of John." Consistent with the time, Fee did not attempt to discern a relationship between the article and personal names. It is likely that he, like his contemporaries, did not believe that one exists. Instead, his goal was to determine if there were circumstantial or syntactical influences governing its use in the Fourth Gospel. Fee begins with the caveat that usage "tended to be marked by

---

[233] Burk, *Articular Infinitives*, 35.
[234] Wallace, *Greek Grammar*, 247.

individual preference, not by generally defined rules."[235] His goal, then, is to identify a particularly Johannine usage.

Fee's first observation is that the anaphoric usage of the article, that is, the rule of "renewed mention," does not apply. Briefly stated, this rule argues that names are frequently first introduced without the article. Subsequent mentions of the name then employ it. Fee argues that only a small minority of occurrences conform to this rule.[236] Instead, he observes that certain names "tend to disregard all other rules and are always (or generally) anarthrous, while others generally have the article."[237] In general, compound names are anarthrous, which Fee interprets as an explanation for the two anarthrous occurrences of πνεῦμα ἅγιον, arguing that "John understands the combination, therefore, as a proper name."[238] The exception of the one articular occurrence is explained by the fact that it stands in apposition to ὁ παράκλητς.[239]

In the end, Fee proposes ten instances in which personal names will be anarthrous, versus four in which they will be articular.[240] All are based on matters of syntax, or at times the case of the name. At no point does he propose or indicate that he even entertains the idea that the article may function as a modifier with personal names.

As Fee did with the Fourth Gospel, Jenny Heimerdinger and Stephen Levinsohn attempt to identify patterns of usage in the book of Acts, focusing in the text in the Codex Bezae. Their first observation is that the problem is exacerbated by the large number of textual variants of the book of Acts involving the presence of absence of the article.[241] Because of this diversity, the authors chose to employ Codices Sinaiticus and Vaticanus as representatives of the Alexandrian tradition and Codex Bezae for the Western tradition.[242]

Heimerdinger and Levinsohn begin their examination with the statement of a general rule: "The unmarked way of mentioning a person by name is with the article. The omission of the article indicates that

---

[235] Fee, "Use of the Definite Article," 168, citing B.L. Gildersleeve, "On the Article with Proper Names," 483–7.

[236] Fee, "Use of the Definite Article," 170.

[237] Fee, "Use of the Definite Article," 170.

[238] Fee, "Use of the Definite Article," 171.

[239] Fee, "Use of the Definite Article," 171. I will argue that this is correct, but for reasons other than Fee's.

[240] Fee, "Use of the Definite Article," 182–3.

[241] Heimerdinger and Levinsohn, "The Use of the Definite Article," 15–16.

[242] Heimerdinger and Levinsohn, "The Use of the Definite Article," 17.

attention is being drawn to the person being named."[243] By arguing that the anarthrous construction represents the marked form, they argue that this form,

> ... draws particular attention to the person in question at that point in the narrative. The purpose of omitting the article frequently is to distinguish the person from other participants or even other possible participants and so the implication is that the person being name is "that one rather than some other".[244]

They believe that this rule explains why a participant's name is anarthrous when first mentioned and is then articular in subsequent occurrences:

> When a participant is first introduced into a story, the author almost always spotlights his initial appearance on stage so that his presence is clearly registered by the audience ... Subsequently, once the participant has entered into the story, he can be referred to as a known factor with the other possibilities already ruled out, and the article is therefore retained.[245]

In conjunction with this usage, the authors argue that the presence or absence of the article performs the discourse function of marking *salience*, which they define as "attention being drawn to a specific participant."[246] They argue that the article is dropped in order to highlight certain characters: "Highlighting, however, occurs when one character or another becomes salient at various other points in the story, too,"[247] not just when they first enter.

The approach employed by Heimerdinger and Levinsohn represents a significant shift from traditional approaches to the article, as they themselves note:

> These are rules which operate not on the level of the sentence, which is the domain of traditional linguistics, but on the level of larger portions of the text such as the paragraph or the episode. For this reason, this type of linguistic analysis which looks beyond the sentence for factors governing the features of language is known as "discourse analysis" or "textlinguistics".[248]

---

[243] Heimerdinger and Levinsohn, "The Use of the Definite Article," 17–18.
[244] Heimerdinger and Levinsohn, "The Use of the Definite Article," 18.
[245] Heimerdinger and Levinsohn, "The Use of the Definite Article," 18.
[246] Heimerdinger and Levinsohn, "The Use of the Definite Article," 20.
[247] Heimerdinger and Levinsohn, "The Use of the Definite Article," 20. Note that this is contrary to Middleton's conclusion that the article is "the symbol of that which is uppermost in the speaker's mind." See above 1.6, 61.
[248] Heimerdinger and Levinsohn, "The Use of the Definite Article," 34.

On the one hand, the authors bring a refreshing new approach to the study of the Greek article's function. It is certainly worth investigating how the article may function at the discourse level. On the other hand, their approach does continue to operate in a manner similar to that of traditional grammarians. They do not attempt to analyze the relationship between the article and the head term, in this case proper names. The approach continues to focus on issues pertaining to structure. However, it is structure operating at a higher level of discourse than clausal syntax. This observation is not meant to denigrate or marginalize such investigation. The article's role in syntax and discourse analysis is relevant and will be addressed below. It is merely an observation that they, like others, do not address the question of the relationship between the article and the head term.

Kent Spielmann also takes up the discourse approach to the article with proper names and using this approach revisits Fee's work in the Gospel of John. Citing the work of Levinsohn, he too argues that, at the discourse level, anarthrous names are marked off as being salient.[249] It is his conclusion that application of Levinsohn's guidelines to an analysis of the fourth Gospel is consistent with and "might explain Fee's observations."[250] Spielmann does not challenge Fee's findings. Rather, he contends that they only tell part of the story:

> This examination of Fee's findings shows that, while they may accurately reflect John's style, they tell us very little about the meanings John's style conveyed to his original readers. This is because Fee does not take into consideration the discourse factors which are the primary criteria governing the use of the definite article. Using discourse considerations, I have shown that there are probably systematic explanations for most, if not all, of Fee's findings.[251]

Thus, Spielmann's approach is to employ the rules set out by Levinsohn. In so doing, he concludes that John's usage of the article is generally consistent with these rules and that examination at the level of discourse provides a more exhaustive explanation than Fee's.

---

[249] Spielmann, "Participant Reference," 47.
[250] Spielmann, "Participant Reference," 51.
[251] Spielmann, "Participant Reference," 60.

e. *Conclusion*

With regard to the matter of the use of the article with personal names, it is encouraging to see scholars moving away from traditional grammatical approaches. As Spielmann writes: "This study has shown that a discourse approach to Koine Greek provides a more consistent description of language phenomena than the more traditional grammatical approach."[252] Without commenting on validity of his conclusions, one must concur with the basic premise which recognizes the limitations of traditional grammatical approaches and the need for new ones. Analysis of the function of the Greek article is certainly appropriate and necessary, and these authors are to be commended for doing so. However, the question of how the article functions as a modifier, in particular with reference to proper names, remains open.

8. THE STATE OF CURRENT RESEARCH

Based on the preceding survey of the treatment of the Greek article over the last 150 years, we can make the following observations. First, until very recently there has been an assumption that the Greek article and both the German and English definite articles performed parallel functions. Specifically, the presence of the article was believed to indicate *definiteness*, just as its English counterpart. This resulted in a methodology that explained the Greek article's function by means of analogy with the English definite article, which served as the norm. When it was observed that the Greek article functioned in a way that was inconsistent with its English counterpart, it was explained as a deviation from this norm. While this correspondence has been (rightly) challenged and rejected, the methodology associated with it has not been entirely overturned. The function of the Greek article is still too often defined and illustrated via analogy with the English definite article. This methodology and its results are unsatisfactory. The grammar of the Greek article must be revisited based on a methodology that is grounded in the Greek language and grows organically from it.

Second, German speaking Greek grammarians observed what they believed to be a parallel between the German and Greek demonstrative, relative and article. They posited that in Greek, just as in German,

---

[252] Spielmann, "Participant Reference," 72.

all three parts of speech may be realized by a single form, concluding that at an early stage in its history the Greek article was a realization of all three forms. This perception was carried into descriptions of its function in the Attic/Classical and Hellenistic/Koine periods. Early English language Greek grammars were either translations of German originals or written by grammarians whose information was based on German work. As a result, this triple function was perpetuated in English grammars for decades. Though it may have been true at an early stage of its use (a debatable point at best), the Greek article clearly developed beyond this triple function, so that by the time of the New Testament it was no longer employed as a demonstrative pronoun, and was employed as a relative pronoun only in a reduced fashion.

Third, the overwhelming consensus is that the Greek article was originally a demonstrative pronoun. Though it is widely recognized that by the classical period (Attic) and into the Hellenistic period (Koine) it was no longer functioning as a demonstrative, grammarians are nearly unified in their assertion that it retained its demonstrative force. For this reason, it had been argued that the presence of the Greek article indicated definiteness. While this perception of definiteness has been recently challenged, the function of the article continues to be defined in light of this association. This is the first point I wish to challenge. Though the article may have indeed begun its life as a demonstrative, and in antiquity so been used, it will be argued below that by the Koine period, it had moved beyond this role. Grammarians frequently recognize it is used as a relative pronoun as well as the article; however this usage does not inform their grammar. With the ascendancy of the demonstratives οὗτος and ἐκεῖνος, the article and the relative pronoun followed new trajectories and were both pressed into new services, with the article representing a reduced or diminished form and function of the relative pronoun. The article and relative pronoun possibly retained a bit of their original demonstrative force, which prevents an exact one for one correlation with the English relative pronoun. However, the article has moved further from this demonstrative origin than has historically been recognized, and is in fact closer in function to the relative pronoun.

Fourth, to an overwhelming degree, the role of the article has been addressed in terms of syntax. This is because no satisfactory description of its function as a modifier could be formulated. Scholars observed no universal patterns of usage that would allow them to formulate a single, overarching description of its function. This left grammarians to analyze the article in terms of a marker of syntax. Yet this analysis also yielded inconsistent results. In the end, it was concluded that the use of the article was a matter of personal idiom, of individual style. As stated above, the despair felt by previous generations of grammarians was the result of inadequate terminology and inaccurate assumptions regarding both the article and the head terms to which it was connected. By revising both terminology and assumptions, it will be possible to articulate a single, comprehensive, internally consistent description of the article's function.

Fifth, though recent studies have brought modern linguistic theory into the analysis of the article's function, there is still much work to be done. Many have attempted to analyze and describe the article's function at the discourse level. They are to be commended for this, and their work should be continued and expanded. However, very little has been done to address the article's basic function as a modifier using the principles of modern linguistics. It is the goal of the remainder of this work to bring those principles to bear on the Greek article in order to formulate a description of its function so that we may, as Rose wrote in his forward to Bishop Middleton's book, "account for all the usages of the Article on one principle."

CHAPTER TWO

THE COMMON FUNCTION OF THE ARTICLE AND
RELATIVE PRONOUNS: METHODOLOGY

As noted above, grammarians have historically given little room for the article to function as a relative pronoun. Most have agreed to a greater or lesser degree with Moulton's assertion that the New Testament "shows no trace of the use of the article as a relative."[1] There have been occasional exceptions, such as Moule, who suggested that the article with a participle functioned like a relative clause.[2] However, Moulton's view was by far the dominant view and continues to this day.[3] By contrast, the following treatment operates from the view that, by the New Testament (and more broadly, Koine) period, the article and relative pronoun had both separated themselves from the historical demonstrative for purposes that are most closely analogous to the English relative pronoun. To adapt the words of Moulton and Howard, the article and relative pronoun have detached themselves for special functions answering generally to those of our own *who*, or more specifically, *the one who*.[4] That this is the case may be demonstrated first by their similar morphology, and second by the fact that the two items are employed in similar constructions. The purpose of the following chapters is to illustrate these similarities. First, we will examine participial clauses that employ the article in order to determine whether they perform the same function as defining and non-defining relative clauses, as well as relative clauses that function as subject and object. It will be demonstrated that articular participial clauses do indeed perform the same function as relative clauses. This, in turn, will demonstrate that, in the case of defining and non-defining relative clauses and corresponding articular participial clauses, the article and relative pronoun are employed to indicate that the speaker or writer is providing information that is to be used for the purpose of further identifying the head term. In the case of relative clauses and articular participial clauses

---

[1] Moulton, *Prolegomena*, 81.

[2] Moule, *Idiom Book*, 106.

[3] As noted above, Wallace rejects the notion that the article bears the semantic force of the relative pronoun, *Greek Grammar*, 214.

[4] "The Article has detached itself for special functions answering generally to those of our own *the*," Moulton and Howard, *Accidence and Word Formation*, 117.

that function as subject or compliment, the article and relative pronoun indicate that information is being provided that is to be used as the identifying characteristic of an extra-linguistic referent, rather than a head term. Unlike demonstratives, which direct the recipient to the information necessary for identification, or the English definite article, which indicates that the recipient already possesses the information necessary for identification, the Greek article and relative pronouns indicate that this information is being provided by the speaker. Thus, they orient identification of the referent to the speaker, not the recipient. Next, we will examine the use of relative pronouns and the article in μέν … δέ constructions, as well as independent μέν and δέ constructions. The results of this analysis will confirm that the Greek article and relative pronoun belong to a common category, which we will designate *Ho-* items (ὁ-items).

Second, the information from this examination will be employed to formulate a description of the article's function with other parts of speech, both individual lexical items and group structures. It will be argued that with all parts of speech the article is employed to indicate that the information grammaticalized by the head term is being provided by the speaker to the recipient, which he or she is to use for the purpose of identifying the referent. The article is used to subjectively characterize the head term as *concrete*, as belonging to experience of an actual person or thing, or as a specific instance. With regard to nouns, it will also be argued that when the article is not employed, the head term is characterized as *abstract*, as not belonging to experience of an actual person or thing, or a specific instance. Various discourse motives for such characterization will also be examined.

1. The Semantic Function of ὁ-items

To begin, it is necessary to categorize the article and relative pronoun as parts of speech that operate within a larger system of classification. In his grammar, Halliday places the English definite article under the general category *TH-item*. Lexical items in this category share distinctive traits both in morphology and function and consist of demonstrative pronouns and the definite article. Closely related are *WH-items*, which consist of relative pronouns. Each group is part "of a wider set embracing both WH- and TH- forms, which taken together fulfill a *deictic* or 'pointing out' function."[5] These items are listed categorically in the chart below:[6]

---

    [5] Halliday, *Functional Grammar*, 86.
    [6] Halliday, *Functional Grammar*, 87.

	TH-Items	WH-Items
nominal	the this that	which what who whose
adverbial	there then thus	where when how/why
	[thence thither]	[whence whither]
	there- fore/by etc.	where- fore/by etc.

Halliday illustrates the function of these items using the following chart:[7]

		Meaning	Deictic type	Example
(1)		I'm telling you which	TH-	I saw the one, this/that (one)
(2)		I'm not telling you which	WH-	
	(a)	I'm asking you (bounded)	int. def.	which/who/what did you see?
	(b)	I'm asking you (unbounded)	int. indef.	whichever etc. did you see?
	(c)	I'm not concerned	rel. indef.	whichever etc. you saw
	(d)	I'm telling you about something else	rel. def.	the one which/who I saw

The function of deictic elements is to indicate "whether or not some specific subset of the Thing is intended, and if so, which."[8] These operate within a system of *determination*, within which Halliday distinguishes between specific and non-specific determiners: non-specific being *a(n)*, *one*, *no*, and *each*; specific being *the, those, his, her, whose* and *the chief's*.[9] The elements *the, this, these, that* and *those* are demonstrative determiners, which means that their distinctive deictic feature is that of *proximity* to the speaker or writer.[10] The English definite article *the* is unique among the determiners:

> The word *the* is a specific, determinative Deictic of a peculiar kind: it means 'the subset in question is identifiable; but this will not tell you how to identify it—the information is somewhere around, where you can recover it'…Hence *the* is usually accompanied by some other element which supplies the information required…If there is no such information supplied,

---

[7] Halliday, *Functional Grammar*, 87.
[8] Halliday, *Functional Grammar*, 312.
[9] Halliday, *Functional Grammar*, 312.
[10] Halliday, *Functional Grammar*, 314.

the subset in question will either be obvious from the situation, or else will have been referred to already in the discourse.[11]

The two most important pieces of information to focus on regarding the English definite article are *proximity* and *recoverability*. When a head term is modified by the English definite article, it will be something that is proximate in the discourse and recoverable from the discourse, whether implicitly or explicitly. Consider that following example, which is a common formula used in jokes: "A horse walks into a bar. The bartender says to the horse, 'Why the long face?'" When the participant *horse* is first introduced, it is not known to the recipients. Its identity is not recoverable in the discourse, nor is it obvious from the discourse. Therefore, it cannot be modified by the definite article. Conversely, subsequent references do employ the article because both the speaker and the recipients share common information regarding the identity of the participant. The speaker, by employing the definite article, indicates to the recipient, "You know which horse I am talking about," because its identity is recoverable from the discourse. By contrast, the identity of the *bartender* is not recoverable from the discourse, even though this participant is first introduced using the definite article. This is because the speaker and the recipients share common information necessary for identification. The opening statement locates the participants in *a bar*. Since one expects to encounter bartenders in a bar, the identity of the participant is obvious from the situation. It is not necessary to establish the bartender's identity, since it is assumed based on the context of the situation that there will be at least one bartender present. Even the bartender's question, "Why the long face?" assumes that he and the horse share the necessary information to identify *the long face* in question without further specification. If this were not true, he would have had to rephrase the question, "Why do you have a long face?" However, this does not work as well for the purpose of the joke.

WH- items stand in contrast to demonstrative determiners:

> The category of WH- element opens up this semantic space, of an identity that is established by interrogation, perhaps with an element of challenge or disbelief, or put aside as irrelevant; or established relative to some other entity.[12]

---

[11] Halliday, *Functional Grammar*, 314.
[12] Halliday, *Functional Grammar*, 86.

Thus, "These two values, interrogative and relative, are themselves related at a deeper level, through the general sense of 'identity to be retrieved from elsewhere.' "[13] If, as will be argued below, the Greek article is more closely analogous to WH- items than TH- items, analogy with the English definite article breaks down due to two major problems: proximity and recoverability.[14] When modifying a head term, the Greek article will not indicate proximity within the discourse, nor will it indicate that the identity of the head term is recoverable from the discourse. Rather, the article will indicate that the identity of the head term is recoverable "from some other place." This does not mean that the thing identified by the article has not previously been a participant in the discourse, it may very well have. What it does mean is that the information necessary for identification is not a matter of proximity or recoverability. Rather, the speaker or writer employs the article to indicate that the information necessary for identification is "from some other place." Specifically, it indicates that he or she is providing this information. Unlike the English definite article, which indicates that the speaker and recipient share the necessary information in common, the Greek article orients identification to the speaker alone.[15] The information the speaker provides must be accepted by the recipient as the basis for identification.

Using the information outlined above, we can already begin to understand the difficulties that arise when grammarians attempt to define and to describe the Greek article by means of analogy with the English definite article. If the Greek article is closely related to the Greek relative pronoun, it is more closely analogous to WH- items in English, rather than TH- items under which the English definite article is found. Rather than being "cumbersome," as Wallace puts it, this is in fact the very function it

---

[13] Halliday, *Functional Grammar*, 86, referring to interrogative and relative pronouns.

[14] The use of WH- items throughout excludes the interrogative forms.

[15] When an English speaker employs the definite article, the speaker assumes that the recipient possesses the same information that he or she does. If this assumption is false, the recipient experiences cognitive dissonance. When a speaker says, "Please pass the salt," it is assumed that the recipient possesses the information necessary for identifying the salt to which the speaker is referring. It the recipient does not, he or she will respond, "What salt?" In this way, the recipient indicates that assumption is false, that the information is not shared and more information is required. In contrast, the Greek article does not make this assumption. It gives no indication that the speaker and recipient share information. It does not indicate that they do not; indeed they may or may not. It simply makes no comment in this regard. The speaker provides the information necessary for identification, irrespective of whether the recipient already possessed it and without comment on the matter.

performs in Greek. The numerous examples that will be provided below will illustrate that the function of the Greek article is most closely analogous to the "defining relative clause" in meaning, as in Halliday's chart above: (2)(d), "I'm telling you about something else."

At first glance, one immediately notices a strong similarity between (2)(d) and the TH- deictic type, "I saw the one, this/that (one)." However, it is important to note the distinction:

> The 'defining relative clause' (d) is anomalous, in that, while it does not itself identify the thing or person seen, it uses the fact of my seeing for the purpose of identification. This is why there is an alternative form using a TH- item as relative: *the one that I saw.*[16]

This distinction is fundamental for understanding the dissonance that analogy with the English definite article produces. In English, to employ the definite article is to say, "I'm telling you which," meaning "I saw the one, this/that one." The speaker or writer, through the use of the definite article, indicates to the recipient that the identity of the thing is proximate and recoverable, or is at least obvious from the situation. These statements, by their very nature, indicate *definiteness*, because the item so defined is recoverable, and thus available, to the listener or reader. In contrast, WH- elements are not necessarily immediately recoverable, and thus available, to the reader or listener: "While it does not itself identify the thing or person seen, it uses the fact of my seeing for the purpose of identification." The referent of a WH- element may or may not be available to the recipient. Either way it is immaterial, because the speaker or writer is indicating that the recipient must accept his or her word that "such a thing exists and I am identifying it to you." Additionally, while the function of the WH- item in a defining relative clause is the closest analogy to the function of the Greek article, it is not an absolute one-for-one correspondence. For example, in English WH- items frequently function as interrogatives, while in Greek, this function is performed by other lexical items such as τίς, τί. Thus, we must strive to allow the Greek article to speak for itself, resisting the urge to force it into absolute conformity with a category from a foreign language. Rather, the categories must be allowed to grow organically from the Greek language. The use of English categories must serve merely as point of departure. While there will certainly be instances of parallel usage between English and Greek, the analyst must

---

[16] Halliday, *Functional Grammar*, 86.

resist the temptation to force conformity where it does not exist, allowing the two languages to depart from one another as well. By emphasizing Greek patterns of usage, this methodology allows the researcher, on the one hand, to observe general characteristics possessed by both the article and relative pronouns, while at the same time observing how the article and relative pronouns are functionally distinct.

Following Halliday's lead, we will employ the category *Ho-* items [ὁ- items]. Like TH- items and WH- items in English, *Ho-* items are grouped together because they share traits in both morphology and function. We may begin to organize these lexical items using the following chart:

ὁ-item	*Deictic Type*
ὁ, ἡ, τό	art.
ὅς, ἥ, ὅ	rel. def.
ὅστις, ἥτις, ὅτι	rel. def./indef.[17]
οὗ, ὅπου	rel. def.

This is not the first attempt to employ such an organization. Thomas Robinson employs a chart based on "Cognate Groups" that is very similar,[18]

ὁ ἡ τό
the / who / which

ὁ ἡ τό	the	adj
ὅδε ἥδε τόδε	this	adj
ὅς ἥ ὅ	who, which, what	pron
ὅσπερ ἥπερ ὅπερ	who, which	pron

Robinson's glosses suggest he maintains a close association with a demonstrative function for the article. In spite of this, his organization represents a view that associates the article and relative pronoun from at least a morphological perspective.

Before engaging in a focused description of the Greek article's function (this will be taken up in chapter 6), it is necessary to establish the points of connection between the article and the relative pronoun as elements of the general category of ὁ-items. By doing so, it will be demonstrated

---

[17] This categorization recognizes that the distinct indefinite usage was breaking down, though not wholly absent in the Koine era.

[18] Robinson, *Mastering New Testament Greek*, 11.

that it is correct to place these items in the same category, while also demonstrating the fallacy of association of Greek demonstratives and English TH- items. To this end, numerous samples will be examined that illustrate how the article functions in a manner similar to the relative pronoun, and that certain constructions that employ the article function in a manner similar to relative clauses. In this, it will be observed that ὁ-items are used to produce structures that are functionally parallel. In chapter 3 we will observe that articular participial groups perform the same function as defining relative clauses, which identify the head term by locating it within a subset, by specifying it as a particular subset of a general class.[19] This is accomplished by means of elaboration, where the head term is further specified or described; extension, where something new is added to the head term; or enhancement, where the head term is qualified "by reference to time, place, manner, cause or condition."[20]

The statement "functionally parallel" must itself be qualified. Any unit of discourse at any hierarchal level may perform a variety of functions simultaneously. Halliday identifies three *metafunctions* of language: ideational, interpersonal, and textual. Regarding the first two metafunctions, he summarizes by saying, "every message is both about something and addressing someone."[21] The function of the ideational metafunction is to construe human experience by using language to name things, "thus construing them into categories."[22] At the same time, language enacts "our personal and social relationships with the other people around us."[23] This is the domain of the interpersonal metafunction, by which we use language to "inform or question, give an order or make an offer, and express our appraisal of and attitude towards whoever we are addressing and what we are talking about."[24]

The third metafunction, *textual*, "relates to the construction of text."[25] The textual metafunction,

> . . . can be regarded as an enabling or facilitating function, since both the others—construing experience and enacting personal relations—depend on being able to build up sequences of discourse, organizing the discursive flow and creating cohesion and continuity as it moves along.[26]

---

[19] Halliday, *Functional Grammar*, 400.
[20] Halliday, *Functional Grammar*, 396–410.
[21] Halliday, *Functional Grammar*, 30.
[22] Halliday, *Functional Grammar*, 29.
[23] Halliday, *Functional Grammar*, 29.
[24] Halliday, *Functional Grammar*, 29.
[25] Halliday, *Functional Grammar*, 30.
[26] Halliday, *Functional Grammar*, 30.

In the following analysis, we are mostly concerned with this third meta-function. We are specifically concerned with how Greek speakers use structures that employ ό-items "to build up sequences of discourse." These structures are used by Greek speakers for the purpose of *realization*. The creation of text is the means by which a speaker or writer makes information accessible to his or her audience: "Realization comes in because what becomes accessible to us is the text *as realized* in sound or writing."[27] That which a speaker or writer wants to make accessible may be realized by a variety of structures. The option to choose between one structure or another is part of the process of realization:

> Structural operations—inserting elements, ordering elements and so on—are explained as *realizing* systemic choices...When we speak of structural features as 'realizing' systemic choices, this is one manifestation of a general relationship that pervades every quarter of language. Realization derives from the fact that a language is a stratified system.[28]

In this sense, certain structures may said to be functionally parallel. *Ho-*items are used to produce structures for the purpose of realization. While different structures may be used to fill the same syntactical slot, they function at different hierarchal levels, or strata. It will be argued that the article functions as a form similar to that of the relative pronoun because it is demonstrable that the article is used to produce structures that fill the same slot as relative clauses. This represents a system of choice, whereby a Greek speaker may choose one form or the other. With regard to the production of text, both structures fill the same slot, and thus perform the same function. However, with regard to both the ideational and interpersonal metafunctions, the choice of one structure over the other reflects a difference in meaning, and thus they are not in this sense functionally parallel. The statement *functionally parallel* in the following analysis applies to the textual metafunction only. The limited scope of this term must be stressed, with the recognition that the structures examined below, at other levels of linguistic operation, are not at all functionally parallel.

2. The Discourse Function of 'ο-items

The presence of two structures that perform the same function provides the speaker with a choice in the production of text. Determining the

---

[27] Halliday, *Functional Grammar*, 33, emphasis his.
[28] Halliday, *Functional Grammar*, 24.

motivation behind the choice of one structure over the other provides insight into the meaning the speaker assigns to the structure.

In language, one observes that there are typical patterns of realization. However, as Halliday observes so often happens in language, "in contrast with the typical pattern there is a standing-out or *marked* alternative."[29] In relative terms, markedness theory is a fairly recent field of inquiry within linguistics. The principles of markedness theory have their origins in the Prague School of linguistics based on the pioneering work of Nikolai Trubetzkoy and Roman Jakobson in the early twentieth century.[30] However, extensive work on markedness did not take off until the second half of the century. Despite its youth, markedness theory has seen substantial development, such that there is now significant diversity of theories, each of which has expanded upon and introduced substantial modifications to its original form.

From the beginning, at the core of markedness theory has been the concept of polar or binary opposition of features, with one pole representing that which is *marked*, and the other *unmarked*. It is this polarity that is at the heart of markedness theory. As the various schools of linguistics began to adopt markedness theory and incorporate it into their system, each gave it a form of expression consistent with its own goals and interests while essentially retaining the core principle of opposition. Today, though one may not always encounter the terms polarity or binary opposition, the influence of these terms and the views that underpin them may still be perceived.

In the 1986 publication simply titled *Markedness*, Moravcsik and Wirth illustrate the basic principles of markedness through the use of analogy. On the one hand, they argue, there is a correlation between familiarity and variability. Things that are common or familiar such as everyday clothes or food exhibit greater variability, whereas holiday foods and festive attire exhibit less variability.[31] In contrast to this is structural complexity. They argue "the more common an object is in our experience, the more simple it is perceived or created to be."[32] They conclude that there is a three-way correlation between familiarity, variability, and complexity: "Closer

---

[29] Halliday, *Functional Grammar*, 70.
[30] Battistella, *Markedness*, 1. "Roman Jakobson first discovered the relation of *marked* and *unmarked* terms in 1921, although it was Nikolai Trubetzkoy who first used the term *priznak* (Russian 'mark') for this particular type of opposition." Andrews, *Markedness Theory*, 1.
[31] Moravcsik and Wirth, "Markedness: An Overview," 1–2.
[32] Moravcsik and Wirth, "Markedness: An Overview," 2.

familiarity tends to be paired with simpler structure and greater variability; less frequent occurrence in human experience goes with increased structural complexity and diminished variability."[33] It is their argument that this applies to language as well, which "constitutes the classic form of markedness theory."[34] Unmarked forms are those that have one or more of the characteristics of wide distribution, simple structure, and/or rich elaboration.[35]

Building on the work of the Prague school, Edwin Battistella defines *markedness* in terms of polar opposites. Though he is primarily concerned with semantic markedness, his theory has implications for the broader field of markedness theory:

> The term *markedness* refers to the relationship between the two poles of an opposition; the terms *marked* and *unmarked* refer to the evaluation of the poles; the simpler, more general pole is the unmarked term of the opposition while the more complex and focused pole is the marked term.[36]

Battistella latter writes:

> Distribution within a language plays an important role in the determination of language-particular markedness values. Unmarked terms are distinguished from their marked counterparts by having greater freedom of occurrence and a greater ability to combine with other linguistic elements.[37]

Working within the "functionalist" school (though in practice heavily cognitivistic), Givón offers three criteria that may be used to distinguish marked and unmarked categories: structural complexity, where the marked structure tends to be larger or more complex than the unmarked structure; frequency distribution, where the marked structure tends to be less frequent and more cognitively salient; and cognitive complexity, where the marked structure engenders greater attention, mental effort or processing time.[38] He notes that structural complexity has traditionally been the criterion of markedness, but that this is "often useless without substantial help from [frequency distribution] and [cognitive complexity]."[39]

---

[33] Moravcsik and Wirth, "Markedness: An Overview," 2.
[34] Moravcsik and Wirth, "Markedness: An Overview," 3.
[35] Moravcsik and Wirth, "Markedness: An Overview," 3.
[36] Battistella, *Markedness*, 1.
[37] Battistella, *Markedness*, 26.
[38] Givón, *Syntax, Vol. 2*, 947.
[39] Givón, *Syntax, Vol. 2*, 947, also *Functionalism and Grammar*, 25.

While markedness theory has been the object of significant interest and development over the last several decades, it is not without its detractors. Martin Haspelmath argues that the term is "superfluous, because some of the concepts that it denotes are not helpful, and others are better expressed by more straightforward, less ambiguous terms."[40] Haspelmath lists 12 senses of markedness arranged into four classes: markedness as complexity, markedness as difficulty, markedness as abnormality, markedness as multidimensional correlation.[41] It is this plethora of senses that leads him to question the usefulness of the term. Despite his objections, most linguists continue to employ the term.

Prominence is related to markedness but is distinguished from it. Markedness is a matter of the production of text. It is simply a matter of the identification of a particular structure, without comment upon function or significance. Thus, it may be said that markedness is a matter of the textual metafunction only. Prominence, however, has to do with the significance assigned to a particular structure, which is the domain of both the informational and interpersonal metafunctions.

Regarding prominence theory, Reed writes:

> One way to build thematic structure in discourse is by creating *prominence* (also known as emphasis, grounding, relevance, salience), i.e. by drawing the listener/reader's attention to topics and motifs which are important to the speaker/author and by supporting those topics with other less significant material.[42]

He continues by defining prominence as

> semantic and grammatical elements of discourse that serve to set aside certain subjects, ideas, or motifs of the author as more or less semantically and pragmatically significant than others.[43]

Porter quotes Halliday's definition of prominence as "the phenomenon of linguistic highlighting, whereby some feature of the language of a text stands out in some way."[44] He observes in Halliday an important qualification that we, too, must maintain:

---

[40] Haspelmath, "Against Markedness," 25.
[41] Haspelmath, "Against Markedness," 25–26.
[42] Reed, "Identifying Theme in the New Testament," 75.
[43] Reed, "Identifying Theme in the New Testament," 76.
[44] Porter, "Prominence: An Overview," 52, quoting Halliday, "Linguistic Function," 340; *Explorations*, 113.

> [Halliday] phrases his definition in such a way to avoid characterizing prominence in terms of simply departure or deviance, and sees prominence in terms of motivation to create foregrounding. Nevertheless, it is hard to deny that there are departures from expected syntactical or paradigmatic patterns, many of which may not appear to be prominent in discourse.[45]

It is for this reason that we must resist an appeal to simple departure or deviation as the basis for an argument for prominence. Instead, there must also be evidence that such a departure or deviation is a demonstrably motivated deviation.

With regard to the function of ό-items, it will be demonstrated that an analysis of certain structures that employ these items will reveal that they may be categorized in terms of marked and unmarked forms. One of the most common characterisitics of marked forms is *structural complexity*. We will observe that relative clauses generally represent a more structurally complex form than articular participial clauses. In instances where a speaker or writer may choose between a relative clause and articular participial clause where both are equally suited for the production of text, the relative clause represents a marked form. Based on this, it will be argued that, at times, marked forms are employed to produce prominence or indicate salience. Specifically, we will observe that, in certain instances, when a speaker may choose between a relative clause and articular pariticipial clause, the choice of the relative clause will indicate the speaker's desire to make that element prominent.

3. Selection and Organization of Sample Texts

There are far too many occurrences of the relative pronoun and relative clauses, to say nothing of the article, to engage in an exhaustive treatment of each individual occurrence. The choice of each example used throughout this work and their arrangement are based on several factors. Passages have been chosen to illustrate the usage of individual authors such as Paul, John, Luke, et al. While the arrangement generally follows a canonical order, authorship overrides canon. Thus, the Johannine corpus is grouped together; so too Luke-Acts. Sub-corpora are also grouped. The deutero-Pauline letters are separated from the accepted letters and sub-catergorized into Ephesians/Colossians and the Pastorals, though it is recognized that even these distinctions and groupings may be disputed.

---

[45] Porter, "Prominence: An Overview," 52.

The question of source material necessitates that the synoptic Gospels be treated both in terms of individual authors and as a single sub-corpora. Hebrews and James stand alone. 1 and 2 Peter and Jude present unique issues. 1 and 2 Peter claim to have been the work of a single author, while at the same time suggesting different hands (such as different scribes). The connections between 2 Peter and Jude are well documented. In all arrangements, the author has chosen to follow the views of the broadest general consensus. In addition, it must be recognized that instances of each type of relative clause, for example, will not necessarily occur in every New Testament book.

CHAPTER THREE

DEFINING AND NON-DEFINING RELATIVE CLAUSES

1. Introduction

In this chapter, we will examine how both relative clauses and articular participial clauses are used interchangeably to perform similar functions. It will be seen that both fill the same syntactical slot. In these instances, both function to define or provide further characterization of a head term. The purpose of this examination is to illustrate how the article and relative pronouns are employed to perform similar functions. This, in turn, provides justification for categorizing them together, as well for distinguishing the article from the demonstrative pronoun and from determiners in general.

Within a given discourse, the clauses that make up the discourse enter into various relationships with one another. At the most basic level, a clause is either *primary* or *secondary*. Relative clauses are secondary in function, in that they are a continuation of a primary clause and are thus dependent.[1] Relative clauses may be both embedded and non-embedded. As an embedded element, the function of the relative clause will be either that of a modifier/qualifier of the head of the group or it may function as the actual head of the group.[2] Non-embedded relative clauses do not function as qualifiers but typically add "further characterization of something that is taken to be already fully specific."[3]

It has long been observed that the Greek language, like English, employs relative clauses, which are set apart through the use of the relative pronoun.[4] In English, "WH- items also function as *relatives*, marking a 'relative clause'—one that is structurally related to another by hypotaxis or embedding."[5] As stated above, a relative clause may perform a variety

---

[1] Halliday, *Functional Grammar*, 376.

[2] Halliday, *Functional Grammar*, 426.

[3] Halliday, *Functional Grammar*, 400.

[4] For classic treatments see Dana & Mantey, *Manual Grammer*, 270–73; Robertson, *Grammar*, 711, 953–62. More recently: Porter, *Idioms*, 244–53.

[5] Halliday, *Functional Grammar*, 85, emphasis his. "Parataxis is the linking of elements of equal status," while "Hypotaxis is the binding of elements of unequal status," *Fuctional Grammar*, 384.

of functions: head of a group, qualifier of a head, or a clause that provides further characterization of a head. In Greek, relative clauses perform these same functions. However, one will also observe that ὁ-items
in general, both the article and relative pronouns, are used to produce
structures that perform these functions.[6] On the one hand, the relative
pronoun is employed with finite verbs; while on the other hand, the article
is employed with non-finite verbs, in this case, participles. Nevertheless,
both are employed to produce structures that function in similar ways, as
will be demonstrated below. It is in this that we observe one of the first
serious deviations in function from the English definite article specifically,
and TH- items in general. As Moule observed, though did not elaborate
upon, the article often functions as a relative pronoun, with its adjoining
word group functioning as a relative clause.[7] In English, Halliday distinguishes between defining and non-defining relative clauses, as well as the
relative clause as head of a group. We will examine the Greek language to
determine if these descriptors are appropriate for it as well.

2. Defining Relative Clauses

While clauses in general may perform a variety of functions, one of the
functions of a relative clause is that of *expansion*. In expansion, "The
secondary clause expands the primary clause, by (a) elaborating it, (b)
extending it or (c) enhancing it."[8] This notion of expansion may be illustrated by means of analogy with mathematics:

elaborating	=	('equals')
extending	+	('is added to')
enhancing	×	('is multiplied by')[9]

Such clauses are categorized as *defining relative clauses*. In English, Halliday writes that a defining relative clause functions as a qualifier that
is embedded in the nominal group.[10] In embedding, a phrase or clause

---

[6] Robertson observes "The article with the participle is very common as the equivalent of a relative clause," *Grammar*, 764. Moule, as noted above, makes a similar observation, "[The article] also offers (when used before a participle or adjective) a neat way of
expressing what would otherwise have to be expressed by a relative clause," *Idiom Book*,
106. Despite these observations, they do not give priority to the relationship between the
article and the relative pronoun.

[7] Moule, *Idiom Book*, 106.

[8] Halliday, *Functional Grammar*, 377. See also Reed, *Philippians*, 90–93.

[9] Halliday, *Functional Grammar*, 377.

[10] Halliday, *Functional Grammar*, 324–25.

"comes to function as a constituent *within* the structure of a group, which itself is a constituent of a clause."[11] As a qualifier, a defining relative clause identifies the head term by locating it within a subset, by specifying it as a particular subset of a general class.[12] For the purposes of the present analysis, what is most important is that ὁ-items, both the article and relative pronoun, are used by the speaker or writer to introduce new information that the recipient is to use for the purpose of identifying a head term by locating it within a subset.

In English, within the nominal group, a qualifier is an element that follows the Thing (often, though not universally, the head term) and is either a phrase or a clause.[13] In Greek, the definition of qualifier must be modified due to the syntactical flexibility of the language (qualifiers may precede the head term) and the presence of grammatical elements not found in English: "A qualifier is a modifier that in some way limits or constrains the scope of the word it modifies. Common examples of qualifiers are words in the genitive and dative case."[14] In Greek, qualifiers may be individual words or larger units such as groups and clauses. The sub-categories employed by Halliday are a useful point of departure for examining Greek relative clauses. As will be seen, there are general points of continuity between Greek and English, as well as areas of discontinuity. Both will be examined below.

a. *Elaboration*

In elaboration, the defining relative clause elaborates on the meaning of the head term "by further specifying or describing it."[15] This function is common in the New Testament. We will first observe this as a function of relative clauses, then as a function of articular participial clauses.[16] In both instances, the speaker or writer does not indicate that the information necessary for identification is recoverable or obvious from the discourse, nor is the recipient directed to the necessary information. Instead, this

---

[11] Halliday, *Functional Grammar*, 426.

[12] Halliday, *Functional Grammar*, 400.

[13] Halliday, *Functional Grammar*, 323. *Thing* is the term employed by Halliday. We will use *head term*, which refers to the head of a nominal group.

[14] "OpenText.org Annotation Model," lines 38–39.

[15] Halliday, *Functional Grammar*, 396.

[16] The use of the designation *participial clause* is based on the definition of *clause* employed by OpenText.org. Among the basic components of the clause is the *predicate*, which "includes both finite and infinite (participle and infinitive) verb forms," "OpenText. org Clause Level Annotation Specification," lines 40–41 (2. Definitions [d4] the Predicate).

information is provided by the speaker or writer, to whom identification of the referent is oriented.

a.1. *Elaborating Relative Clauses*

In Matt 2:16, the author makes reference to a particular χρόνος, *time*. However, the exact nature of this *time* requires further specification. This function of the relative clause is to further specify the *time* to which the author refers:

> κατὰ τὸν χρόνον ὃν ἠκρίβωσεν παρὰ τῶν μάγων.
>
> …according to the time *which he learned from the magi.*

The embedded relative clause is graphically illustrated in the OpenText. org clause annotation:[17]

A			
κατὰ τὸν χρόνον			
	C	P	A
Mat.c2_79	ὃν	ἠκρίβωσεν	παρὰ τῶν μάγων

The *time* to which the author makes reference is further specified by means of the embedded defining relative clause. It is the specific time that King Herod *learned from the Magi*. Time is a very broad, general class. The time *which he learned from the magi* is a subset within this class. By employing a relative pronoun, the writer indicates that he is providing information to the reader that he or she is to use to more specifically identify *the time*. Because this information is known and provided by the writer, the identification of the referent is oriented to him.

In Luke 2:11, the author employs a relative clause to elaborate on σωτήρ, *savior*. In this instance, the relative clause further describes him:

> ὅτι ἐτέχθη ὑμῖν σήμερον σωτὴρ ὅς ἐστιν χριστὸς κύριος ἐν πόλει Δαυίδ.
>
> Because today to you was born in the city of David a savior, *who is Christ the Lord.*

---

[17] This type of clause level annotation of the entire New Testament may be viewed at www.opentext.org, from which this and the following examples are taken.

	cj	P	C	A	S				A
	ὅτι	ἐτέχθη	ὑμῖν	σήμερον	σωτὴρ				ἐν
Luk.c2_34									πόλει
⌐c2_32						S	P	C	Δαυίδ
					Luk.c2_35	ὅς	ἐστιν	Χριστός κύριος	

The head of the group is *savior*, which also functions as the subject of the clause. The head is further described by the relative clause and thus it establishes its identity: the savior is *Christ the Lord*. The head may also be viewed as a class, *savior*, since there are many whose activities would qualify for inclusion into this group. *Christ the Lord* is a subset of one within this class. Once again, the speaker provides the information necessary for identification. There is no indication that both the speaker and the recipient share this information, nor does the speaker direct the recipient to the information. He provides the information, thus orienting the identification of the referent to him.

The apostle Paul employs a defining relative clause in Rom 10:8 to elaborate on the nature of τὸ ῥῆμα τῆς πίστεως, *the word of faith*:

τὸ ῥῆμα τῆς πίστεως ὃ κηρύσσομεν.

The word of faith, *which we proclaim.*

	C		
Rom.c10_24	τὸ ῥῆμα τῆς πίστεως		
⌐c10_22		C	P
	Rom.c10_25	ὃ	κηρύσσομεν

The function of the relative clause may be interpreted as either further specifying or further describing the *word of faith* to which Paul refers. It is the one which Paul and his companions proclaim. This is its distinguishing feature. For Paul, any *word of faith* which is not consistent with the one *which we proclaim* is false. This characterization identifies this particular *word of faith* as a subset within a broader class. The information necessary to make this identification is provided by Paul.

Paul's use of a defining relative clause may be observed again in 1 Cor 10:16:

τὸ ποτήριον τῆς εὐλογίας ὃ εὐλογοῦμεν, οὐχὶ κοινωνία ἐστὶν τοῦ αἵματος τοῦ Χριστοῦ; τὸν ἄρτον ὃν κλῶμεν, οὐχὶ κοινωνία τοῦ σώματος τοῦ Χριτοῦ ἐστιν;

Is not the cup of blessing, *which we bless,* associated with the blood of Christ?
Is not the bread, *which we break,* associated with the body of Christ?

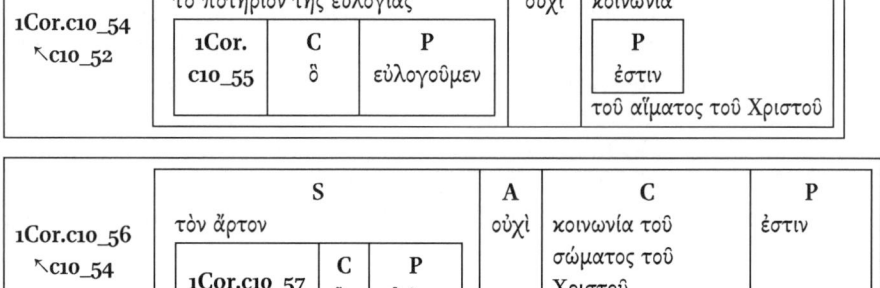

Instead of additional specification, these embedded relative clauses provide further description of the both *the cup* and *the bread*: the former is that *which we bless,* the latter is that *which we break.* There are certainly many cups and many loaves of bread one encounters in daily life. These embedded relative clauses specifically identify them through the implied association with the Eucharist (blessing and breaking being the associative words). *Cup* and *bread* are general classes. The *cup which we bless* and the *bread which we break* are specific subsets within this general class.

Col 1:4 provides an opportunity to observe both an embedded defining relative clause and an embedded participial clause that functions as a reduced defining relative clause. This example illustrates the manner in which ὅ-items, relative pronouns and the article may share a common function.

ἀκούσαντες τὴν πίστιν ὑμῶν ἐν Χριστῷ Ἰησοῦ καὶ τὴν ἀγάπην ἣν ἔχετε εἰς πάντας τοὺς ἁγίους διὰ τὴν ἐλπίδα τὴν ἀποκειμένην ὑμῖν ἐν τοῖς οὐρανοῖς.

Hearing about your faith in Christ Jesus and the love *which you have in all the saints because of the hope which is stored for you in the heavens.*

	P ἀκούσαντες	**C** τὴν πίστιν ὑμῶν ἐν Χριστῷ Ἰησοῦ καὶ τὴν ἀγάπην				
Col.c1_5		**Col.c1_6**	**C** ἦν	**P** ἔχετε	**A** εἰς πάντας τοὺς ἁγίους	**A** διὰ τὴν ἐλπίδα

Inner table under A (διὰ τὴν ἐλπίδα):

	P	**C**	**A**
Col. c1_7	τὴν ἀποκειμένην	ὑμῖν	ἐν τοῖς οὐρανοῖς

Love is a very broad notion. For Paul, there is a very specific manifestation of love in operation in Colossae that he is pleased to hear about. Within the class of *love* is the specific subset for which Paul commends his audience. The nature of this subset is characterized by a particular quality: it is the one *which you have*. Additionally, they have this love *because of hope*. However, it is not *hope* in a generic sense. Paul has in mind a specific subset of *hope*. Therefore, he further specifies *hope*. In this instance, rather than use a defining relative clause, Paul employs a participial clause. The sub-set of *hope* that Paul has in view is characterized by the fact that it is *the one stored up for you in heaven*. In this we observe that both the relative pronoun and the article are elements that establish a relation in structures that perform the same function. In both instances, the relative pronoun and the article indicate that the writer is providing the information necessary for identification. There is no indication that the recipients share this information with the writer or that the information is recoverable or obvious in the discourse, nor does he direct them to where the information may be found, as would be the case with the English definite article or demonstrative pronouns. Thus, identification of the referent is oriented to the writer.

James also employs the defining relative clause for the purpose of elaboration. In Jas 1:12 we read:

μακάριος ἀνὴρ ὃς ὑπομένει πειρασμόν.

Blessed is the man *who endures testing*.

Jam.c1_32 ⌐c1_31	**C** μακάριος	**S** ἀνὴρ			
		Jam. c1_33	**S** ὅς	**P** ὑπομένει	**C** πειρασμόν

Through the use of an embedded relative clause, James elaborates on the person who is blessed by further describing him. *Blessed person* is a very general class of thing. Within this class is the subset of the one *who endures testing.*

John, too, makes use of the defining relative clause. In each instance, the writer does not direct the reader to the information necessary for identification, nor does he indicate that it is available to the reader. Instead, he provides the information that the reader is to use for the purpose of identification. Several examples may be cited. First, in 1 John 2:7 the author explains the nature of the *new commandment* to his audience:

ἡ ἐντολὴ ἡ παλαιά ἐστιν ὁ λόγος ὃν ἠκούσατε.

The old commandment is the word *which you heard.*

1Joh.c2_28 ↖c2_26	S ἡ ἐντολὴ ἡ παλαιά	P ἐστιν	C		
			ὁ λόγος		
			1J h.c2_29	C ὃν	P ἠκούσατε

The *word* to which the author makes reference is further specified; it is the word *which you heard.* For purposes of this letter, this qualification is extremely important, as the author goes to great lengths to contrast himself and his teaching with his opponents and their teachings. The recipients of the letter have received many words. These words are a general class (we may narrow them by using the term *teaching*). Within this class is the subset of word or teaching that is defined as the one *which you heard.*

Later, the author elaborates on the nature of a specific *promise.* Thus, in 1 John 2:25 we read:

καὶ αὕτη ἐστὶν ἡ ἐπαγγελία ἣν αὐτὸς ἐπηγγείλατο ἡμῖν,

And this is the promise, *which he himself promised to us.*

1Joh.c2_105 ↖c2_104	cj καὶ	C αὕτη	P ἐστὶν	S				
				ἡ ἐπαγγελία				
				1Joh. c2_106	C ἣν	S αὐτὸς	P ἐπηγγείλατο	C ἡμῖν

The general class of *promise* is further specified. It is not just any promise, but specifically the one *which he himself promised to us*. The nature of the promise is further defined by the fact that it was promised by God.

At one point, the author needs to make a distinction between sub-classes of *spirit*. Once again, this is accomplished by means of defining relative clauses. In 1 John 4:2-3 we read:

πᾶν πνεῦμα ὃ ὁμολογεῖ Ἰησοῦν Χριστὸν ἐν σαρκὶ ἐληλυθότα ἐκ τοῦ θεοῦ ἐστιν,
καὶ πᾶν πνεῦμα ὃ μὴ ὁμολογεῖ τὸν Ἰησοῦν ἐκ τοῦ θεοῦ οὐκ ἔστιν.

Every spirit *which confesses that Jesus Christ has come in the flesh* is from God;
and each spirit *that does not confess Jesus* is not from God.

				S				A	P
	πᾶν πνεῦμα							ἐκ τοῦ θεοῦ	ἐστιν
1Joh.c4_6 ⌐c4_5	1Joh. c4_7	S ὃ	P ὁμολογεῖ	C Ἰησοῦν Χριστὸν					
					1Joh. c4_8	A ἐν σαρκὶ	P ἐληλυθότα		

	cj		S					A	A	P
	καὶ	πᾶν πνεῦμα						ἐκ τοῦ θεοῦ	οὐκ	ἔστιν
1Joh.c4_9 ⌐c4_6		1Joh. c4_10	S ὃ	A μὴ	P ὁμολογεῖ	C τὸν Ἰησοῦν				

The embedded relative clauses in these two verses both specify and define which spirits the author is talking about. In the first instance, the spirit that is from God is the one *who confesses that Jesus Christ has come in the flesh*. In the second instance, the spirit that is not from God is the one *who does not confess Jesus*.

a.2. *Elaborating Participial Clause*
In addition to the defining relative clause, an articular participial clause may also be employed to qualify a head term. In these instances, the article, like the relative pronoun, establishes a relation between the head term and a participial clause. Correspondingly, the participial clause qualifies

the head term and characterizes it as a subset within a class.[18] In this we observe how two different structures are used to fill the same slot. This also illustrates how the article, like the relative pronoun, is employed to indicate that the speaker or writer is providing the information necessary for identifying the referent. He or she does not indicate that the recipient already possesses this information or that it is recoverable or obvious from the discourse; nor is the recipient directed to this information. This usage is often observed in the so-called second attributive position.

Among first-century Jews, the name Simon was very common. Therefore, the author must further specify which Simon is being referenced. In Matt 4:18 this is accomplished by means of a defining participial clause:

εἶδεν δύο ἀδελφούς, Σίμωνα τὸν λεγόμενον Πέτρον καὶ Ἀδνρέαν τὸν ἀδελφὸν αὐτοῦ.

He saw two brothers, Simon, *who is called Peter*, and Andrew his brother.

εἶδεν	C δύο ἀδελφούς Σίμωνα		
	Matt.c4_65	**P** τὸν λεγόμενον	**C** Πέτρον
	καὶ Ἀνδρέαν τὸν ἀδελφὸν αὐτοῦ		

The word group τὸν λεγόμενον Πέτρον is embedded within the complement. As noted, the name Simon was very common in first century Judea. Because of this fact, the name itself may be understood as a broad class. In this instance, this name is further specified by the fact that he is the one *who is called Peter*, a subset within the class. The writer does not direct the recipient to the information necessary for identification, nor does he

---

[18] The use of the articular participle in place of a relative clause did not go unnoticed by grammarians. Moulton observes: "Relative clauses are frequently ousted by the articular participle, which (as Blass observes) had become synonymous therewith," *Prolegomena*, 228. Robertson agrees: "It is a very common thing in the N.T., as already noted, to have ὁ and the participle where a relative clause is possible," *Grammar*, 1108. The comments of Moule and Wallace on this usage have already been noted. One is left to wonder why this usage has not played a greater role in descriptions of the article's function. In all likelihood, the answer lies in the unswerving association of the Greek article with the demonstrative pronoun, as well as the English article. In contrast to Moulton's assertion that articular participles "had become" synonomous with relative clauses, I argue that they were by their very nature synonomous because of the relationship between the article and relative pronoun.

indicate it is obvious or recoverable from the discourse. He provides this information that the reader is to use to identify the referent.

In Luke 11:27, we again observe an embedded defining relative clause in the same context as an embedded defining participial clause:

μακαρία ἡ κοιλία ἡ βαστάσασά σε καὶ μαστοὶ οὓς ἐθήλασας.

Blessed is the womb *which carried you* and the breasts *which nursed.*

122 ╲c11_120	C μακαρία	S		
		ἡ κοιλία		
		Luk.c11_123	P ἡ βαστάσασά	C σε
		καὶ μαστοὶ		
		Luk.c11_124	C οὓς	P ἐθήλασας

Womb is further specified by the fact that it is the one which *carried you.* As seen in the OpenText.org annotation, ἡ βαστάσασά σε is embedded, just as a typical relative clause would be. *Womb* is a general class. The one *that carried you* is a subset of that class. Immediately following is the more typical embedded relative clause, which further describes *breasts* as *ones that nursed.* Again, the class of *breasts* is defined as a subset by the fact that they are characterized as *the ones that nursed.* Correspondingly, the article is used with a non-finite verb, in this instance a participle, and establishes a relation between a clause and the head term. The relative pronoun is used with a finite verb and also establishes a relation between a clause and the head term. Once again we observe that the two elements perform the same function. This example is particularly useful in that it illustrates how the two structures are both embedded and perform the same function by providing the information necessary for identifying the referent.

The same author employs this structure in Acts 3:2:

τὴν θύραν τοῦ ἱεροῦ τὴν λεγομένην Ὡραίαν.

The temple's enterance, *which is called "beautiful."*

Act.c3_4 ↖c3_2	A		
	πρὸς τὴν θύραν τοῦ ἱεροῦ		
	Act.c3_5	P τὴν λεγομένην	C ὡραίαν

First, *the enterance* is qualified by the fact that it is *the temple's*. Second, it is further specified by its nickname, it is the one *which is called "beautiful."* Both the qualifier and the defining participial clause provide characterization that identifies the head term as a subset within a class. A similar form of specification is observed in Acts 3:11:

ἐπὶ τῇ στοᾷ τῇ καλουμένῃ Σολομῶντος.

... on the porch, *which is called "Solomon's."*

Act.c3_44 ↖c3_41	A		
	ἐπὶ τῇ στοᾷ		
	Act.c3_45	P τῇ καλουμένῃ	C Σολομῶντος

This is another example of specification by means of reference to a nickname. The porch is known as the one *which is called "Solomon's."* For further examples see Acts 4:36, Joseph who is called Barnabas; Acts 12:25, John who is called Mark; Acts 13:1, Simeon who is called Niger; Col 4:11, Jesus who is called Justus.

In Acts 17:24, the author records Paul's speech to the philosophers in Athens. In this speech, the apostle distinguishes the God of Israel from the gods worshipped by the Athenians. He is:

ὁ θεὸς ὁ ποιήσας τὸν κόσμον καὶ πάντα τὰ ἐν αὐτῷ.

The God *who made the world and all things in it.*

Act.c17_103 ↖c17_102	S	
	ὁ θεὸς	
	Act.c17_104	P ὁ ποιήσας	C τὸν κόσμον καὶ πάντα τὰ ἐν αὐτῷ

In the ancient world, there was certainly a plethora of gods. Within this class is the subset of one: the God of Israel. When speaking or writing about God, an aspect of his nature to which the biblical writers frequently appealed was his activity of creation. In contrast to the pagan gods, who were typically depicted as fashioning or bringing order to an existing but chaotic universe, God was personally responsible for its existence. Thus, God has ownership and authority over all created things; he is Lord. As Paul goes on to say, such a god as this does not reside in temples built by human beings or have needs that could be served by them. In this example, the participial clause, which functionally is a defining relative clause, further specifies the God whom Paul preaches as a subset within the general class of *gods*. He is the one *who made the world and all things in it.* Paul provides this information, which his audience is to use for the purpose of identifying the referent, God.

In the Johannine corpus, we also observe the use of defining participial clauses. For example, observe its use in John 5:12:

τίς ἐστιν ὁ ἄνθρωπος ὁ εἰπών σοι· ἆρον καὶ περιπάτει;

Who is the person *who said to you,* "Take up [your mat] and walk"?

	C τίς	P ἐστιν	S		
John.c5_44 ↖c5_43			ὁ ἄνθρωπος		
			John.c5_45	P ὁ εἰπών	C σοι
			John.c5_45		P ἆρον
			John.c5_47	cj καὶ	P περιπάτει

The person in question is specified by means of an embedded participial clause functioning as a defining relative clause, without which the question would be vague. The paralytic might respond, "Which man are you talking about?" Thus, the inquisitors employ a defining participial clause to further specify which man is in view; they provide the information necessary to identify the referent. He is the man *who said to you, "Take up your mat and walk."*

In the Johannine writings, the author distinguishes between those who are begotten of God and those who are not. In 1 John 4:7, he employs a defining participial clause to identify one of the qualities that characterize those who are begotten of God:

καὶ πᾶς ὁ ἀγαπῶν ἐκ τοῦ θεοῦ γεγέννηται.

And each one *who loves* is begotten from God.

1Joh.c4_30 ⌐c4_29	cj καὶ	S πᾶς		A ἐκ τοῦ θεοῦ	P γεγέννηται
		1Joh.c4_31	P ὁ ἀγαπῶν		

In this verse, *each one* is the subject of the clause. However, the subject needs further specification. The phrase ὁ ἀγαπῶν functions as a reduced relative clause, qualifying the subject. It is not each person who is begotten from God, but a subset within this group: each person *who loves* is begotten from God.

The same author uses a defining participial clause in 1 John 5:4 to identify a subset of νίκη, *victory*:

καὶ αὕτη ἐστὶν ἡ νίκη ἡ νικήσασα τὸν κόσμον, ἡ πίστις ἡμῶν.

And this is the victory *which conquers the world*: our faith.

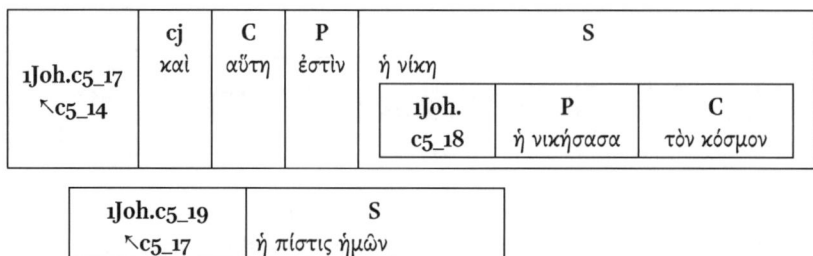

1Joh.c5_17 ⌐c5_14	cj καὶ	C αὕτη	P ἐστὶν	S ἡ νίκη		
					1Joh. c5_18	P ἡ νικήσασα	C τὸν κόσμον

1Joh.c5_19 ⌐c5_17	S ἡ πίστις ἡμῶν

There is a specific *victory* that John has in mind. It is defined by the fact that it is the one *which conquers the world*.

The author of the Apocalypse uses a defining participial clause in Rev 2:20 to further specify an individual:

τὴν γυναῖκα Ἰεζάβελ, ἡ λέγουσα ἑαυτὴν προφῆτιν.

The woman Jezebel *who calls herself "prophet."*

Rev.c2_106 ⤷c2_105	C			
	τὴν γυναῖκα Ἰεζάβελ			
	Rev.c2_107	P ἡ λέγουσα	C ἑαυτὴν	C προφῆτιν

The reader may interpret the seer's reference to Jezebel exclusively as reference to the Old Testament figure who brought Baal worship to Israel. While certainly John means to make this connection, the name is further specified by the fact that she is the one *who calls herself "prophet."* By defining it this way, John hopes the audience will associate the name and activity with a specific "prophetic" member of their congregation and thus reject this person's influence.

The apostle Paul frequently employs the defining participial clause. In Rom 9:5, he further specifies ὁ Χριστὸς in this manner:

καὶ ἐξ ὧν ὁ Χριστὸς τὸ κατὰ σάρκα, ὁ ὢν ἐπὶ πάντων θεὸς ...[19]

And from whom Christ, according to the flesh, *who is God over all things...*

Rom.c9_11 ⤷c9_10	cj καὶ	A ἐξ ὧν	S		
			ὁ Χριστὸς		
			C τὸ κατὰ σάρκα		
			Rom. c9_12	P ὁ ὢν	C ἐπὶ πάντων θεὸς

Just as *god* was a class in the ancient world, so too there were many χριστοί, *anointed ones*, thus the class *Christ*. Jesus is *the Christ* who is defined by the fact that he is the one *who is God over all things*, as subset of the class *Christ*. Paul provided the information necessary for the readers to make this identification.

---

[19] In the participial clause, the OpenText.org annotation associates the article with the participle. However, it is at least possible that the article modifies θεός and that the participle and prepositional phrase constitute an embedded clause.

Just as there were many *anointed ones*, there are also many laws. In Gal 3:21, Paul employs a defining participial clause to identify a subset of *law*:

εἰ γὰρ ἐδόθη νόμος ὁ δυνάμενος ζῳοποιῆσαι...

For if a law was given *which is able to give life*...

Gal.c3_72 ✓c3_75	cj εἰ	cj γὰρ	P ἐδόθη	S				
				νόμος				
					Gal. c3_73	P ὁ δυνάμενος	C	
							Gal. c3_74	P ζῳοποιῆσαι

For the sake of argument, Paul suggests that within the general class of *law*, there may be a subset which is defined by the fact that it is the one *which is able to give life*. Of course, his argument is that such a law does not exist.[20]

One observes numerous instances of the defining participial clause in the General or Catholic Epistles. The author of Hebrews uses this method to further specify the *tent* (σκηνή) to which he refers in 9:3:

μετὰ δὲ τὸ δεύτερον καταπέτασμα σκηνὴ ἡ λεγομένη Ἅγια Ἁγίων.

But after the second curtain, a tent *which is called "Holy of Holies."*

A μετὰ		S		
		σκηνὴ		
	cj δὲ	Heb.c9_6	P ἡ λεγομένη	C ἅγια ἁγίων
τὸ δεύτερον καταπέτασμα				

---

[20] This example is the protasis of a second class conditional, which is often defined as presenting a hypothetical situation for the sake of argument that is contrary to fact. Whether or not the protasis is actually contrary to fact must be determined by context, Porter, *Idioms*, 256–60. In this instance, this is a reasonable conclusion considering Paul's view of the relationship between law and salvation and/or justification.

The tent that is being referred to is further specified, not by an embedded relative clause, but by an embedded participial clause functioning as a relative clause. It is the tent, *which is called "Holy of Holies." Tent* is a class; the tent *which is called "Holy of Holies"* is a subset within that class. We observe this again in the next verse:

ἡ ῥάβδος Ἀαρὼν ἡ βλαστήσασα.

The rod of Aaron, *which spouted leaves.*

	S
	καὶ ἡ ῥάβδος Ἀαρὼν
Heb.c9_9	**Heb.c9_11** / P / ἡ βλαστήσασα

Rod is a general class. On the one hand it is qualified by the genitive *of Aaron,* which restricts the head by reference to ownership or possession. In addition, it is further specified as a subset within a class by the group ἡ βλαστήσασα, *which sprouted leaves.* In both these examples, the relative pronoun has been replaced by the article, the finite verb with a participle. The function of both the articular participial clause and the relative clause are the same, they further specify or describe the head term in some way. The articular participial clause fills the same slot as a relative clause.

Likewise, this usage is observed in 1 Pet 3:5:

οὕτως γάρ ποτε καὶ αἱ ἅγιαι γυναῖκες αἱ ἐλπίζουσαι εἰς θεόν...

For thus also, formerly holy women *who hoped in God...*

	A	cj	A	cj	S		
1Pet.c3_9 ↖**c3_1**	οὕτως	γάρ	ποτε	καὶ	αἱ ἅγιαι γυναῖκες		
					1Pet.c3_10	P / αἱ ἐλπίζουσαι	C / εἰς θεὸν

Within the general class of *women,* you have the subset *holy women.* Within that subset is a further subset of holy women *who hoped in God.* These women are defined by the fact that they are holy and further specified by the fact that they engaged in the activity of hoping.

The author of 1 Peter employs these kinds of embedded participial clauses in very elaborate and complex ways. Observe the example from 1 Pet 1:3:

> Εὐλογητὸς ὁ θεὸς καὶ πατὴρ τοῦ κυρίου ἡμῶν Ἰησοῦ Χριστοῦ, ὁ κατὰ τὸ πολὺ αὐτοῦ ἔλεος ἀναγεννήσας ἡμᾶς...

> Blessed [be] the God and father of our lord Jesus Christ, *who gave us new birth according to his great mercy*...

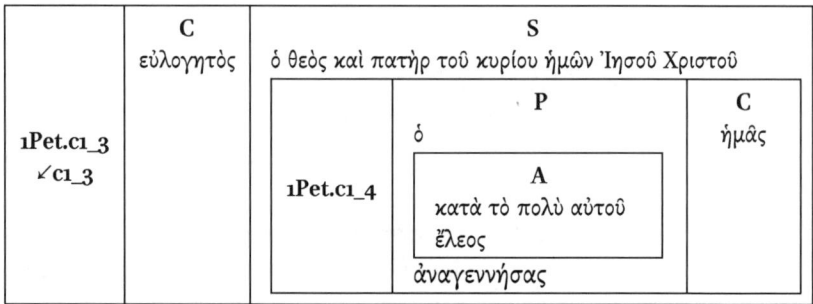

Embedded in the subject is the articular participial clause ὁ κατὰ τὸ πολὺ αὐτοῦ ἔλεος ἀναγεννήσας ἡμᾶς. Embedded with the participial clause is the prepositional group κατὰ τὸ πολὺ αὐτοῦ ἔλεος. The subject, *the God and father of our lord Jesus Christ*, is qualified, that is further defined, by the fact that he is the one *who gave us new birth according to his great mercy*. We again observe this same kind of elaborate embedding in 1 Pet 1:10:

> περὶ ἧς σωτηρίας ἐξεζήτησαν καὶ ἐξηραύνησαν προφῆται οἱ περὶ τῆς εἰς ὑμᾶς χάριτος προφητεύσαντες.

> Concerning which salvation, prophets *who prophesied about the grace in you* searched and inquired.

1Pet.c1_23	A	P
↖c1_18	περὶ ἧς σωτηρίας	ἐξεζήτησαν

	cj καὶ	P ἐξηραύνησαν	S προφῆται		
1Pet.c1_24 ↖c1_23			1Pet.c1_25	P οἱ	
				A περὶ τῆς εἰς ὑμᾶς χάριτος προφητεύσαντες	

The class, *prophets*, to whom the author makes reference, is qualified by the fact that the specific ones being referred to are a subset which is defined as the ones *who prophesied about the grace in you.*

b. *Extension*

Extension takes place when the defining relative clause adds something new to the head term.[21] In English, "The only sense of extension which produces embedded clauses is that of possession, introduced by *whose, of which/which... of* or a 'contact' relative ending with *of*."[22] In Greek, possession may be indicated by means of the genitive case, whereby the identity of the head term is *restricted* by the word in the genitive, indicating "some sort of dependent or derivative status for the governing (head) term in relation to the word in the genitive."[23] Therefore, one would anticipate that, if this type of relative clause appears in Greek, it would employ a relative pronoun in the genitive case. This proposition is problematic because of the reality of *attraction*, whereby a relative pronoun's case mirrors its antecedent rather than being determined by its grammatical function. Thus, many instances of genitive relative pronouns will not indicate possession. In addition, indicating possession is only one of several possible uses of the genitive.[24] Once these factors are taken into consideration, what at first appeared to be a simple proposition is revealed to be

---

[21] Halliday, *Functional Grammar*, 405.

[22] Halliday, *Functional Grammar*, 432.

[23] Porter, *Idioms*, 93. The function of *restriction* is "the essential semantic feature of the genitive case," Porter, *Idioms*, 92.

[24] The genitive may indicate that the head term is "a portion of a larger body denoted by the item in the genitive," it may indicate "ownership or source," or it may be used to "draw a comparison," to name a few, Porter, *Idioms*, 92–97.

anything but simple. Upon examination, attempts to conform Greek usage to this category will be frustrated. In what follows, we will test the category of *extension* to determine if it is applicable to New Testament Greek.

b.1. *Extending Relative Clauses*

The challenge of identifying the category of extension is well illustrated in 1 John 3:24:

καὶ ἐν τούτῳ γινώσκομεν ὅτι μένει ἐν ἡμῖν, ἐκ τοῦ πνεύματος οὗ ἡμῖν ἔδωκεν.

And by this we know that he remains in us, from the spirit *which he gave to us.*

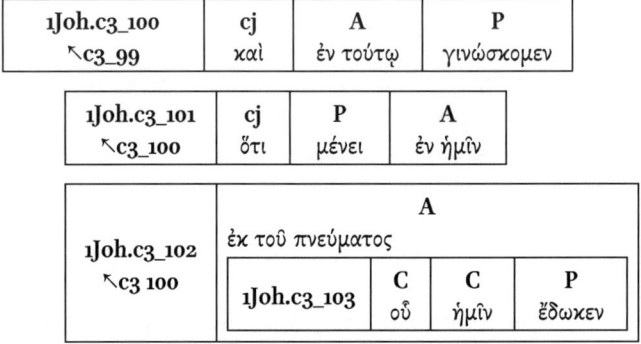

At first glance, this instance appears to fit the criteria of extension: there is an embedded relative clause that employs a relative pronoun in the genitive case. However, in this instance, the function of the genitive case may be explained apart from simple *possession.* On the one hand, the relative pronoun may be in the genitive case due to attraction.[25] On the other hand, it may be employed to indicate the *origin* or *source* of the head term, τοῦ πνεύματος.[26] Thus, while structurally this example fits the pattern outlined above, it varies from the definition laid out by Halliday. This does not render Halliday's category useless, however. We may employ it as a launching point for a categorization that is more organic to the Greek language. As noted above, the basic function of the Greek genitive case

---

[25] Brown, *The Epistles of John,* 466; Smalley, *1,2,3 John,* 212; Culy, *I,II,III John,* 99.
[26] Porter, *Idioms,* 93.

is that of *restriction*.[27] Based on this, it is possible to still view the relative clause as something that adds to the head term by way of extension, but it is the addition of a restriction. Another possible course would be to opt out of Halliday's sub-category altogether in favor of a new sub-category: that of *restriction* instead of *extension*.[28]

Greek speakers did not employ the gentive case only to indicate *possession*, as English speakers understand it. At times they also employed the dative case for this purpose, which grammaticalizes "the semantic feature of relation."[29] As with the genitive, possession was only one of many possible functions. Nevertheless, it presents another option to potentially identify extending relative clauses in Greek. Consider Luke 8:41:

καὶ ἰδοὺ ἦλθεν ἀνὴρ ᾧ ὄνομα Ἰάϊρος

And behold, a man *whose name (was) Jairus* came

Luk.c8_210	cj	P
↖c8_208	καὶ	ἰδοὺ

Luk.c8_211	P	S
↖c8_210	ἦλθεν	ἀνὴρ

Luk.c8_212	S	C
↖c8_211	ᾧ ὄνομα	Ἰάϊρος

A coursory reading of the text suggests that this construction might represent extension. However, as the OpenText.org annotation clearly illustrates, the relative clause is not embedded, which is one of the characteristics of defining relative clauses. While dative relative pronouns are common in the Greek New Testament, by a significant margin their case is due to the fact that they are the object of the preposition ἐν or because they must agree with the case of their head term. Ultimately, examples of extending relative clauses that employ the dative case remain elusive.

---

[27] Porter, *Idioms*, 92.

[28] This, of course, would result in the loss of the convenient alliteration of *elaboration, extension,* and *enhancement.*

[29] Porter, *Idioms*, 97.

b.2. *Extending Articular Participial Clauses*

Examples of the article in a participial clause functioning in this capacity may also be observed. As noted with the relative pronoun, this usage is not entirely consistent with that of English, which is the basis of Halliday's categorization. If we maintain the sub-category of *restriction*, rather than *extension*, we have something more serviceable to the Greek of the New Testament.

In Acts 19:18, the head term is extended by means of additional information that serves to restrict it:

Πολλοί τε τῶν πεπιστευκότων ἤρχοντο.

And many *of the ones who believed* were coming.

	S		P
	πολλοί		ἤρχοντο
Act.c19_72	**cj**		
⌐c19_71	τε		
	Act.c19_73	**P**	
		τῶν πεπιστευκότων	

In this example, the articular participial clause adds new information to the head term, but this information serves to restrict it. The *many* to which the author makes reference are restricted by being characterized as *the ones who believed.*

Likewise, in Rom 8:11, Paul employs an articular participial clause in the genitive case to extend the head term:

εἰ δὲ τὸ πνεῦμα τοῦ ἐγείροντος τὸν Ἰησοῦν ἐκ νεκρῶν οἰκεῖ ἐν ὑμῖν,

But if the spirit *of the one who raised Jesus from the dead* dwells in you,

	cj εἰ	cj δὲ	S				P οἰκεῖ	A ἐν ὑμῖν
Rom.c8_29			τὸ πνεῦμα					
⌐c8_31			**Rom. c8_30**	**P** τοῦ ἐγείραντος	**C** τὸν Ἰησοῦν	**A** ἐκ νεκρῶν		

Additional information is provided regarding *the spirit*. Again, this information restricts *spirit*. In this instance, ownership is indicated. He is the spirit *of the one who raised Jesus from the dead.*

The restriction of the head term in 1 Cor 4:19 is accomplished by means of an articular participial clause:

καὶ γνώσομαι οὐ τὸν λόγον τῶν πεφυσιωμένων ἀλλὰ τὴν δύναμιν·

And I will know not the word *of the ones who are arrogant*, but the power.

1Cor.c4_72 ⌐c4_70	cj καὶ	P γνώσομαι	C οὐ τὸν λόγον	
			1Cor.c4_73	P τῶν πεφυσιωμένων

1Cor.c4_74 ⌐c4_72	cj ἀλλὰ	C τὴν δύναμιν

New information is provided by the participial clause, which indicates who "owns" *the word*. It belongs to *the ones who are arrogant*.[30] The same is true in 1 Pet 1:3:

διὰ τῆς ἐπιγνώσεως τοῦ καλέσαντος ἡμᾶς...

Through the knowledge *of the one who called us*...

2Pet.c1_4 ⌐c1_3	A διὰ τῆς ἐπιγνώσεως		
	2Pet.c1_5	P τοῦ καλέσαντος	C ἡμᾶς

As was the case with dative relative clauses, there are no clear examples of extending participial clauses in the dative case. In instances where the dative case is observed, the participial clause often functions as the head of a nominal group (see chapter 4.2 below), and therefore does not perform

---

[30] Ownership or possession is not the only possibility. Consistent with the description provided by Porter, the genitive may indicate the origin or source of *the word* to which Paul refers.

an extending function. In other instances, the dative case is required to agree with the head term, or is the object of a preposition such as ἐν or σύν.

This attempt to identify extension in Greek illustrates the challenges, and sometimes obstacles, one faces when attempting to categorize grammatical elements in one language using categories from another language. In the case of elaboration, Greek usage is fairly consistent with that of English and so the category proves useful. This is not the case with extension. The notion of *possession*, which is a defining characteristic of the category in English, may be indicated in Greek by means of either *restriction* (the genitive case) or *relation* (the dative case). Neither corresponds exactly with the English usage. In addition, examples of embedded structures, another characteristic of *extension*, are rare. This demonstrates the need for flexibility and adaptability with regard to linguistic description. To force the category of extension onto the Greek lanauge would represent the imposition of a foreign classification (not unlike classifying the Greek article as a "definite article"). The use of *restriction* and/or *relation*, rather than *extension*, while requiring modification of the description to make it conform to Greek usage, would reflect a categorization that is more organic to the language. In the end, we must question the usefulness of this category as a means of describing Greek usage.

c. *Enhancement*

When a defining relative clause enhances the head term, it does so "by qualifying it in one of a number of possible ways: by reference to time, place, manner, cause or condition."[31] Specifically, "the relation between the embedded clause and the Head noun is a circumstantial one of time, place, manner, cause or condition."[32] This usage continues to illustrate that both the relative pronoun and the article indicate that the speaker or writer is providing information that the recipient is to use for the purpose of identification.

c.1. *Enhancing Relative Clauses*
The use of relative clauses for the purpose of enhancement is common in the New Testament. This is observed in Luke 7:37:

---

[31] Halliday, *Functional Grammar*, 410.
[32] Halliday, *Functional Grammar*, 432.

καὶ ἰδοὺ γυνὴ ἥτις ἦν ἐν τῇ πόλει ἁμαρτωλός,

And behold, a sinful woman *who was in the city,*

Luke.c7_174 ↖c7_172	cj καὶ	P ἰδοὺ

Luke.c7_175 ↖c7_174	S γυνὴ				
	Luke. c7_176	S ἥτις	P ἦν	A ἐν τῇ πόλει	C ἁμαρτωλός

The woman in this passage is defined by her circumstances: the place she is in is *the city,* her condition is *sinful.* This situates her as a specific subset within the class, *woman.*

In John 1:30, the circumstances are of a temporal nature:

οὗτος ἐστιν ὑπὲρ οὗ ἐγὼ εἶπον· ὀπίσω μου ἔρχεται ἀνὴρ ὃς ἔμπροσθέν μου γέγονεν, ὅτι πρῶτός μου ἦν.

This one is on behalf of whom I said, "A man is coming after me, *who came to be in front of me,* because he was before me."

S οὗτός	P ἐστιν	C			
		John. c1_105	A ὑπὲρ οὗ	S ἐγὼ	P εἶπον
		John. c1_106	A ὀπίσω μου	P ἔρχεται	S ἀνὴρ
					John. c1_107	S ὃς	A ἔμπροσθέν μου	P γέγονεν
					John. c1_108	cj ὅτι	C πρῶτός μου	P ἦν

In John the Baptist's famous riddle concerning Jesus, he qualifies Jesus by means of a spatial/temporal play on words. Though Jesus is the one

who comes *after* him, he was *ahead of* him because he existed *before* him.
John worded his riddle in a way that needed further specification. *A man
was coming up behind him.* Within this class is a specific subset, which is
defined by the circumstances outlined in the defining relative clause. He
is the one *who came to be in front of me.*

The apostle Paul enhances a head term in 1 Cor 7:20 by reference to a
more general set of circumstances:

ἕκαστος ἐν τῇ κλήσει ᾗ ἐκλήθη, ἐν ταύτῃ μενέτω.

Each one in the role *in which he or she was called*, in this must remain.

1Cor.c7_73 ↖c7_72	S ἕκαστος	A ἐν τῇ κλήσει		
		1Cor.c7_74	A ᾗ	P ἐκλήθη

1Cor.c7_75 ↖c7_73	A ἐν ταύτῃ	P μενέτω

The *role* or *station* in which one may be is not specific enough and therefore must be enhanced upon. It is not any role, but the role *in which he or
she was called*. The relative clause provides additional information regarding the circumstances surrounding the condition in which one is called,
as well as identifying the specific subset of *station* to which Paul makes
reference.

The circumstance to which the apostle makes reference in Eph 2:13,
couched in spatial terms, have spiritual and relational connotations:

νυνὶ δὲ ἐν Χριστῷ Ἰησοῦ ὑμεῖς οἵ ποτε ὄντες μακρὰν ἐγενήθητε ἐγγὺς ἐν τῷ αἵματι
τοῦ Χριστοῦ.

But now you in Christ Jesus, *who were formerly far away*, have become near
by the blood of Christ.

Eph. c2_36 ↖c2_33	A νυνὶ	cj δὲ	A ἐν Χριστῷ Ἰησοῦ	S					P ἐγενήθητε	A ἐγγὺς	A ἐν τῷ αἵματι τοῦ Χριστοῦ
				ὑμεῖς							
				Eph. c2_37	s οἵ	A ποτε	P ὄντες	C μακρὰν			

For the Christians in Ephesus, their previous condition was one of distance from God. The function of the embedded relative clause is to enhance the head term by means of reference to their place (the spatial relationship likely being a metaphorical description of a spiritual state).

The reader observes a causal set of circumstances in 1 Pet 4:11:

εἴ τις διακονεῖ, ὡς ἐξ ἰσχύος ἧς χορηγεῖ ὁ θεός.

If someone serves, as from strength *which God provides.*

1Pet.c4_33 ✓c4_34	cj εἴ	S τις	P διακονεῖ

1Pet.c4_34 ✓c4_32	A			
	ὡς ἐξ ἰσχύος			
	1Pet.c4_35	C ἧς	P χορηγεῖ	S ὁ θεός

The strength to which the author makes reference is qualified with regard to its cause; it is strength *which God provides.* This cause distinguishes this strength from other kinds of strength within the general class of *strength.*

c.2. *Enhancing Articular Participial Clauses*
As observed with the elaborating relative clause, enhancement is also accomplished by means of the article at the level of embedded participial clause. In these instances, the article indicates that the speaker or writer is providing the information necessary for identification. There is no indication that this information is recoverable or obvious in the discourse, nor is the recipient directed to the information. The identity of the referent is oriented solely to the speaker or writer.

This construction is observed in the opening of several of the New Testament letters as a way of identifying the addressees by mean of reference to their place, that is, their location. This is seen in 1 Cor 1:2:

τῇ ἐκκλησίᾳ τοῦ θεοῦ τῇ οὔσῃ ἐν Κορίνθῳ,

To the church of God, *which is in Corinth.*

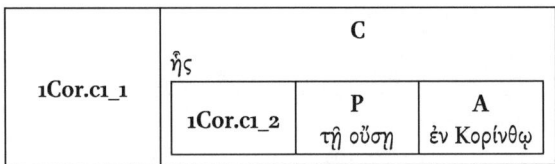

The address in 2 Cor 1:1 is identical to the example above from 1 Cor 1:2. The address in Phil 1:1 follows the same structure:

πᾶσιν τοῖς ἁγίοις ἐν Χριστῷ Ἰησοῦ τοῖς οὖσιν ἐν Φιλίπποις.

To all the saints in Christ Jesus, *who are in Philippi.*

Phil.c1_1	C πᾶσιν τοῖς ἁγίοις ἐν Χριστῷ Ἰησοῦ		
	Phil.c1_2	P τοῖς οὖσιν	A ἐν Φιλίπποις

This is again observed in Eph 1:1:

τοῖς ἁγίοις τοῖς οὖσιν [ἐν Ἐφέσῳ] . . .

To the saints, *who are [in Ephesus]* . . .

Eph.c1_1	C τοῖς ἁγίοις		
	Eph.c1_2	P τοῖς οὖσιν	A ἐν ἐφέσῳ

In each of these examples, the recipients are specified as a subset within a class, whether that class is *church* or *saints*. They are defined by their location.

We observe articular participial clauses routinely employed throughout the New Testament for the purpose of enhancement. In Acts 10:14, *the men* are identified with regard to their condition:

οἱ ἄνδρες οἱ ἀπεσταλμένοι ὑπὸ τοῦ Κορνηλίου.

The men, *who were sent by Cornelius*

Act.c10_57 ⌐c10_56	S		
	οἱ ἄνδρες		
	Act.c10_58	P οἱ ἀπεσταλμένοι	A ὑπὸ τοῦ Κορνηλίου

The condition of these men is defined by the fact that they were *sent by Cornelius*. Later, in Acts 16:3, another group is identified in terms of location by means of an enhancing articular participial clause:

καὶ λαβὼν περιέτεμεν αὐτὸν διὰ τοὺς Ἰουδαίους τοὺς ὄντας ἐν τοῖς τόποις ἐκείνοις.

And taking [him], he circumcised him because of the Jews, *who were in those regions.*

Act.c16_8 ⌐c16_6	cj καὶ	A		P περιέτεμεν	C αὐτὸν	A		
		Act. c16_9	P λαβὼν			διὰ τοὺς Ἰουδαίους		
						Act. c16_10	P τοὺς ὄντας	A ἐν τοῖς τόποις ἐκείνοις

The designation *Jew* is a class of people. Within this class are subsets. In this case, the Jews to which the author makes reference are a subset that is further specified by their location: they are the ones *who were in those regions.*

Enhancing participial clauses are employed in the Johannine corpus. In John 1:18, Jesus is also identified with reference to his circumstances:

μονογενὴς θεὸς ὁ ὢν εἰς τὸν κόλπον τοῦ πατρὸς.

The one and only God, *who is in the bosom of the father.*

John.c1_50 ⌐c1_49	S		
	μονογενὴς θεὸς		
	John.c1_51	P ὁ ὢν	A εἰς τὸν κόλπον τοῦ πατρὸς

Embedded within the subject is the articular participial clause ὁ ὢν εἰς τὸν κόλπον τοῦ πατρὸς. It further qualifies who the *one and only God* is by means of reference to his circumstances, specifically his place. He is the one *who is in the bosom of the father.*

In Rev 1:8, God's own self-description is realized by means of enhancement through the use of embedded articular participial clauses that reference his circumstances:

Ἐγώ εἰμι τὸ ἄλφα καὶ τὸ ὦ, λέγει κύριος ὁ θεός, ὁ ὢν καὶ ὁ ἦν καὶ ὁ ἐρχόμενος.

"I am the alpha and the omega," says the Lord [who is] God, *"the one who is and the one who was and the one coming."*

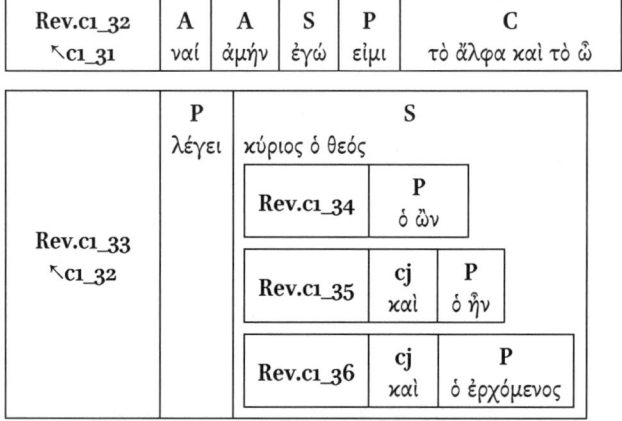

As Paul wrote, "there are many gods and many lords," (1 Cor 8:5). Within these classes of *gods* and *lords*, God defines himself as a subset. The head term *Lord God* is enhanced by means of reference to his circumstances, which in this instance are temporal in nature. Rather than employ a relative clause, the author uses two embedded articular participial clauses. Again, the article, functioning like the relative pronoun, introduces participial clauses that function as relative clauses. In addition, one interesting observation regarding ὁ ἦν must be made. Typically, a relative pronoun is employed in clauses with a finite verb, while the article is employed in clauses with non-finite verbs such as participles and infinitive. In two of the qualifiers above, this is the case. In the other, the article actually modifies a finite verb, ἦν. On the one hand, this instance illustrates the wide variety of head terms to which the article may be affixed (which we will discuss below). On the other hand, it also illustrates that structure is not

an either/or proposition: relative clause or articular participial clause. If
the article is being employed as a relative pronoun, then this is a relative
clause. If the article is functioning as a true article, then the verb is occu-
pying a position not usually reserved for finite verbs. This demonstrates
the flexibility inherent in the system. Relative clauses and articular participial phrases are not opposed in an absolute sense. Rather they stand at
opposite ends of a scale or cline, with structures such as this one falling
somewhere in between. Most importantly, it illustrates that the article
and relative pronoun were viewed as somewhat interchangeable, confirm-
ing that they are categorically and functionally similar.

Enhancement through reference to condition is observed in Rev 2:17:

δώσω αὐτῷ τοῦ μάννα τοῦ κεκρυμμένου.

I will give to him from the manna, *which is hidden.*

Rev.c2_91 ↖c2_89	P δώσω	C αὐτῷ	C τοῦ μάννα	
			Rev.c2_92	P τοῦ κεκρυμμένου

This manna is defined by its condition; it is in a hidden state.

The apostle Paul frequently employs articular participial clauses for the
purpose of enhancement in his letters. Note this usage in Rom 1:3:

περὶ τοῦ υἱοῦ αὐτοῦ τοῦ γενομένου ἐκ σπέρματος Δαυὶδ κατὰ σάρκα.

Concerning his son, *who came into being from the seed of David according
to the flesh.*

Rom.c1_3	A περὶ τοῦ υἱοῦ αὐτοῦ			
	Rom.c1_4	P τοῦ γενομένου	A ἐκ σπέρματος Δαυὶδ	A κατὰ σάρκα

The son is defined in terms of causation, that is, with regard to his origin.
He is the one *who came into being from the seed of David according to the
flesh.*

Similar to the condition of origin is the condition of cause, which is observed in Gal. 2:9:

καὶ γνόντες τὴν χάριν τὴν δοθεῖσάν μοι,

And knowing the grace, *which was given to me,*

	cj καὶ	P γνόντες	C		
Gal.c2_34			τὴν χάριν		
			Gal.c2_35	P τὴν δοθεῖσάν	C μοι

The head term *grace* is enhanced by means of reference to its condition based on its cause. Paul writes that it is the grace *which was given to me.* Once again, the embedded articular participial clause functions as a defining relative clause.

Examples abound in the general epistles as well. A few examples are sufficient to illustrate this usage. Observe, first, the author of Hebrews in Heb 2:5:

Οὐ γὰρ ἀγγέλοις ὑπέταξεν τὴν οἰκουμένην τὴν μέλλουσαν.

For he did not subject to angels the world, *which is coming.*

	A οὐ	cj γὰρ	C ἀγγέλοις	P ὑπέταξεν	C	
Heb.c2_15 ↖c2_8					τὴν οἰκουμένην	
					Heb.c2_16	P τὴν μέλλουσαν

The circumstances of *the world* are defined in temporal and conditional terms: it is the world *which is coming* [lit. *about to be/become/come to pass*].

The usage is found in Jas 2:7:

οὐκ αὐτοὶ βλασφημοῦσιν τὸ καλὸν ὄνομα τὸ ἐπικληθὲν ἐφ᾽ ὑμᾶς;

Are they not blaspheming the good name, *which was given to you?*

Jam.c2_20 ↖c2_19	A οὐκ	S αὐτοὶ	P βλασφημοῦσιν	C		
				τὸ καλὸν ὄνομα		
				Jam.c2_21	P τὸ ἐπικληθὲν	P ἐφ᾽ ὑμᾶς

Further description of their name is provided by this embedded articular participial clause by means of appeal to origin as well as current condition: it is the name *which was given to you*. The obvious implication is that this name was given by God himself. Thus, the significance of their name, the honor associated with that name, and the seriousness of the blasphemy, is enhanced.

Lastly, observe the usage in 1 Pet 1:25:

τοῦτο δέ ἐστιν τὸ ῥῆμα τὸ εὐαγγελισθὲν εἰς ὑμᾶς.

And this is the word, *that was proclaimed to you.*

1Pet.c1_71 ↖c1_60	S τοῦτο	cj δέ	P ἐστιν	C		
				τὸ ῥῆμα		
				1Pet.c1_72	P τὸ εὐαγγελισθὲν	A εἰς ὑμᾶς

The word to which the author makes reference is further defined by appeal to its origin: it is the word *that was proclaimed to you. This* is deictic, pointing back to the previous statement, which is a quotation of Isaiah 40:6-9, "The word of the Lord remains forever." Defining it this way enhances the status of *this word.*

3. Non-defining Relative Clauses

According to Halliday, a non-defining relative clause "functions as a kind of descriptive gloss to the main clause."[33] He continues:

As far as the meaning is concerned, the clauses do not define subsets, in the way that a defining relative clause does... A non-defining relative clause...

---

[33] Halliday, *Functional Grammar*, 399.

adds a further characterization of something that is taken to be already fully specific.[34]

These clauses are not embedded but stand in hypotactic relation, which Halliday defines thus:

> Degree of interdependency is known technically as *taxis*; and the two different degrees of interdependency as *parataxis* (equal status) and *hypotaxis* (unequal status). *Hypotaxis* is the relation between a dependent element and its dominant, the element on which it is dependent.[35]

These types of non-embedded, dependent clauses abound in the New Testament.

In Matt 10:26, the subject of the main clause may be interpreted as fully specific; it does not need to be further defined by locating it within a subset of a general class:

οὐδὲν γάρ ἐστιν κεκαλυμμένον ὃ οὐκ ἀποκαλυφθήσεται καὶ κρυπτὸν ὃ οὐ γνωσθήσεται.

For nothing is hidden, *which* will not be revealed; and [nothing is] secret, *which* will not be known.

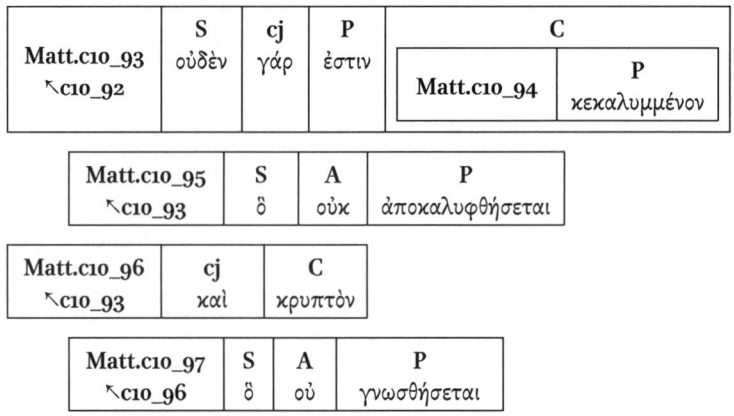

In this passage, the main clause *nothing is hidden/secret* is fully specific, needing no further definition. However, this is not all there is to say. The relative clauses, which are clearly not embedded as seen in the OpenText.

---

34 Halliday, *Functional Grammar*, 400.
35 Halliday, *Functional Grammar*, 374.

org annotation, provide additional information, as Halliday says, "a descriptive gloss." Both relative clauses are dependent upon the main clause, and thus are in hypotactic relation. Not only is there *nothing hidden*, such hidden things *will be revealed.* Likewise, secret things *will be known.*

This "further characterization" is observed in Luke 5:10:

ὁμοίως δὲ καὶ Ἰάκωβον καὶ Ἰωάννην υἱοὺς Ζεβεδαίου, οἳ ἦσαν κοινωνοὶ τῷ Σίμωνι,

Likewise, and also James and John, sons of Zebedee, *who were partners with Simon.*

Luke.c5_42 ↖c5_40	A ὁμοίως	cj δὲ	cj καὶ	C Ἰάκωβον καὶ Ἰωάννην υἱοὺς Ζεβεδαίου

Luke.c5_43 ↖c5_42	S οἳ	P ἦσαν	C κοινωνοὶ τῷ Σίμωνι

Again, the relative clause in this example is not embedded. In this passage, the individuals James and John are already fully specific; they do not need to be further defined by being located within a subset of a general class. However, the author chooses to add further characterization, which was accomplished by means of a non-defining relative clause.

Like his fellow writers, Paul employs non-defining relative clauses, as is seen in Rom 1:1-2:

ἀφωρισμένος εἰς εὐαγγέλιον θεοῦ, ὃ προεπηγγείλατο διὰ τῶν προφητῶν αὐτοῦ...

Having been set apart for the good news of God, *which was promised beforehand through his prophets...*

Rom.c1_2	P ἀφωρισμένος	A εἰς εὐαγγέλιον θεοῦ

Rom.c1_3	C ὃ	P προεπηγγείλατο	A διὰ τῶν προφητῶν αὐτοῦ

In this instance, *good news of God* is also fully specific, but is further characterized by the fact that it was *promised beforehand through his prophets.* Again, we observe this usage in Rom 3:30:

εἴπερ εἷς ὁ θεὸς ὃς δικαιώσει περιτομὴν ἐκ πίστεως καὶ ἀκροβυστίαν διὰ τῆς πίστεως.

If indeed God is one, *who will justify the circumcised by faith and the uncircumcised through faith.*

Rom.c3_90 ⤻c3_89	cj εἴπερ	C εἷς	S ὁ θεός	

Rom.c3_91 ⤻c3_90	S ὅς	P δικαιώσει	C περιτομὴν	A ἐκ πίστεως

Rom.c3_92 ⤻c3_91	cj καὶ	C ἀκροβυστίαν	A διὰ τῆς πίστεως

The subject, *God*, is certainly fully specific. However, Paul chooses to add further characterization: God is *the one who will justify both the circumcised and uncircumcised by faith.*

In 1 Cor 1:30, Paul provides further characterization of Christ Jesus:

ἐξ αὐτοῦ δὲ ὑμεῖς ἐστε ἐν Χριστῷ Ἰησοῦ, ὃς ἐγενήθη σοφία ἡμῖν ἀπὸ θεοῦ,

But you are from him, in Christ Jesus, *who became wisdom to us from God.*

1Cor.c1_82 ⤻c1_76	A ἐξ αὐτοῦ	cj δὲ	S ὑμεῖς	P ἐστε	A ἐν Χριστῷ Ἰησοῦ

1Cor.c1_83 ⤻c1_82	S ὅς	P ἐγενήθη	C σοφία ἡμῖν ἀπὸ θεοῦ

Christ Jesus is fully specific. He does not need to be further defined by being located within a subset of a general class. The descriptive gloss provided by the relative clause ties *Christ Jesus* to the larger discourse of the first part of the letter, in which Paul challenges the Corinthians' pretensions of wisdom and knowledge. Jesus is *the one who became wisdom to us from God.* Later, in 1 Cor 15:1, Paul's characterization of the gospel is tied to general point he wishes to make in this section of the letter:

γνωρίζω δὲ ὑμῖν, ἀδελφοί, τὸ εὐαγγέλιον ὃ εὐηγγελισάμην ὑμῖν, ὃ καὶ παρελάβετε.

But I make known to you, brothers, the gospel, *which I preached to you, which you indeed received.*

1Cor.c15_1	P γνωρίζω	cj δὲ	C ὑμῖν	add ἀδελφοί	C τὸ εὐαγγέλιον

1Cor.c15_2 ⌐c15_1	cj ὃ	P εὐηγγελισάμην		C ὑμῖν

1Cor.c15_2 ⌐c15_1	cj ὃ	cj καὶ	P παρελάβετε

In this instance, *the gospel* is fully specific; it does not need to be further defined by locating it within a subset of a general class. Nevertheless, Paul chooses to add further characterization. For the purpose of his current argument, the gospel to which he refers is characterized by the fact that it is the one *which he proclaimed* to them and the one *which you received*. Central to his argument is the fact that the resurrection is a core component of the gospel, the same gospel the apostle first preached to the Christians in Corinth. To deny the resurrection is to deny the gospel that is the foundation of their faith, their religious identity. Thus, the relative clauses do not locate *the gospel* within a subset, but provide elaboration, which forms the basis of Paul's argument that the resurrection has been a component of the gospel from the beginning. If the Corinthians believers accepted the gospel Paul originally proclaimed, they accepted the resurrection.[36]

Another example from Paul's writings may be observed in Gal 4:26:

ἡ δὲ ἄνω Ἰερουσαλὴμ ἐλευθέρα ἐστίν, ἥτις ἐστὶν μήτηρ ἡμῶν·

But the Jerusalem above is free, *which is our mother.*

Gal.c4_62 ⌐c4_76	S ἡ / cj δὲ / ἄνω Ἰερουσαλὴμ	C ἐλευθέρα	P ἐστίν

---

[36] "Paul is not here setting out to *prove* the resurrection of Jesus. Rather, he is reasserting the commonly held ground *from which* he will argue against their assertion that there is no resurrection of the dead," Fee, *The First Epistle to the Corinthians*, 718.

Gal.c4_83	S	P	C
↖c4_82	ἥτις	ἐστὶν	μήτηρ ἡμῶν

The descriptive gloss of Jerusalem as that *which is our mother* does not define the city, but is a characterization that serves to tie it to the immediate discourse regarding Hagar and Sarah. Both are significant mother figures from the Torah, whom Paul uses allegorically. Likewise, Jerusalem is used as an allegorical mother figure.

This usage is found in the General Epistles as well, as is seen in Heb. 9:7:

οὐ χωρὶς αἵματος ὃ προσφέρει ὑπὲρ ἑαυτοῦ...

Not without blood, *which he presents on behalf of himself*...

Heb.c9_19	A	A
↖c9_18	οὐ	χωρὶς αἵματος

Heb.c9_20	cj	P	A
↖c9_19	ὃ	προσφέρει	ὑπὲρ ἑαυτοῦ

In this instance, the relative clause provides a descriptive gloss of the head term. With regard to the blood the priest offers, it is that *which he presents on behalf of himself.*

As demonstrated in the examples cited above, Greek speakers and writers also employed non-defining relative clauses. However, unlike defining relative clauses, which are paralleled by defining articular participial clauses, there are no instances of a non-defining articular participial clause, which by definition occurs in a non-embedded structure. However, these may be found in an embedded structure, which perform a parallel function. See, for example, Col 1:7–8:

καθὼς ἐμάθετε ἀπὸ Ἐπαφρᾶ τοῦ ἀγαπητοῦ συνδούλου ἡμῶν, ὅς ἐστιν πιστὸς ὑπὲρ ὑμῶν διάκονος τοῦ Χριστοῦ, ὁ καὶ δηλώσας ἡμῖν τὴν ὑμῶν ἀγάπην ἐν πνεύματι.

Even as you learned from Epaphras our beloved fellow servant, *who is a faithful servant of Christ for your sake, who also made known to us your love in spirit.*

Col.c1_16	cj	P	A
↖c1_15	καθὼς	ἐμάθετε	ἀπὸ Ἐπαφρᾶ τοῦ ἀγαπητοῦ συνδούλου ἡμῶν

	S	P	C			
	ὅς	ἐστιν	πιστὸς ὑπὲρ ὑμῶν διάκονος τοῦ Χριστοῦ			
Col.c1_17 ⌐c1_16				P	C	C	A

		P	C	C	A
Col. c1_18	ὁ cj και δηλώσας		ἡμῖν	τὴν ὑμῶν ἀγάπην	ἐν πνεύματι

The first relative clause, *who is a faithful servant of Christ for your sake*, does not define Epaphras as a subset. Instead, it provides further characterization of him. Likewise, the articular participial clause *who also made known to us your love in spirit* does not function to define Epaphras as a subset, but also provides further characterization of him. However, because it is a participial clause, it must operate as an embedded element.

4. Conclusion

Based on an analysis of the examples cited above, several conclusions may be drawn regarding ὁ-items. First, the use of relative clauses and articular participial clauses to fill the same syntactical slot and perform similar functions demonstrates that the article and relative pronoun have a far greater grammatical and functional relationship than has been historically acknowledged. This relationship is demonstrated by the fact that they frequently operate within structures that function as embedded qualifiers. Both indicate that the speaker or writer is providing information that the recipient is to use for the purpose of identification. In no instance is there any indication that the information is recoverable or obvious in the discourse, nor is the recipient directed to the necessary information, as in the case of the English definite article or demonstrative pronouns respectively. This supports the argument that the article and the relative pronoun are grammatically and functionally related parts of speech.

Second, while the function of embedded defining relative clauses may be paralleled by embedded articular participial clauses, non-defining relative clauses will not be paralleled by non-defining articular participial clauses in a non-embedded structure. Instead, while such relative clauses will be non-embedded, articular participial clauses that perform a parallel function will only be found in an embedded structure.

Third, while Halliday's categories of defining and non-defining relative clauses generally translate well to the Greek language, it must be recognized that this correspondence is not exact. This was observed in regard to *extension*, which we suggested must be expanded in definition and/or renamed as *restriction/relation* in order to be faithful to Greek usage and grammar. However, it was also acknowledged that, even with modification, this particular category may not be useful for the purpose of describing Greek usage.

CHAPTER FOUR

RELATIVE CLAUSES AS THE HEAD OF A NOMINAL GROUP

While relative clauses often function as a qualifier within a group, they may also function as the subject or object of the verb. The relative pronoun is "widely used to bring clauses into relation to each other."[1] However, its function in Greek extends beyond that of the English relative pronoun. It is also employed to construct clauses that function as the subject or object of a clause. When so employed, its force is more akin to *the one who* or *that which*. As Halliday notes, in English this is realized by means of an alternate form of relative clause which uses a TH- item as relative *"the one that I saw"* or *"the one I saw."*[2] In Greek, this is realized by means of the same forms of the ὁ-items. Clauses of this type are embedded within the main clause.

In these instances, the question of the identity of the subject is not merely a matter of whether it is recoverable from the text.[3] As noted above, when using a ὁ-item, the speaker or writer is not saying, "I'm telling which," in the sense that he or she is directing the recipient to the information necessary for identification. Instead, the speaker or writer is indicating "I'm telling you about something else."[4] The information necessary for identification is being provided by the speaker or writer. The identity of the referent established by the relative clause is introduced to the discourse by the speaker or writer. Thus, the deixis of the relative pronoun is *exophoric*, it points "outward from the text."[5] This stands in contrast

---

[1] Porter, *Idioms*, 132.

[2] Halliday, *Functional Grammar*, 86.

[3] In his chapter on relative clauses, Porter includes the sub-category *Substantival Relative Clause*. He notes in these instances that "the pronoun does not have a specific referent but it must be inferred from the context," *Idioms*, 245. He later notes: "In nearly 500 instances in the Greek of the NT, *a relative pronoun standing alone (without an accompanying preposition) takes on a meaning apart from its normal relational usage (e.g. adverbial) or assumes an unspecified referent,*" *Idioms*, 251. It is my argument that, in these circumstances, the function of the relative pronoun, as well as the article, is to indicate that a class is in view whose identifying characteristic(s) are provided by the speaker or writer. Though the referent may be non-specific, in that no actual person or thing is in view, it is characterized as such a person or thing that may or does exist.

[4] Halliday, *Functional Grammar*, 87.

[5] Halliday, *Functional Grammar*, 534–35.

to the function of *the* in English, which signals "You know which one I mean," because the information is available to the recipient.[6] The English definite article and demonstratives perform the same specifying function. However, the demonstratives "state explicitly how the identity is to be established" by directing the recipient toward the necessary information.[7] Conversely, the English definite article does not direct the attention of the recipient, but simply indicates that the identity is indeed known. In the case of the relative clause, the speaker gives no indication that the identity of the referent is known to the recipient; it may or may not be. From the perspective of the speaker this is immaterial. By employing a relative clause in this manner, the identity of the thing or person so referred to is defined by what is predicated about it by the clause, either as a process or state. As with defining relative clauses, this function is paralleled in articular participial clauses. Like the relative pronoun, the Greek article indicates that the process or state grammaticalized by the pariticiple is to be used as for the purpose of identification. It does not indicate that the recipient already possesses this information, nor is the recipient directed to this information. Rather, it indicates that this information is being provided by the speaker or writer, to whom identification of the referent is soleloy oriented.

At this point, it is necessary to consider how the referent in these constructions is characterized. As noted in the historical overview, it was long asserted that the Greek article was used to make the head term definite. Over time, this view has been rejected in light of considerable evidence to the contrary. Some have adopted the term *substantivize*, which generally means that the article may turn a part of speech into a *substantive*. In this usage, the term *substantive* is generally synonymous with *noun*.[8] This, of course, begs the question of how the article functions with nouns (this will be addressed below). Rather than attempt to redefine *substantive*, the term that will be employed herein is *concrete*. Among its many definitions, *Webster's Ninth New Collegiate Dictionary* provides the following definition of *concrete*: "characterized by or belonging to immediate experience of actual things or events."[9] Similarly, *Webster's New World Dictionary, Second College Edition* provides the following definitions:

---

[6] Halliday, *Functional Grammar*, 558.
[7] Halliday, *Functional Grammar*, 558.
[8] See Wallace's usage of the term, *Greek Grammar*, 231.
[9] Webster's Collegiate Dictionary, "Concrete," 273.

2. Having material, perceptible existence; of, belonging to, or characterized by things or events that can be perceived by the senses; real; actual 3. referring to a particular; specific, not general or abstract ... 5. designating a thing or class of things that can be perceived by the senses: opposed to abstract *–n.* 1.a concrete thing condition, idea, etc.[10]

Using these basic definitions, we may formulate a description of the how the referent is characterized in the following relative and participial clauses. In these instances, the referent is characterized as *concrete*, that is, it is characterized as belonging to experience of an actual person or thing. It must be emphasized that this is a *characterization*. It does not mean that an actual person or thing is grammaticalized in a definite sense. It is merely characterized as *such a person or thing*. If an actual person or thing is in view, this will be established by other linguistic features. In addition, it is a *subjective* characterization; the characterization is based on a choice made by the speaker. By employing a ὁ-item, the speaker indicates that he or she is providing the information necessary for the recipient to identify the referent.

Lastly, we must consider the significance of the speaker's choice to employ one clause type in favor of the other. In certain instances, it is arguable that either a relative clause or an articular participial clause would be equally suited for the production of text. In other instances, we will observe a shift from one clause type to another. It is unlikely that the choice made in these instances is merely arbitrary. Instead, it represents a meaningful choice. Drawing upon work done in fields of markedness and prominence, we may posit an explanation for such choices as they are observed in the examples below.

1. The Relative Clause as Subject or Object

Observe, for example, the use of the relative clause as subject in Matt 5:19:

ὃς ἐὰν οὖν λύσῃ μίαν τῶν ἐντολῶν τούτων τῶν ἐλαχίστων καὶ διδάξῃ οὕτως τοὺς ἀνθρώπους, ἐλάχιστος κληθήσεται ἐν τῇ βασιλείᾳ τῶν οὐρανῶν.

Therefore, *whoever breaks the least of these commandments and teaches people thus* will be called least in the kingdom of heaven.

---

[10] Webster's New World Dictionary, "Concrete," 294–5.

Matt.c5_66 ⌐c5_64	S				C	P	A
	Matt. c5_67	**S** ὅς	**A** ἐάν	**P** λύσῃ	**C** μίαν τῶν ἐντολῶν τούτων τῶν ἐλαχίστων	ἐλάχιστος	κληθήσεται	ἐν τῇ βασιλ ίᾳ τῶν οὐρανῶν
	**cj** οὖν						
	Matt. c5_68	**cj** καί	**P** διδάξῃ	**A** οὕτως	**C** τοὺς ἀνθρώπους		

In this instance, the relative pronoun does not function to bring the clause in which it is used in relation to another clause. Instead, the relative clause functions as the subject of the main clause. By employing a relative clause this way, the identity of the referent is defined by a process in which he or she engages; the subject is *the one who destroys the least of these commandments and teaches people thus.* The referent is characterized as *concrete,* as belonging to experience of an actual person. For the purpose of the discourse, he or she is *such a person* whose sole identifying characteristic is the process grammaticalized by the clause. By characterizing the referent in this way, the speaker may hold it out for examination, for the recipient's consideration, as someone who belongs to reality. However, there is no indication that the referent is an actual person. In fact, the use of the subjunctive mood indicates that referent is characterized as hypothetical. Thus, while the ὅ-item characterizes the referent as *concrete,* the additional linguistic feature of the subjunctive mood indicates its condition with regard to *definiteness,* or in this instance, *indefiniteness.* In addition, the ὅ-item orients the identity of the referent to the speaker. It does not direct the recipient to the information necessary for identification, nor does it indicate that the recipient already possesses this information. Rather, it indicates that the speaker is providing this information to the recipient.

In Matt 10:27, two relative clauses are employed as complement rather than subject.

ὃ λέγω ὑμῖν ἐν τῇ σκοτίᾳ εἴπατε ἐν τῷ φωτί,

That which I say to you in the darkness, speak in the light,

καὶ ὃ εἰς τὸ οὖς ἀκούετε κηρύξατε ἐπὶ τῶν δομάτων.

and *that which you hear in the ear*, proclaim on the rooftops.

Matt.c10_98 ⌐c10_96	C					P	A
	Matt. c10_99	C ὃ	P λέγω	C ὑμῖν	A ἐν τῇ σκοτίᾳ	εἴπατε	ἐν τῷ φωτί

Matt.c10_100 ⌐c10_98	cj καὶ	C				P κηρύξατε	A ἐπὶ τῶν δωμάτων
		Matt. c10_101	C ὃ	A εἰς τὸ οὖς	P ἀκούετε		

As in the previous example, the identity of each complement is defined by a process: in the first instance it is *that which I say to you*, in the second instance it is *that which you hear*. Once again, the referents are characterized as concrete, as belonging to experience of an actual event. On the one hand, it is not hypothetical, as in the previous example. The use of a verb in the indicative mood indicates that the predicate is characterized as belonging to the realm of a real process. On the other hand, there is nothing to indicate that a specific speech event is in view in a definite sense. Instead, *that which I say to you* probably refers to the whole of what Jesus spoke over the course of his ministry. Though it refers to things actually spoken, in all likelihood it also refers to the content of future teaching as yet unspoken. This illustrates that, while ὅ-items will characterize something as *concrete, definiteness* is established by other linguistic elements.

The use of a relative clause as subject is observed in Luke 7:23:

καὶ μακάριός ἐστιν ὃς ἐὰν μὴ σκανδαλισθῇ ἐν ἐμοί.

And blessed is *the one who is not offended by me*.

Luke.c7_113 ⌐c7_112	cj καὶ	C μακάριός	P ἐστιν	S					
				Luke. c7_114	S ὃς	A ἐὰν	A μὴ	P σκανδαλισθῇ	A ἐν ἐμοί

As seen earlier, the use of ἐάν and the subjunctive mood form indicates
that the referent is hypothetical, that it is one who is held out for the
audience's consideration (allowing for the possible translation choice
whoever). At the same time, this only works if the subject is characterized
as concrete, as belonging to the realm of experience of an actual person,
thus available for examination and consideration.

The apostle Paul, in Rom 7:15, employs a relative clause to identify an
activity, which he presents to the recipients:

δ γὰρ κατεργάζομαι οὐ γινώσκω·

For I do not know *that which I am doing.*

Rom.c7_59 ᐟc7_55	C				A	P
	Rom. c7_60	C δ	cj γὰρ	P κατεργάζομαι	οὐ	γινώσκω

The identity of the referent is realized by means of a relative clause. It is
identified by what is predicated about it: it is *that which I am doing.* This
information is provided by Paul and is based upon his "seeing," to use
Halliday's wording.[11] The recipients are fully dependent upon Paul provision of this information for the purpose of identification. The referent is
concrete in that is it characterized as belonging to the realm of an actual
event. However, there is no indication that it makes reference to any specific or definite event.

In 1 Cor 11:27, Paul employs a relative clause as subject:

Ὥστε ὃς ἂν ἐσθίῃ τὸν ἄρτον ἢ πίνῃ τὸ ποτήριον τοῦ κυρίου ἀναξίως, ἔνοχος ἔσται
τοῦ σώματος καὶ τοῦ αἵματος τοῦ κυρίου.

So that *whoever eats the bread or drinks the cup of the Lord unworthily* will be
guilty of the body and blood of the Lord.

---

[11] Halliday, *Functional Grammar,* 86. See chapter 2.1 above.

	cj ὥστε	S					C
1Cor. c11_100 ↖c11_98		1Cor. c11_101	S ὃς	A ἂν	P ἐσθίῃ	C τὸν ἄρτον	ἔνοχος P ἔσται τοῦ σώματος καὶ τοῦ αἵματος τοῦ κυρίου
		1Cor. c11_102	cj ἢ	P πίνῃ	C τὸ ποτήριον τοῦ κυρίου	A ἀναξίως	

The relative clause does not indicate that a specific individual in view. The referent is characterized as concrete. It is held out for the consideration of the audience as someone who could indeed exist. In fact, Paul has already made clear there are those in Corinth who are indeed eating and drinking unworthily. However, by employing a relative clause of this type, Paul is able to introduce this individual into the discourse as a new participant. He creates a sense of distance, of separation, between those who are guilty of sin in Corinth and this hypothetical individual. Rhetorically, this allows the apostle to challenge the guilty individuals in a non-confrontational manner. The onus is upon the recipients to examine themselves and determine if their behavior or attitudes conform to this individual.

In Jas 2:10, the author employs a relative clause to hold out a hypothetical individual for the audience's consideration:

ὅστις γὰρ ὅλον τὸν νόμον τηρήσῃ πταίσῃ δὲ ἐν ἑνί, γέγονεν πάντων ἔνοχος.

For *whoever keeps the whole law, but stumbles in one part*, becomes guilty of [breaking] all.

	S				P γέγονεν	C πάντων ἔνοχος
Jam.c2_29 ↖c2_27	Jam. c2_30	S ὅστις	C ὅλον τὸν νόμον	P τηρήσῃ		
	cj γὰρ					
	Jam. c2_31	P πταίσῃ	cj δὲ	A ἐν ἑνί		

Up to this point in the discourse, James had been speaking to his audience directly, repeatedly using the second person plural. Now he introduces a new participant into the discourse. The identity of this person is characterized by the fact that he or she is one *who keeps the whole law but stumbles in one part* it. As with previous examples, the referent is characterized as *concrete*. A person may or may not exist; James makes no comment either way, but characterizes the individual as one who does exist for the sake of his argument.

2. Articular Participial Clauses as Relative Clauses

There are a number of examples that illustrate how an articular participial clause is used to fill the same slot as a relative clause as the subject or complement of a clause in the New Testament. As with the relative pronoun, in these instances the article indicates that the speaker or writer is providing the information necessary for identifying the referent. Unlike the English definite article, there is no indication that this information is recoverable or obvious in the discourse.

Consider, first, the use of a relative clause as subject in Mark 4:9:

ὃς ἔχει ὦτα ἀκούειν ἀκουέτω.

The one who has ears to hear must hear.

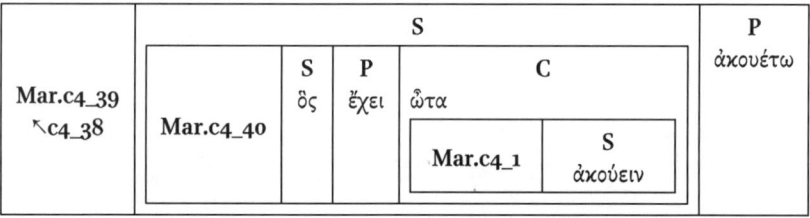

The identity of the referent is established by what is predicated about it: he or she has ears to hear. The speaker/writer presents this individual as someone concrete, yet non-definite; as such a person who exists, yet not associated with an individual who could be singled out by name or face by the audience. It is noteworthy that in the parallel account in Matt 13:9 this expression is realized by an articular participial clause rather than a relative clause:

ὁ ἔχων ὦτα ἀκουέτω (also 13:43).

The one who has ears must hear.

Mat.c13_33 ⌐c13_32	S			P ἀκουέτω
	Mat.c13_34	P ὁ ἔχων	S ὦτα	

As observed in the previous sections on relative clauses, articular participial clauses function in the same manner as relative clauses. As such, they may also serve as the subject or object of a clause. Below are several examples where both articular participial clauses and relative clauses appear in close proximity, illustrating their parallel function.

Matt 10:37–38, Ὁ φιλῶν πατέρα ἢ μητέρα ὑπὲρ ἐμὲ οὐκ ἔστιν μου ἄξιος, καὶ ὁ φιλῶν υἱὸν ἢ θυγατέρα ὑπὲρ ἐμὲ οὐκ ἔστιν μου ἄξιος· καὶ ὃς οὐ λαμβάναι τὸν σταυρὸν αὐτοῦ καὶ ἀκολουθεῖ ὀπίσω μου, οὐκ ἔστιν μου ἄξιος.

The one who loves father or mother above me is not worthy of me. And *the one who loves son or daughter above me* is not worthy of me. And *the one who does not take his cross and follow after me* is not worthy of me.

Matt. c10_131 ⌐c10_130	S				A οὐκ	P ἔστιν	μου ἄξιος
	Matt. c10_132	P ὁ φιλῶν	C πατέρα ἢ μητέρα	A ὑπὲρ ἐμὲ			

Matt. c10_133 ⌐c10_131	cj καὶ	S				A οὐκ	P ἔστιν	C μου ἄξιος
		Matt. c10_134	P ὁ φιλῶν	C υἱὸν ἢ θυγατέρα	A ὑπὲρ ἐμὲ			

Matt. c10_135 ⌐c10_133	cj καὶ	S					A οὐκ	P ἔστιν	C μου ἄξιος
		Matt. c10_136	S ὃς	A οὐ	P λαμβάνει	C τὸν σταυρὸν αὐτοῦ			
		Matt. c10_137	cj καὶ	P ἀκολουθεῖ	A ὀπίσω μου				

Note the parallel constructions. All three clauses employ the same verb, which is negated by οὐκ, and the same complement μου ἄξιος. In clause one and two, the subjects are realized by articular participial clauses incorporating the word group ὁ φιλῶν, which may be translated *the one who loves* or *the one loving*, followed by a complement the elements of which are from the same semantic domain; the first phrase incorporating parents, the second children.[12] Each phrase then incorporates the same adjunct: the prepositional phrase ὑπὲρ ἐμέ. As with the relative clauses in the examples cited above, the identity of the subject is established by means of reference to what is predicated about him or her, in this instance, the activity of loving. The subject is presented as someone concrete, yet non-definite; there is no indication that a specific individual identifiable by name or face is in view. The structure of the third clause is consistent with those cited above, employing a standard relative clause as subject. In all three instances, though employing different clause types, the functions of the clauses are the same. This example affords an excellent opportunity to observe the article operating within a participial clause that performs the same function as a relative clause, but is a reduced form. In addition, the choice to employ articular participial clauses in the first two main clauses and a relative clause in the third main clause may have been motivated by a desire to give the third clause *prominence*, indicating to the recipient that the content of the third clause captures Jesus' main point. It may function as a summary statement of the material beginning in v. 34.[13] As noted above, the content and structure of the first two clauses is very similar, nearly identical, as the OpenText.org clause annotation clearly illustrates. In terms of both content and structure, the third clause represents a significant shift. Not only is there a shift from articular participial clause to relative clause, it is arguable that the relative clause is also structurally more complex. On the one hand, participles do not grammaticalize mood.[14] In this instance, the processes grammaticalized by the participles function as the identifying characteristics of the referents. On the other hand, in the relative clause, the use of the indicative mood form indicates the speaker's choice to grammaticalize his perspective of the verbal action with regard to its relation to reality.[15] When all these factors are brought

---

[12] See Louw and Nida, *Greek/English Lexicon*, Domain 10 Kinship Terms, Sub-Domain B Kinship Relations Involving Successive Generations.

[13] Nolland's comments on 10:38 suggest such an interpretation, but not quite as explicitly as I have, "This final statement both interprets and generalizes the preceeding two, and with its fresh image of suffering to be faced integrates the material here with that of vv. 34–36," *The Gospel of Matthew*, 440. However, he does not note the shift from participial clause to relative clause. This illustrates the exegetical value of attending to ὁ-items.

[14] Porter, *Idioms*, 181.

[15] Porter, *Idioms*, 50.

together, it is reasonable to conclude that the shift to the relative clause represents a motivated choice to make that element more prominent.

In Rom 2:21–23, Paul employs a series of five successive clauses of parallel structure. The first four incorporate an articular participial clause as subject; the fifth a relative clause:

ὁ οὖν διδάσκων ἕτερον σεαυτὸν οὐ διδάσκεις; ὁ κηρύσσων μὴ κλέπτειν κλέπτεις; ὁ λέγων μὴ μοιχεύειν μοιχεύεις; ὁ βδελυσσόμενος τὰ εἴδωλα ἱεροσυλεῖς; ὃς ἐν νόμῳ καυχᾶσαι, διὰ τῆς παραβάσεως τοῦ νόμου τὸν θεὸν ἀτιμάζεις;

The one who teaches others, do you teach yourself? *The one who preaches, "Do not steal,"* do you steal? *The one who says, "Do not commit adultery,"* do you commit adultery? *The one who detests idols,* do you desecrate temples? *The one who has confidence in law,* do you dishonor God by breaking the law?*

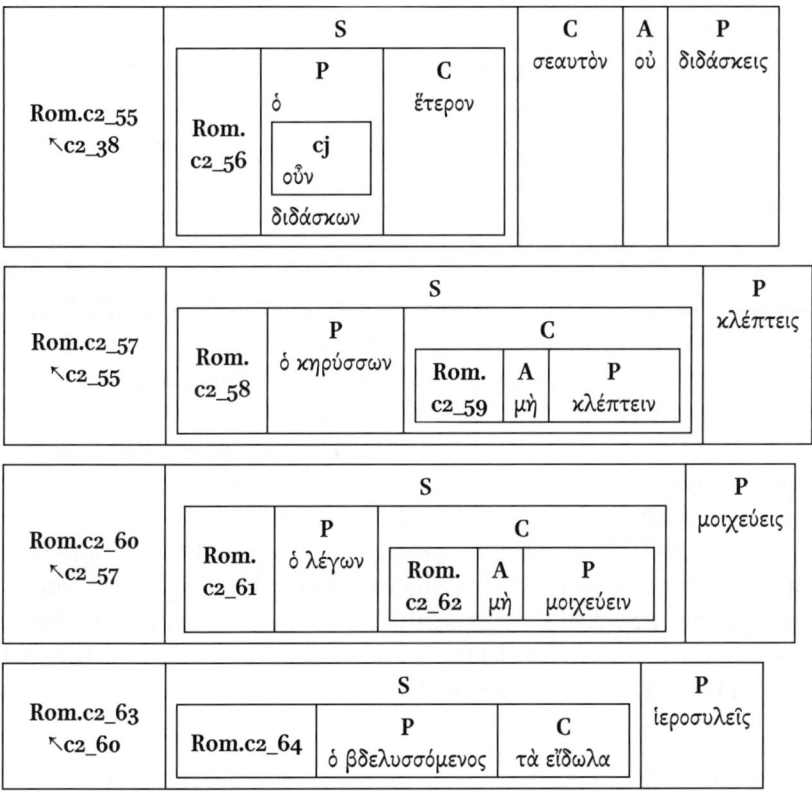

	S				A	C	P
Rom.c2_65 ↖c2_63	Rom. c2_66	S ὅς	A ἐν νόμῳ	P καυχᾶσαι	διὰ τῆς παραβάσεως τοῦ νόμου	τὸν θεὸν	ἀτιμάζεις

This rather lengthy example helps again to illustrate the use of the article and relative pronoun in a way that is functionally parallel. Paul had been, up to this point, speaking directly to Jews both by name and through the use of the second person. Now, he introduces new participants into the discourse. While the following interrogation may indeed be leveled at the Jewish audience, the wording Paul employs does so in a roundabout way, as observed above in 1 Cor 11:27. The accusations are leveled at imaginary interlocutors, who are characterized as though they are in reality present, that is, *concrete*. Once again, the apostle does not confront the recipients directly, but holds out an unnamed individual as an example of the kind of behavior he is confronting. The recipients now have the responsibility of examining themselves to determine if they are guilty of these transgressions.The subjects of the first four clauses are all realized through the use of an articular participle clause. The last clause has as its subject a standard relative clause. In each, the identity of the subject is established by what it predicated about him or her: *the one who teaches, the one who preaches, the one who says, the one who detests,* and *the one who has confidence.* Though realized by different clause types, in terms of the production of text they are functionally equivalent. As with the previous example, one must ask why the apostle shifts from the articular participial clauses to a relative clause. Once again, the answer may lie in his desire to make this element prominent. Like the example from Matthew above, the relative clause represents a break in an established pattern. It is also, arguably, a more complex structure. In terms of the larger co-text of Romans, the fifth clause is a summary statement of Paul's overarching challenge in the epistle to those who confidence is based on law. Thus, it may also be viewed as a comprehensive statement of a general problem, of which the previous four clauses provide specific examples.[16] This would explain Paul's choice to make this element more prominent.

---

[16] Moo seems to draw a similar conclusion. Though he takes the fifth clause to be a statement, rather than question, he suggests that it "brings home to Paul's Jewish addressee the accusation developed in vv. 17–22," *The Epistle to the Romans,* 165. Moo makes no reference to the shift from participial phrase to relative clause. Morris suggests that "this accusation hits at the heart of his religious understanding," *The Epistle to the Romans,* 138. Once again, we observe the exegetical value of attending to ὁ-items.

1 John 4:6 provides another example of this parallel structure:

ἡμεῖς ἐκ τοῦ θεοῦ ἐσμεν, ὁ γινώσκων τὸν θεὸν ἀκούει ἡμῶν, ὃς οὐκ ἔστιν ἐκ τοῦ θεοῦ οὐκ ἀκούει ἡμῶν.

We are from God. *The one who knows God* hears us. *The one who is not from God* does not hear us.

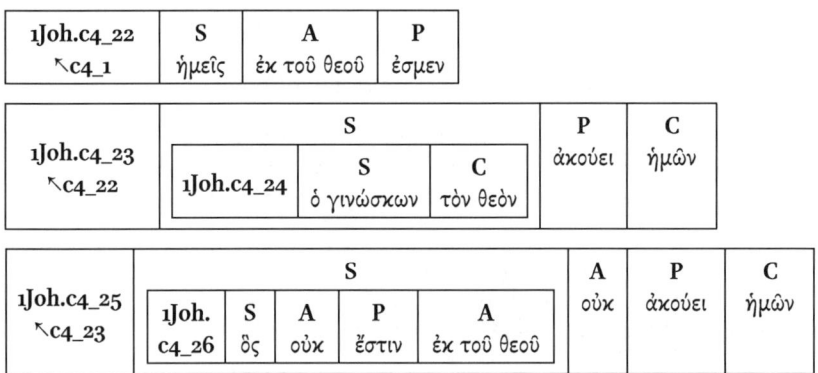

In this example, the author contrasts two classes of individual. Note the use of the same predicator and complement that creates the sense of parallelism, as well as the contrast in the construction of the subjects. The first clause in the parallel construction employs an articular participial clause functioning as a relative clause as subject, while the second clause employs a standard relative clause. Both function as the subject of the main clause. Up to this point, John has moved back and forth between the first and second person, speaking about himself and his associates, as well as directly speaking to his audience. Now he introduces two new participants into the discourse for his audience to consider. In order to be held out for examination, these participants must be characterized as concrete, as something that may be examined. However, there is no indication that definite, specific individuals are in view. The identity of the first participant is defined by a single characteristic: he or she is the one *who knows God.* Such a person listens to John and his confederates. The obvious implication is that his audience should emulate such a person. This person stands in contrast with the next participant, *the one who is not from God.* This person is also held up for the audience's consideration. Such a person does not listen to John and his confederates. As with previous examples, this places the recipient in the position of self-examination to determine to which class he or she belongs. In addition, the author has shifted from an articular participial clause to a relative clause. Based on the previous examples, there is mounting evidence to support the argument that, when all other factors are equal, the relative clause represents a marked form. If this is true, then in this instance the author's choice to employ a relative clause indicates his desire to make this element more prominent.[17] His motivation may be to emphasize to his readers the true nature of such people so that they, the readers, will avoid them.

The previous examples followed a similar pattern of clauses employing articular participial clauses followed by a relative clause. The following example, taken from Matt 5:31–32, employs a different structure:

Ἐρρέθη δέ· ὃς ἂν ἀπολύσῃ τὴν γυναῖκα αὐτοῦ, δότω αὐτῇ ἀποστάσιον. ἐγὼ δὲ λέγω ὑμῖν ὅτι πᾶς ὁ ἀπολύων τὴν γυναῖκα αὐτοῦ παρεκτὸς λόγου πορνείας ποιεῖ αὐτὴν μοιχευθῆναι, καὶ ὃς ἐὰν ἀπολελυμένην γαμήσῃ, μοιχᾶται.

It is said, *whoever divorces his wife* must give her a written notice of divorce. But I say to you, *each one who divorces his wife, except for sexual immorality*, causes her to commit adultery. And *whoever marries one having been so divorced*, commits adultery.

Matt.c5_125 ᴷc5_109	P ἐρρέθη	cj δέ

Matt.c5_126 ᴷc5_125	S					P δότω	C αὐτῇ	C ἀποστάσιον
	Matt. c5_127	S ὃς	A ἂν	P ἀπολύσῃ	C τὴν γυναῖκα αὐτοῦ			

Matt.c5_128 ᴷc5_125	S ἐγὼ	cj δὲ	P λέγω	C ὑμῖν

Matt. c5_129 ᴷc _128	cj ὅτι	S				P ποιεῖ	C αὐτὴν	C	
		Matt. c5_130	P πᾶς ὁ ἀπολύων	C τὴν γυναῖκα αὐτοῦ	A παρεκτὸς λόγου πορνείας			Matt. c5_131	P μοιχευθῆναι

---

[17] Brown notes the shift from participle to relative pronoun, but gives no indication that he attaches significance to it, Brown, *The Epistles of John*, 499–500.

	cj	S							P
Matt. c5_132 ⌐c5_129	καί								μοιχᾶται

			S	A	C			P	
		Matt. c5_133	ὅς	ἐάν				γαμήσῃ	

						P	
					Matt.c _134	ἀπολελυμένην	

This example begins with a clause of saying, which is followed by a clause that provides the content of what was spoken. The subject of this content clause is realized by means of a relative clause. This is followed by another clause of saying, which is followed by two clauses that also provide the content of what was spoken. The first employs an articular participial clause as subject; the second a relative clause. The clauses, *whoever divorces his wife, the one who divorces his wife except for sexual immorality* and *whoever marries one having been so divorced,* each introduce a new participant into the discourse. By establishing their identity by means of ὁ-items, each of these participants is characterized as someone concrete, as such a person who may exist, who may be held out for examination. However, they are non-definite; individuals that may be identified by name or face are not indicated. By employing such a construction, the speaker indicates to the recipient, "You do not know, specifically, which one(s) I mean. You have to take the fact of my seeing for the purpose of identification," to expand on Halliday's wording. The recipient must use the information provided by the speaker for the purpose of identification.

The motivation for the use of relative clauses in this example likely differs from that of the previous examples. In both instances, the relative clauses employ the subjunctive mood form, as well as ὅς ἄν/ἐάν. Such a construction is not available as a form realized by an articular participial claues. Therefore, the speaker was constrained to use the only form available.

3. Articular Participial Clauses as Subject or Complement

The previous examples were drawn from passages in which both an articular participial clause and a relative clause were employed, functioning in parallel. Articular participial clauses that function either as subject or complement are exceedingly common. In these instances, the referent is identified as a member of a class whose identifying characteristic is a process, which is realized by the participle. As always, the information necessary for identification is provided by the speaker or writer.

In Matt 4:14, an articular participial clause functions as the subject of
a clause:

ἵνα πληρωθῇ τὸ ῥηθὲν διὰ Ἠσαΐου τοῦ προφήτου λέγοντος·

In order that *that which was spoken though Isaiah the prophet* may be fulfilled, saying...

Matt.c4_50 ⌐c4_47	cj ἵνα	P πληρωθῇ	S			
			Matt. c4_51	P τὸ ῥηθὲν	A διὰ Ἠσαΐου τοῦ προφήτου	
					Matt. c4_52	P λέγοντος

The subject is identified by what is predicated about it; it is *that which
was spoken.* The subject is characterized as concrete, though the group
τὸ ῥηθὲν by itself is not definite. The fact that it is qualified by the prepositional group *through the prophet Isaiah* indicates that the class in view
is not presented as *such a thing that exists* or *may exist,* but does indeed
belong to the actual realm of reality. The prepositional group characterizes the class as something that was spoken by a real person in time and
space. Thus, this sense of definiteness is not established by the presence
of the article, but by the qualifier.

Articular participial clauses function as both subject and complement
in Matt 7:8:

πᾶς γὰρ ὁ αἰτῶν λαμβάνει καὶ ὁ ζητῶν εὑρίσκει καὶ τῷ κρούοντι ἀνοιγήσεται.

Each one who asks receives, and *the one who seeks* finds, and *to the one who
knocks,* it will be opened.

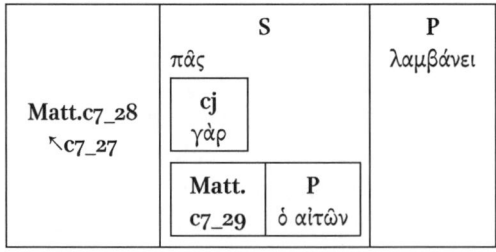

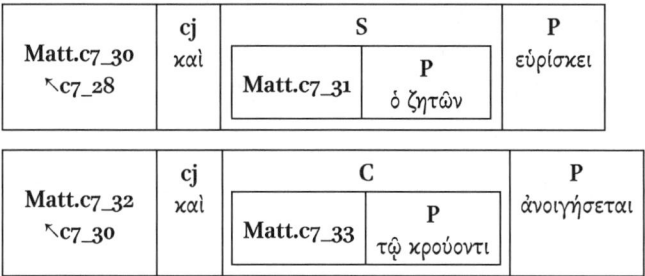

Matt.c7_30 ⌐c7_28	cj καί	S		P εὑρίσκει
		Matt.c7_31	P ὁ ζητῶν	

Matt.c7_32 ⌐c7_30	cj καί	C		P ἀνοιγήσεται
		Matt.c7_33	P τῷ κρούοντι	

In the first two clauses, an articular participial clause functions as a component of the subject of the main clause. In the third, the participial clause functions as a component of the complement of the main clause. As observed with relative clauses above, the identities of the referents are characterized as concrete, yet non-definite. The nature of their identity is based on what is predicated about them: *the one who asks, the one who seeks, the one who knocks.* As is typically seen, there is no indication that specific individuals are in view. Each is held out for the recipient's examination. The speaker is saying (as seen before), "You do not know, specifically, which one(s) I mean. You have to take the fact of my seeing for the purpose of identification." The information necessary for identification is provided by the speaker.

An articular participial clause is employed in Matt 10:20 to identify a class with whom Jesus' disciples are not associated:

οὐ γὰρ ὑμεῖς ἐστε οἱ λαλοῦντες…

For you will not be *the ones who are speaking*…

Matt.c10_67 ⌐c10_65	A οὐ	cj γὰρ	S ὑμεῖς	P ἐστε	C	
					Matt.c10_68	P οἱ λαλοῦντες

In this example of Jesus' reported speech, *the ones who are speaking* are a class whose identity is based solely on the fact of their *speaking*. By employing the article, the speaker indicates to the recipients that he is providing the information necessary to identify this class in the form of the participle.

Two separate articular participial clauses function as components of subjects in Luke 5:31. The first simply employs an articular participle; the second an articular participle and an adverbial adjunct:

οὐ χρείαν ἔχουσιν οἱ ὑγιαίνοντες ἰατροῦ ἀλλὰ οἱ κακῶς ἔχοντες·

The ones who are well have no need of a doctor, but *the ones who have sickness.*

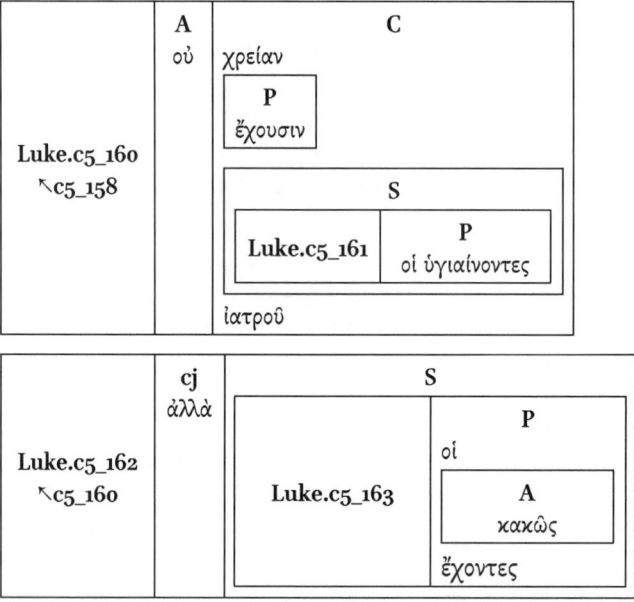

As with previous examples, the first articular participial clause denotes a class whose identity is based solely on the fact that they *are well*. The second articular participial clause denotes a class whose identity is not established by the process of the participle alone: *having*. It is what they are *having* that the speaker offers as the identifying feature of this class: they are *having badly*, an idiom that means "to be in a bad state, to be ill."[18] While neither class refers to a specific group in a *definite* sense, they are characterized as *concrete*, as belonging to experience of actual things that

---

[18] Louw and Nida, *Greek-English Lexicon*, 270.

do exist. Such people as this do exist, even if specific individuals identifiable by name and face are not in view.

In Luke 11:23, slightly more developed articular participial clauses that include prepositional phrases as adjuncts are employed:

Ὁ μὴ ὢν μετ᾽ ἐμοῦ κατ᾽ ἐμοῦ ἐστιν, καὶ ὁ μὴ συνάγων μετ᾽ ἐμοῦ σκορπίζει.

The one who is not with me is against me, and *the one who does not gather with me*, scatters.

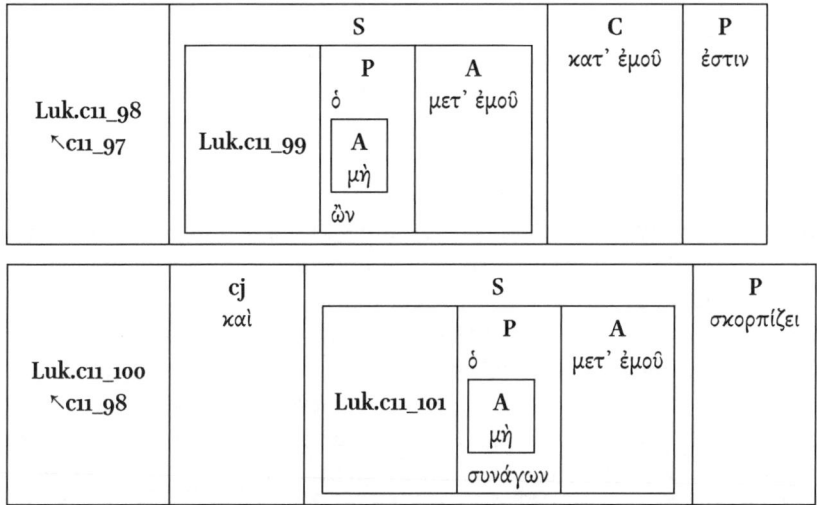

Both *the one who is not with me* and *the one who does not gather with me* are identified by what is predicated about them. However, this identity has more to do than simply *being* or *gathering*. They are not *with me* [that is, Jesus], nor do they gather *with me* [again, Jesus]. The article indicates to the recipients that they are to use this information, which the speaker has provided them, for the purpose of identifying these classes. Whether or not these classes are known to the recipients is not indicated. There is no indication that the identity may be recovered from the text or is obvious from the text (as would be the case with the English definite article).

In Acts 2:44, the question of identity that may be recovered from the text is illustrated in the use of an articular participial clause:

πάντες δὲ οἱ πιστεύοντες ἦσαν ἐπὶ τὸ αὐτό.

And *all the ones believing* were unified.

Act.c2_148 ⌐c2_147	S		P ἦσαν	A ἐπὶ τὸ αὐτὸ
	Act.c2_149	P πάντες οἱ πιστεύοντες		
	cj δὲ			

Immediately preceding this clause, the author makes reference to those in Jerusalem who were afraid. Next, he makes reference to the signs and wonders performed by the apostles. *All the ones believing* are introduced as new participants. Certainly the reader senses an implicit, logical connection between *all the ones believing* and those mentioned earlier in verse 42 who gave themselves to the teaching of the apostles and to fellowship. However, the use of the article does not make this identification explicit. The function of the article is not to indicate to the recipient that the identity of this class is recoverable in the text or is even obvious. Any connection between these people and those previously mentioned must be made by the recipient by logically associating *all the ones believing* with those previously mentioned in v. 42. Such a connection, though legitimate, is not grammatically indicated. The information that the writer provides regarding the class, *all the ones believing*, is the only identifying feature of this class, even if the recipient may be able to logically associate this class with another class previously mentioned.

In this instance, *all the ones believing* may be understood as definite. However, this definiteness is not established by the article. Rather, it is the combination of a class that is characterized as concrete with processes that are presented as actual events occurring in the real world in the narrative. By first characterizing the class as concrete, the writer may place this element into a narrative environment that produces a further characterization of definiteness. Thus, definiteness is not the function of the article, but additional co-textual features.

The apostle Paul employs articular participial clauses to provide the identifying characteristics of certain classes of individuals in Romans 8:

Rom 8:5, οἱ γὰρ κατὰ σάρκα ὄντες τὰ τῆς σαρκὸς φρονοῦσιν,

For *the ones who are based on flesh* think about the things of the flesh.

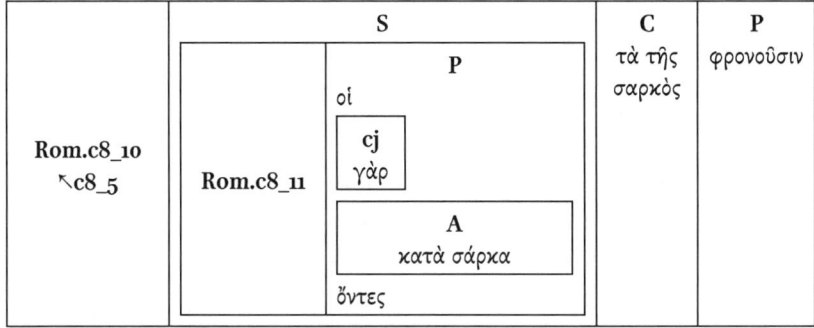

Rom 8:8, οἱ δὲ ἐν σαρκὶ ὄντες θεῷ ἀρέσαι οὐ δύνανται.

But *the ones who are fleshly* are unable to please God.

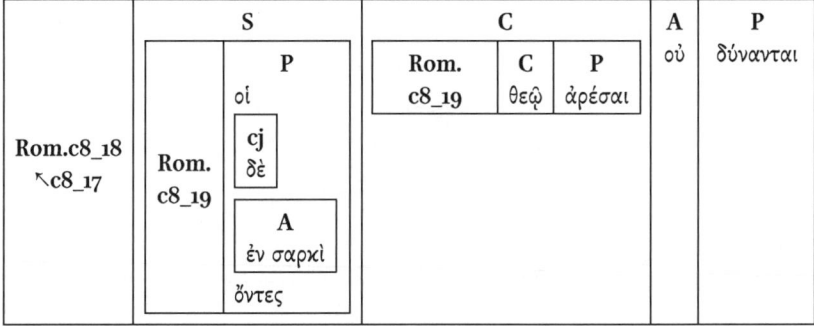

In the larger co-text of Rom 8:5–8, Paul introduces several participants into the discourse. Each participant's identity is established by a particular state. In the first clause presented above, the participants' identity is defined by the fact that they are those *who are according to the flesh*. In the second clause, the participants are defined by a similar, yet slightly different state: they are those *who are in the flesh*. In both instances, the author, through the use of an articular participle, indicates that identification is based on information he is providing. He is not directing the reader to the identity of the referent, nor does he indicate that the reader knows the identity. The reader must accept Paul's "seeing" of these individuals for the purpose of identification. The apostle is telling them about someone else, in the sense of "these people that I see I am now making known to you." It is possible to argue that the identity of the first class, *the ones according to the flesh*, is the same as the second, *the ones*

in the flesh. As seen above, this may be an appropriate logical association. However, Paul's characterization presents each as a grammatically distinct class. Whether or not the two individuals are synonymous is immaterial for the present purpose. Paul presents them as distinct classes because of the roles they perform in their own clauses. While presented as concrete, there is nothing that suggests that the identities of these individuals are specific or definite. For the sake of Paul's argument, they are simply presented as such a person who does or may exist, and are held out for the audience's examination.

Paul records in Gal 1:23 that he himself was identified by a particular process at one time, that being *persecution*:

μόνον δὲ ἀκούοντες ἦσαν ὅτι ὁ διώκων ἡμᾶς ποτε νῦν εὐαγγελίζεται τὴν πίστιν ἣν ποτε ἐπόρθει.

But they were hearing, *"The one who was persecuting us* is now proclaiming as good news the faith that he attacked."

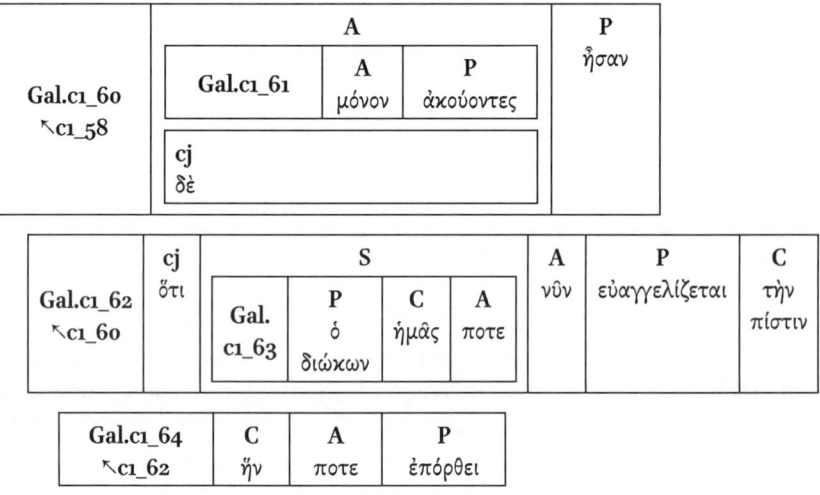

Paul's former activity is used as an identifying characteristic; he is characterized as ὁ διώκων ἡμᾶς ποτε, *the one formerly persecuting us.* Once again, the speakers whose words Paul records employ the article to indicate that they are providing the information necessary for identification. The identity of the referent is defined solely by the process grammaticalized by the participle. For the immediate purpose of the discourse, the referent has no other identifying characteristics. As with other examples, the referent may be interpreted as definite, but this is established by other co-textual features, in this instance, its presence in an account that purports to narrate the activity of an actual person.

Gal 6:6 offers an interesting example in that it employs two articular participial clauses that employ the same verb, but in different voices:

Κοινωνείτω δὲ ὁ κατηχούμενος τὸν λόγον τῷ κατηχοῦντι ἐν πᾶσιν ἀγαθοῖς.

The one who is taught the word must share in all good things *with the one who teaches.*

Gal. c6_15 ⌐c6_14	P κοινωνείτω	cj δὲ		S			C		A ἐν πᾶσιν ἀγαθοῖς
			Gal. c6_16	P ὁ κατηχούμενος	C τὸν λόγον	Gal. c6_17	P τῷ κατηχοῦντι		

At this point in the letter, Paul's topic moves from teaching about correcting others and bearing others' burdens to a short statement about supporting teachers. Thus, *the one who is taught the word* and *the one who teaches* are new participants in the discourse. The use of the same verb, κατηχέω, for both serves the obvious rhetorical function of connecting the two participants by means of their shared participation in a single process: that of teaching. This is the only identifying characteristic offered for each participant. For the purposes of the discourse, it is their participation in this process that defines them. However, they are distinguished by the fact that one is the giver, the other the recipient, as indicated by the voice forms. While Paul may have specific individuals in mind (that is, specific teachers operating within the Christian communities in Galatia whom he could identify by name), there is nothing to indicate this in the grammar. He is not saying, "The one who teaches (you know who I am talking about)," which would indicate definiteness. At best, we may conclude that Paul is not speaking of hypothetical individuals who may or may not exist. Rather, his characterization indicates that he is referring to such individuals who exist, "The one who teaches (I'm telling you about the sort of person I am talking about)." There is no demonstrative to indicate where the recipient may find the necessary information for identification, nor is it assumed that the recipient already possesses the necessary information for identification. He or she is dependent upon Paul's seeing for the purpose of identification.

In 1 Thess 5:7, Paul introduces participants into the discourse whose sole identifying traits are *sleep* and *drunkenness*:

Οἱ γὰρ καθεύδοντες νυκτὸς καθεύδουσιν καὶ οἱ μεθυσκόμενοι νυκτὸς μεθύουσιν·

For *the ones who sleep* sleep at night, and *the ones who get drunk* get drunk at night.

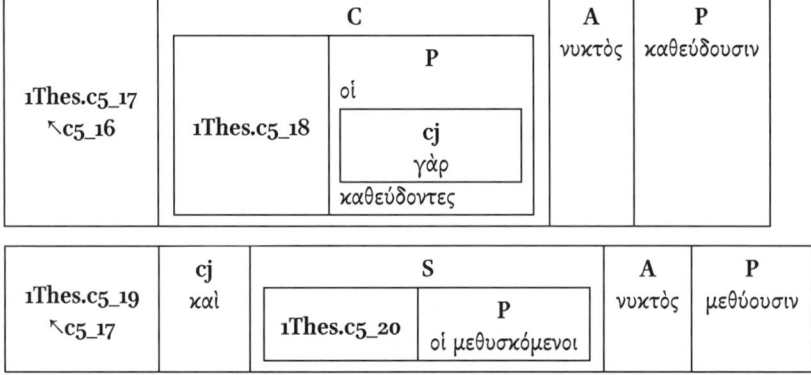

In the previous verses, Paul states that the Thessalonian Christians "are not in darkness." They are "children of light and children of day." He and they are not "of the night nor of the darkness." Paul and the Thessalonian Christians are not asleep like others, but are "alert and sober." In contrast, he next introduces new participants into the discourse, those *who are sleeping* and those *who are drunk.* As with previous examples, it is their participation in these processes that are the sole identifying characteristics of these participants. Likewise, though not definite, they are characterized as concrete, as belonging to experience of actual people. Such people as these exist, even if specific individuals are not in view.

In 1 Tim 5:6, Paul holds out another individual whose identity is characterized solely by her actions for the consideration of Timothy:

ἡ δὲ σπαταλῶσα ζῶσα τέθνηκεν.

But *the one living indulgently*, though living, is dead.

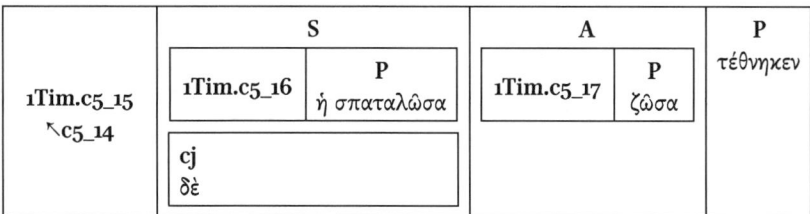

In his discussion of widows, Paul introduces a particular kind of widow to Timothy. This person is defined by her lifestyle; she is the one *who lives indulgently*. From Timothy's perspective, he must accept this information, which is provided by Paul, as the basis of identification. The referent is not recoverable from the discourse, nor is it obvious. Timothy must base his identification of this woman on the fact of Paul's seeing.

On a more positive note, the author of Hebrews introduces a participant in 4:10 whose sole identifying characteristic is *rest*:

ὁ γὰρ εἰσελθὼν εἰς τὴν κατάπουσιν αὐτοῦ καὶ αὐτὸς κατέπαυσεν ἀπὸ τῶν ἔργων αὐτοῦ.

For *the one who has entered into his rest* also himself rests from his work.

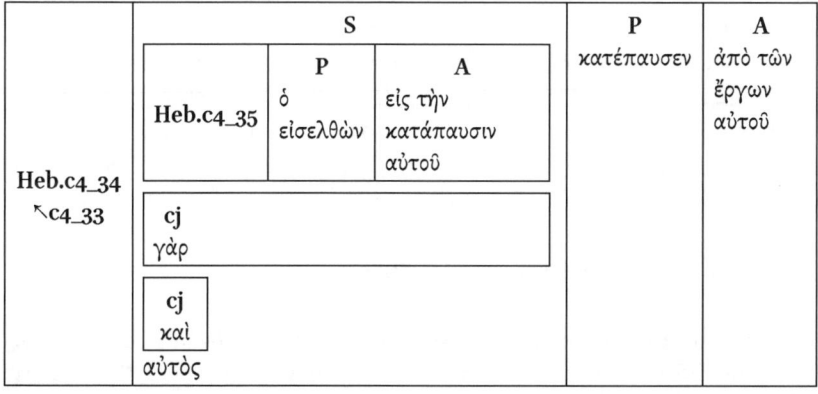

In the previous clause, the author states that there is yet "a Sabbath rest for the people of God." To illustrate his point, he holds up for examination an individual who is identified as *the one who has entered into his rest*. While this person is held up as a concrete example, there is no indication that a specific individual, identifiable by name and face, is in view, at least from the perspective of the audience.

Engaging in the process of *slander* or *judging* is the identifying characteristic of certain individuals in Jas 4:11:

Μὴ καταλαλεῖτε ἀλλήλων, ἀδελφοί. ὁ καταλαλῶν ἀδελφοῦ ἢ κρίνων τὸν ἀδελφὸν αὐτοῦ καταλαλεῖ νόμου.

Do not slander one another, brothers. *The one who slanders a brother or judges his brother* slanders law.

Jam.c4_46 ⌐c4_45	A μὴ	P καταλαλεῖτε	C ἀλλήλων	add ἀδελφοί

		S			P καταλαλεῖ	C νόμου
Jam.c4_47 ⌐c4_46	Jam.c4_48	P ὁ καταλαλῶν	C ἀδελφοῦ			
	Jam.c4_49	cj ἢ	P κρίνων	C τὸν ἀδελφὸν αὐτοῦ		

To reinforce his command, *do not slander one another,* James holds out for his audience's consideration the example of *the one who slanders a brother or [the one who] judges his brother.* In order to function as something that may be examined by the audience, this person must be characterized as concrete. However, as with many other examples, James does not choose to present this person as definite. While such people may indeed exist, and likely do, the rhetorical function of this person is simply to serve as a hypothetical example. His or her slander of the law should chill the hearts of the letter's audience, providing further motivation to heed the author's command.

The author of the Johannine epistles is particularly fond of this construction. Variations of the example below are used by the author no less than 40 times throughout the three letters.

1 John 4:8, ὁ μὴ ἀγαπῶν οὐκ ἔγνω τὸν θεόν.

The one who does not love does not know God.

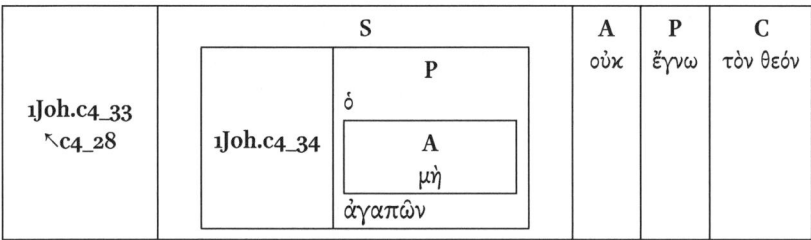

1Joh.c4_33 \c4_28		S			A oὐκ	P ἔγνω	C τὸν θεόν
	1Joh.c4_34		P ὁ				
				A μὴ			
			ἀγαπῶν				

In addition to multiple instances of ὁ ἀγαπῶν/μὴ ἀγαπῶν, *the one who loves/ does not love* (2:10, 3:10, 3:14, 4:7, 4:20–21, 5:1), the author repeatedly makes reference to individuals who are defined as ὁ μισῶν, *the one who hates* (2:11, 3:15); ὁ πιστεύων/μὴ πιστεύων, *the one who believes/does not believe* (5:1, 5, 10, 13); ὁ μενῶν/μὴ μενῶν, *the one who remains/does not remain* (3:6, 15, 4:16, 2 John 2, 9), to name but a few.

   2 John 1, καὶ οὐκ ἐγὼ ἀλλὰ καὶ πάντες οἱ ἐγνωκότες τὴν ἀλήθειαν,

   And not only I, but also *all the ones who know the truth*.

2Joh.c1_3 \c1_2	cj καὶ	A οὐκ	S ἐγὼ	A μόνος

2Joh.c1_4 \c1_3	cj ἀλλὰ	cj καὶ		S	
			2Joh.c1_5	P πάντες οἱ ἐγνωκότες	C τὴν ἀλήθειαν

The author addresses this letter to "the chosen lady and her children, whom I love in truth." However, he is not the only one who loves these people this way. In addition, *all the ones who know the truth* also love the recipients. These additional individuals are presented as unknown to the letters recipients. Their identity is only known to the author, who chooses to identify them only in terms of what is predicated about them: they are *the ones who know the truth*. As far as the text is concerned, their identity cannot be recovered; nor does the author direct the recipients to where the identity may be found. While presented as concrete individuals, they are non-definite as far as the text is concerned. It is reasonable to suggest that the author does indeed have specific individuals in mind, which he could identify by name and face. However, from the point of view of the recipients (and we the present readers), their identity indeterminate, as it is limited to the author's perspective alone. We, along with the original recipients, must accept the information he provides as the basis of their identity. There is nothing to suggest that the author is saying, "You know which ones I am talking about."

4. CONCLUSION

The use of articular participial clauses as a component of a subject or complement is yet another example of how such clauses fill the same slot and perform a similar function as a relative clause. As stated in the conclusion of the previous chapter, this further supports the hypothesis that the article and relative pronoun are morphologically, grammatically, and functionally related. These two structures are part of a system that provides the speaker with a choice of how he or she may produce text, construe experience, and indicate an appraisal of or attitude toward what is being communicated.[19]

In structures of this type, the speaker or writer employs a ὁ-item to indicate the he or she is providing the recipient with the information necessary for identifying the referent. Thus, the identity of the referent is oriented to the speaker or writer. There is no indication that the recipient already possesses this information. While he or she may, the article does not indicate this. By employing a ὁ-item, the speaker or writer characterizes the referent as concrete, as belonging to experience of an actual person or thing. However, the ὁ-item gives no indication of *definiteness*, which is established by other linguistic elements.

---

[19] Halliday, *Functional Grammar*, 29–31. See chapter 2.1 above.

ὁ-ITEMS IN μὲν ... δὲ STRUCTURES

In addition to relative clauses, another structure illustrates the parallel function of ὁ-items: the μὲν ... δὲ construction. In this construction, we again observe the article filling the same slot as the relative pronoun. The μὲν ... δὲ construction is used to mark "sets of items in contrast with one another—'on the one hand ... but on the other hand.' "[1] It is also used when "two or more items which are additively related and thematically parallel—'some ... others, first ... then.' "[2] Numerous examples of structures using both the relative pronoun and the article are found in the New Testament. The use of ὁ-items in these constructions does not always conform to that of WH- items in English and illustrates the lack of absolute parallel across the two languages.

Historically, it has been asserted that relative pronouns and the article, when employed in this structure, function as different parts of speech. Robertson classifies them both as demonstratives.[3] No doubt, this was, at least to some degree, influenced by translation rather than Greek usage, as Dana and Mantey write: "When [μέν] is used with the article, the expression may be translated as a pronoun."[4] Turner writes, "There is no instance of the article as a relative pronoun in the NT."[5] He equates ὁ δὲ with *but he*, and ὁ μὲν with *now he*.[6] Likewise, Wallace categorizes the article as a personal pronoun (he, she, it) when used in the μὲν ... δὲ structure.[7] There is no doubt that the translator, when faced with this construction, will be forced to use other English pronouns in the place occupied by the article or relative pronoun in Greek in order to conform to the English idiom. However, this in no way indicates a one-for-one correlation. When the function of ὅς, ἥ, ὅ is expanded beyond *who, which* to include the alternative relative *the one who, that which* as well (as seen above), additional

---

[1] Louw and Nida, *Greek-English Lexicon*, 795.
[2] Louw and Nida, *Greek-English Lexicon*, 791.
[3] Robertson, *Grammar*, 290, 694–95.
[4] Dana & Mantey, *Manual Grammar*, 261.
[5] Turner, *Syntax*, 37.
[6] Turner, *Syntax*, 36.
[7] Wallace, *Greek Grammar*, 211.

categorization as a demonstrative is no longer necessary.[8] This usage is comparable to the use of a relative clause or articular participial clause as a component of a subject or object. In both instances, the speaker or writer employs a ὁ-item to indicate, "I am telling you about someone/ something else." The recipient is not directed to the information neces-sary for identification, as is the case with demonstrative pronouns; nor does the speaker indicate that the recipient already has the informa-tion necessary for identification, as with the English definite article. The speaker and recipient do not share the information necessary for identi-fication, which is the case with personal pronouns or the English definite article. Instead, with μὲν ... δὲ structures, this information is provided by the speaker or writer. At times, the referent has virtually no identity apart from the simple fact of its *being*. In certain situations, ὁ-items will indicate that the referent is a subset of a class previously mentioned, which is con-sistent with their general function in defining relative clauses.[9] However, sometimes no class is indicated. In these instances, the referent is simply identified as someone or something that *is*, which is consistent with rela-tive clauses as subject or object.

With regard to the article, it will be argued that in μὲν ... δὲ structures, as well as with μὲν and δὲ independently, its function is not that of a demonstrative or personal pronoun, as believed by previous grammarians. Instead, it either functions like the relative pronoun, or in certain circum-stances, due to ellipsis of its head term, the article itself is elevated to the role of head. For Greek speakers, there was a tendency to use the article with the particles μὲν and δὲ as a type of short hand, where there is an additional element present by means of ellipsis. The use of ellipsis "makes it possible to leave out parts of a structure when they can be presumed from what has gone before."[10] This statement may be further elaborated:

---

[8] As a general rule it is, in fact, more accurate to say that ὁ-items are more closely analogous to the alternate English WH- form that employs a TH- item as a relative rather than a simple relative pronoun such as *who* or *which*. In English, this is realized by the form *the one that I saw*, as well as "a 'contact' type which avoids choosing either, *the one I saw*," Halliday, *Functional Grammar*, 86. In this way, the Greek language employs a single form for a variety of functions, while English employs different forms for such functions. By recognizing that Greek relative pronouns function not only like English relative pronouns, but also like the alternate English WH- form using a TH- item, we are able to provide a fuller and more accurate description of its function.

[9] As demonstrated above with regard to defining relative clauses, which identify the head term by locating it within a subset, by specifying it as a particular subset of a general class.

[10] Halliday, *Functional Grammar*, 535.

The starting point of the discussion of ellipsis can be the familiar notion that it is 'something left unsaid'. There is no implication here that what is unsaid is not understood; on the contrary, 'unsaid' implies 'but understood nevertheless', and another way of referring to ellipsis is in fact as SOME-THING UNDERSTOOD, where *understood* is used in the special sense of 'going without saying.'[11]

Halliday and Hasan go on to write:

We can take as a general guide the notion that ellipsis occurs when something that is structurally necessary is left unsaid; there is a sense of incompleteness associated with it.[12]

The structure of the nominal group consists of the head term along with optional modifiers.[13] Ellipsis in the nominal group is realized when a word that would normally function as a modifier is upgraded to function as the head term.[14] In Greek, both μὲν and δὲ are postpositive, thus it is frequently the case that the article is separated from its head term by one of these particles. Over time, Greek speakers appear to have begun using ὁ μὲν and ὁ δὲ as a contracted form or short hand, with the head term elided and the article upgraded to function as the head term.[15]

1. THE RELATIVE PRONOUN IN ὅς μὲν ... ὅς δὲ STRUCTURES

When ὅς, ἥ, ὅ are rigidly and exclusively equated with *who, which*, no small amount of cognitive dissonance occurs when they are used in structures that do not conform to English patterns of usage. The historical tendency (as noted above) has been to expand their categorization to include other types of pronouns such as demonstratives and personal pronouns. As we have already observed, the Greek relative pronoun has a broader range of function than English WH- relatives. It also functions like the alternate TH- form of the WH- element, *the one (who)*.[16] As when the relative clause functions as head, we also observe this function in the ὅς μὲν ... ὅς δὲ structure.

---

[11] Halliday and Hasan, *Cohesion*, 142.
[12] Halliday and Hasan, *Cohesion*, 144.
[13] Halliday and Hasan, *Cohesion*, 147.
[14] Halliday and Hasan, *Cohesion*, 148.
[15] This is in contrast with Robertson's interpretation of this construction, in which the article is demonstrative in force, "where ὁ δέ, ἡ δέ, οἱ δέ refer to persons already mentioned in an oblique case," *Grammar*, 695.
[16] Halliday, *Functional Grammar*, 86.

Technically, ὅ-items in this construction do not have an antecedent; they do not correspond with a previously mentioned referent in a one-for-one manner, as in the case of a defining or non-defining relative clause. In certain instances, they are characterized merely by the fact that they are a person or thing that *is*, with no other identifying characteristics. In other instances, they will be used to identify a subset of a particular referent, with which they will usually (though not always) agree in gender only. Thus, the speaker still indicates that he or she is "telling you about something else," but that this person or thing is related to something already mentioned. In this way, they stand between defining and non-defining relative clauses, in which the ὅ-item has an antecedent, and an independent relative clause that functions as a subject or object, in which it has no antecedent.

In Matt 13:23, it is demonstrable that the function of the relative pronoun does indeed correspond more closely to the alternate WH- form that uses a TH- item:

ὃς δὴ καρποφορεῖ καὶ ποιεῖ ὃ μὲν ἑκατόν, ὃ δὲ ἑξήκοντα, ὃ δὲ τριάκοντα

...who bears fruit and produces *some* one-hundred, *another* sixty, *and another* thirty.[17]

Mat.c13_112	S	A	P
⬉c13_109	ὃς	δὴ	καρποφορεῖ

Mat.c13_113	cj	P
⬉c13_112	καὶ	ποιεῖ

Mat.c13_114	S	cj	A
⬉c13_113	ὃ	μὲν	ἑκατόν

Mat.c13_115	S	cj	A
⬉c13_114	ὃ	δὲ	ἑξήκοντα

Mat.c13_116	S	cj	A
⬉c13_115	ὃ	δὲ	τριάκοντα

---

[17] The OpenText.org annotation identifies the relative pronouns as subjects. However, it is entirely possible that they are complements, rather than subjects. The translation above reflects this interpretation.

Based on the OpenText.org annotation, this μὲν ... δὲ structure is part of a non-defining relative clause, which provides further characterization of *the one who hears the word*. As seen above, an attempt to conform the translation of the μὲν ... δὲ structure literally to the Greek produces a somewhat strained English rendering. Using Louw and Nida's suggestion, it may be translated: *who bears fruit and produces, some one-hundred, another sixty, and another thirty.*[18] However, it is imperative to recognize that, though this is the English idiom, it must not be read back into the Greek. In Greek, writers and speakers employ different grammatical elements than those using English to perform similar functions. When the semantic space of Greek relative pronouns is limited to *who* or *which*, the resulting "literal" translation is almost unintelligible. When an alternate WH- form is employed, the "literal" translation, as seen above, is much less difficult, even if it still requires some accommodation to the English idiom.

In this instance, the ὁ-items in the μὲν ... δὲ structure do not have an antecedent; there is no element with which they agree in gender.[19] They function like an independent relative clause. The speaker provides the information necessary for identification, though merely characterizing the referent as something that *is*. The referent is not known to the recipients; the speaker is "telling them about something else." They must accept that fact of the speaker's "seeing" of these things for the purpose of identification.

The use of ὁ-items in a manner analogous to alternate WH- items is again observed in Matt 21:35:

καὶ λαβόντες οἱ γεωργοὶ τοὺς δούλους αὐτοῦ ὃν μὲν ἔδειραν, ὃν δὲ ἀπέκτειναν, ὃν δὲ ἐλιθοβόλησαν.

And the farmers, taking his servants, on the one hand beat *the one*, killed *the one*, and stoned *the one*.

---

[18] Louw and Nida, *Greek-English Lexicon*, 791.

[19] Nolland sees the shift to the neuter as a move to "break away from the focus on a single individual that has characterized the main part of the replacement narrative," *Matthew*, 542.

	cj	A			C	cj	P
Matt.c21_173 ⤡c21_171	καί	**Matt.** **c21_174**	**P** λαβόντες	**C** τοὺς δούλους αὐτοῦ	ὅν	μέν	ἔδειραν
		S οἱ γεωργοί					

	C	cj	P
Matt.c21_175 ⤡c21_173	ὅν	δέ	ἀπέκτειναν

	C	cj	P
Matt. **c21_176** ⤡c21_175	ὅν	δέ	ἐλιθοβόλησαν

In this example, the referents of the ὁ-items in the μέν … δέ are a subset of the class τοὺς δούλους αὐτοῦ, as evidenced by the agreement in gender. However, just as in the previous example, they have no other identifying characteristics apart from the fact that they simply *are*. Each is "seen" by the speaker. The recipients must accept the fact of the speaker's "seeing" of these individuals as the basis of identification. This is consistent with the use of ὁ-items to indicate, "I am telling you about something else." The speaker is no longer speaking of the broad group of τοὺς δούλους αὐτοῦ. He is now talking about individual members of that group.

The following example from Matt 22:5 begins with an article that functions as subject, which is followed by a μέν … δέ construction that introduces new participants, each of whom is a subset of the subject:

> οἱ δὲ ἀμελήσαντες ἀπῆλθον, ὃς μὲν εἰς τὸν ἴδιον ἀγρόν, ὃς δὲ ἐπὶ τὴν ἐμπορίαν αὐτοῦ·

> But the ones disregarding [the invitation] went away, *the one* to his own field, *the one* to his business.

	S	cj	A		P
Matt.c22_21 ⤡c22_11	οἱ	δέ	**Matt.c22_22**	**P** ἀμελήσαντες	ἀπῆλθον

Matt.c22_23 ↖c22_21	S ὅς	cj μὲν	A εἰς τὸν ἴδιον ἀγρόν

Matt.c22_24 ↖c22_23	S ὅς	cj δὲ	A ἐπὶ τὴν ἐμπορίαν αὐτοῦ

Once again there is gender agreement between the ὁ-items in the μὲν ... δὲ construction and the subject, οἱ ἀμελήσαντες.[20] However, there is not number agreement. Each member of the μὲν ... δὲ construction is a sub-set of this general class of οἱ ἀμελήσαντες, *the ones who disregard [the invitation]*.[21]

Mark 12:5 incorporates a slight variation of the ὃς μὲν ... ὃς δὲ construction:[22]

καὶ πολλοὺς ἄλλους, οὓς μὲν δέροντες, οὓς δὲ ἀποκτέννοντες.

... and many others, beating *the ones*, killing *the ones*.

	cj καὶ	C πολλοὺς ἄλλους	A			
Mar.c12_19 ↖c12_18			**Mar.** c12_20	**C** οὓς	**cj** μὲν	**P** δέροντες
			Mar. c12_21	**C** οὓς	**cj** δὲ	**P** ἀποκτέννοντες

---

[20] The OpenText.org annotation identifies the article alone as subject. The agreement between the article and the participle suggests that this is an articular participial clause functioning as a component of the subject. Were the two elements not separated by the post-positive *δέ*, this would be certain. It is also possible that there is, instead, an elided element. The only logical candidate for this element would be τοὺς κεκλημένους εἰς τοὺς γάμους, *the ones called to the wedding*, in v. 3, and simply τοῖς κεκλημένοις, *[to] the ones called*, in v. 4. One could argue that this is, indeed the case. However, the answer to the question of whether or not this element "goes without saying," to quote Halliday and Hasan, is subjective, which is frequently the case with elision in general. A good argument could be made for either elision or an articular participial clause.

[21] Robertson designates this partitive or distributional apposition, "when the words in apposition do not correspond to the whole," *Grammar*, 399. He also cites this instance as an example of the demonstrative use of ὅς, *Grammar*, 695. However, as individuals, they are new participants. This would argue against a demonstrative force for the pro-noun. Instead, the speaker is providing the recipients with the necessary information for identification, not directing them to it. Though associated with the previously mentioned *servants*, each is identified by means of "further characterization." This is more consistent with the use of the relative pronoun.

[22] Robertson also cites this as example of the demonstrative use of ὅς, *Grammar*, 696.

Mark's usage is different than the previous examples. The μὲν...δὲ structure is embedded in the adjunct, which is similar to a defining relative clause. However, the ὁ-items do not define the head as a subset, but are themselves as subset of the head. At first glance, it appears that there is concord between the ὁ-items and πολλοὺς ἄλλους. However, in the examples previously cited, as well as those that follow, this type of concord rarely occurs. This suggests that what at first appears to be concord is not. Rather, the accusative case is employed because the relative pronouns are the complements of the participles, and the plural form is employed because the subsets themselves are groups, not individuals.

Rom 9:21 also incorporates an embedded μὲν...δὲ structure:

ἢ οὐκ ἔχει ἐξουσίαν ὁ κεραμεὺς τοῦ πηλοῦ ἐκ τοῦ αὐτοῦ φυράματος ποιῆσαι ὃ μὲν εἰς τιμὴν σκεῦος ὃ δὲ εἰς ἀτιμίαν;

Or doesn't the potter have the right to make from the same lump of clay *the one* into an honorable vessel *but the one* into a dishonorable?

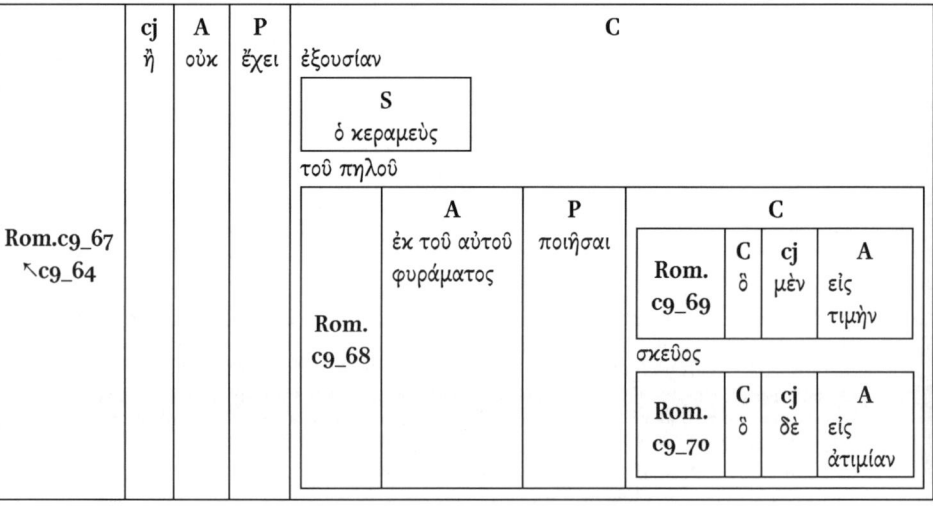

The ὁ-items in the μὲν...δὲ; structure are embedded in the complement. While they do agree with σκεῦος in number and gender, they are not part of a defining relative clause. The ὁ-items do not identify the head term σκεῦος as a subset, but are themselves a subset of the broader class of σκεῦος.[23] As with the previous examples, their only identifying character-istic is that they *are*.

In Rom 14:5, Paul uses ό-items in a μὲν ... δὲ construction in a manner consistent with a relative clause as subject:

ὃς μὲν [γὰρ] κρίνει ἡμέραν παρ' ἡμέραν, ὃς δὲ κρίνει πᾶσαν ἡμέραν·

The one distinguishes one day from another, *but the one* considers each day [the same].

Rom. C14_22 ⟋C14_20	S ὃς	cj μὲν	cj γὰρ	P κρίνει	C ἡμέραν	A παρ' ἡμέραν

Rom. C14_23 ⟋C14_22	S ὃς	cj δὲ	P κρίνει	C πᾶσαν ἡμέραν

In his discourse on *the weak* and *the strong*, Paul has not yet made mention of these specific individuals; they are introduced as new participants.[24] Each of the ό-items functions independently as the subject of its own clause. While the usage bears certain similarities with the use of a relative clause as subject or object, this structure is distinguished from other relative clauses in that the ό-items are independent; they do not introduce a relative clause. If these items were functioning as demonstra-tives, as Robertson suggests, Paul would be directing the recipients to the identity of the referents.[25] While the recipients may indeed be able to say "I know someone like that," this is not realized from the text. The apostle is not directing the recipients to the information necessary for identifica-tion. Rather, he is providing that information, albeit in the broadest, most generic terms. Each is identified merely as such a person who *is*; thus, *the one*.

The very simple μὲν ... δὲ structure 1 Cor 11:21 again illustrates how new participants are introduced into the discourse:

---

[23] This is, once again, in contrast to Robertson, who categorizes these pronouns as demonstratives, *Grammar*, 695.

[24] While it is possible to associate the views of these two participants regarding the value of certain days with the "weak" and the "strong," Paul does not make this explicit, Moo, *Romans*, 841–42.

[25] Robertson, *Grammar*, 290. See also Morris, *Romans*, 480, footnote 17.

1 Cor 11:21, ἕκαστος γὰρ ἴδιον δεῖπνον προλαμβάνει ἐν τῷ φαγεῖν, καὶ ὃς μὲν πεινᾷ ὃς δὲ μεθύει.

For each goes ahead while eating his own meal, and *the one* is hungry, *but the one* gets drunk.

1Cor.c11_68 ⌐c11_66	S ἕκαστος	cj γὰρ	C τὸ ἴδιον δεῖπνον	P προλαμβάνει	A	
					1Cor. c11_69	P ἐν τῷ φαγεῖν

1Cor.c11_70 ⌐c11_68	cj καὶ	S ὃς	cj μὲν	P πεινᾷ

1Cor.c11_71 ⌐c11_70	S ὃς	cj δὲ	P μεθύει

The ὁ-items in this instance introduce participants who are a subset of the previously mentioned ἕκαστος, *each*. In his criticism of abuse of the Lord's Supper, Paul identifies a disparity in the meal experience among the participants. He holds out for consideration the examples of, on the one hand, *the one [who] goes hungry*, and on the other hand, *the one [who] gets drunk*. There is no indication that it is Paul's intention to identify specific individuals who are guilty of this kind of selfish and inconsiderate behavior. However, this does not mean there are not individuals in Corinth who may be identified with either of these two subsets. The fact that Paul is writing to address such a situation suggests otherwise. However, Paul does not make this specific identification. Each is characterized as such a person who exists, *the one*. However, there is nothing grammatical that would direct the Corinthians to the information that would enable them to make a specific identification. This allows Paul to challenge these individuals in an oblique, less confrontational manner. By doing so, he places the onus upon the recipients to examine themselves and determine to which category they belong.

In 2 Tim 2:20, the μὲν ... δὲ construction is employed to identify subsets within multiple subsets:

Ἐν μεγάλῃ δὲ οἰκίᾳ οὐκ ἔστιν μόνον σκεύη χρυσᾶ καὶ ἀργυρᾶ ἀλλὰ καὶ ξύλινα καὶ ὀστράκινα, καὶ ἃ μὲν εἰς τιμὴν ἃ δὲ εἰς ἀτιμίαν·

In a large house there are not only gold and silver vessels but also wood and clay, *the ones* for honor, *but the ones* for dishonor.

2Tim.c2_59 ↖c2_53	**A** ἐν μεγάλῃ **cj δὲ** οἰκίᾳ	**A** οὐκ	**P** ἔστιν	**A** μόνον	**S** σκεύη χρυσᾶ καὶ ἀργυρᾶ

2Tim.c2_60 ↖c2_59	cj ἀλλὰ	cj καὶ	**S** ξύλινα καὶ ὀστράκινα		

2Tim.c2_61 ↖c2_60	cj καὶ	**S** ἃ	cj μὲν	**A** εἰς τιμὴν

2Tim.c2_62 ↖c2_61	**S** ἃ	cj δὲ	**A** εἰς ἀτιμίαν

Paul identifies several subsets of *vessels*: those of *gold and silver*, and those of *wood and clay*. The μὲν … δὲ construction is used to introduce subsets of these various types of vessels: *the ones* that are used for *honorable* purposes and *the ones* that are used for *dishonorable* purposes.[26]

The only instance of a μὲν … δὲ construction that employs relative pronouns in the General Epistles is found in Jude 21–23:

ἑαυτοὺς ἐν ἀγάπῃ θεοῦ τηρήσατε προσδεχόμενοι τὸ ἔλεος τοῦ κυρίου ἡμῶν Ἰησοῦ Χριστοῦ εἰς ζωὴν αἰώνιον. Καὶ οὓς μὲν ἐλεᾶτε διακρινομένους, οὓς δὲ σῴζετε ἐκ πυρὸς ἁρπάζοντες, οὓς δὲ ἐλεᾶτε ἐν φόβῳ μισοῦντες καὶ τὸν ἀπὸ τῆς σαρκὸς ἐσπιλωμένον χιτῶνα.

Keep guard over yourselves in the love of God, awaiting the mercy of our Lord Jesus Christ into eternal life. Show mercy to *the ones* doubting, but save *the ones* snatching from fire, but show mercy to *the ones*, in fear hating the garment defiled by the flesh.

---

[26] Knight classifies this as a demonstrative use of the relative pronoun, *The Pastoral Epistles*, 418.

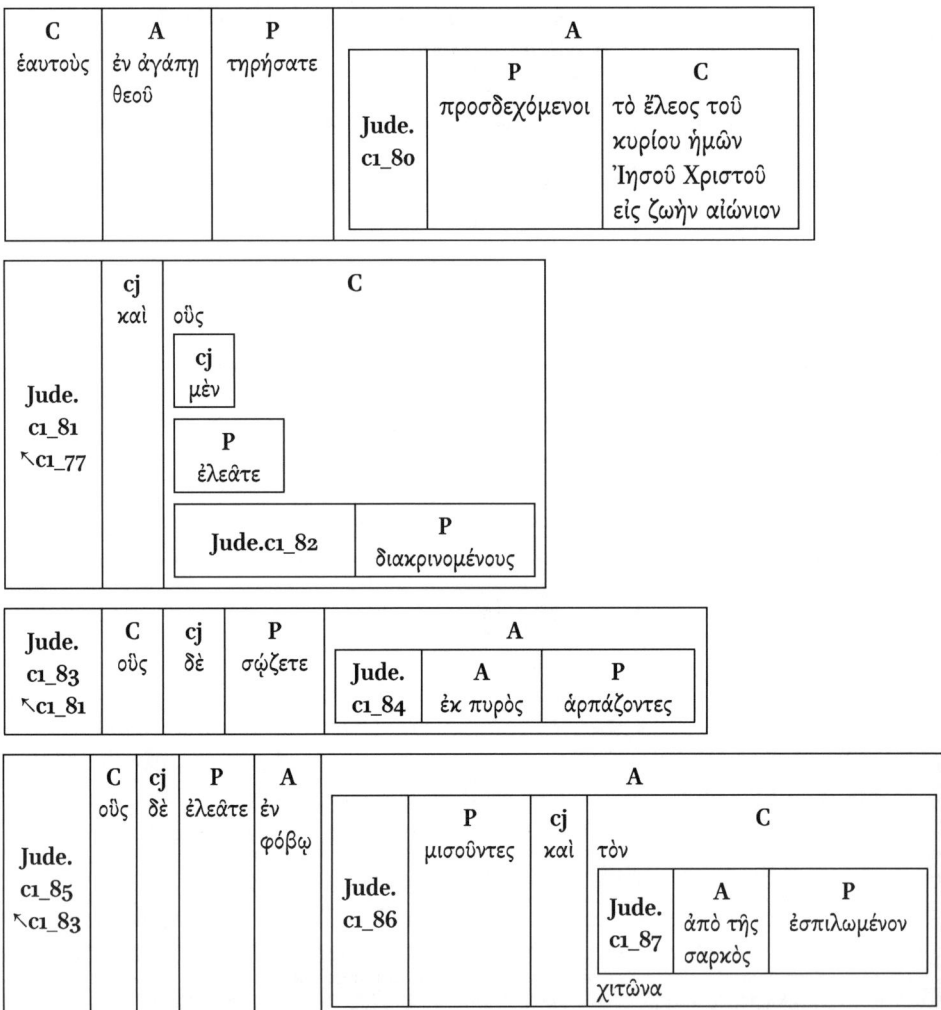

The ὁ-items in this construction function like the relative clause as complement. However, instead of introducing a clause, they function independently. As participants, they have no identifying characteristics apart from *being*. As with previous examples, the referents are not identified as specific individuals, identifiable to the recipients by name and face. They are characterized as *such people*.

2. The Article in ὁ μὲν … ὁ δὲ Structures

The use of the article by itself in μὲν … δὲ constructions appears to have arisen from two distinct yet complementary factors. The first of these is the obvious connection with the relative pronoun. As a ό-item, we have observed that the article is frequently used in constructions that parallel uses of the relative pronoun, though often at a different hierarchal level. It should come as no surprise, then, that Greek speakers would employ the article in μὲν … δὲ constructions as well. Just as an articular participial clause may fill the same slot as a relative clause, the article alone may fill the same slot as a relative pronoun. The second factor, as argued above, was the use of ὁ μὲν and ὁ δὲ as a form of shorthand, where the head term is elided and the article is elevated to the role of head term. These two factors combined likely explain how the article came to be used in this construction.

As an example of both items filling the same slot, consider the use of both the relative pronoun and the article in Rom 14:2:

ὃς μὲν πιστεύει φαγεῖν πάντα, ὁ δὲ ἀσθενῶν λάχανα ἐσθίει.

The one believes [it is right] to eat all things, *but the one who is weak* eats vegetables.

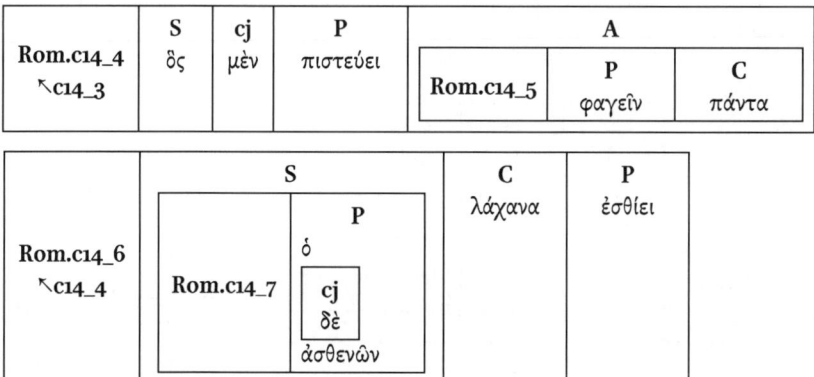

This passage affords an excellent opportunity to observe the parallel use of ό-items in the μὲν … δὲ construction. In the first clause, the μὲν half of the construction, the subject is simply the ό-item ὅς. This pronoun does not have an antecedent, but introduces a new participant who stands in contrast to τὸν ἀσθενοῦντα, *the weak* mentioned in the previous clause as well is in the μὲν ... δὲ structure. The identity of this participant is non-specific; he or she is characterized merely as someone who *is*, as such a person. The reason for this may be that this participant's role is simply to serve as a foil for ὁ ἀσθενῶν, with whom Paul is primarily concerned.[27] Additionally, since relative pronouns typically operate at the clause level, it is to be expected that it will be employed as the subject of an indicative verb.

A component of the subject of the δέ half of the construction is the articular participial clause ὁ ἀσθενῶν, *the one who is weak*. Unlike the former participant, this participant's identity is established by a single defining characteristic: he or she is *weak*. As is often the case, this articular participial clause is functioning as a relative clause. On the one hand, the parallel between the μὲν section and the δὲ section is not exact; the article is not used independently like the relative pronoun. On the other hand, the entire μὲν ... δὲ construction is complete through the use of alternate ὁ-items.

Matt 16:14 provides an opportunity to examine multiple factors involving the use of the article in μὲν ... δὲ constructions:

> οἱ δὲ εἶπαν· οἱ μὲν Ἰωάννην τὸν βαπτιστήν, ἄλλοι δὲ Ἐλίαν, ἕτεροι δὲ Ἰερεμίαν ἢ ἕνα τῶν προφητῶν.

> But they said, "*The ones* John the Baptist, but others Elijah, and others Jeremiah or one of the prophets."

Matt.c16_55 ⤓c16_50	S οἱ	cj δὲ	P εἶπαν

Matt.c16_56 ⤓c16_55	S οἱ	cj μὲν	C

			Matt.c16_57	C Ἰωάννην τὸν βαπτιστήν

Matt.c16_58 ⤓c16_56	S ἄλλοι	cj δὲ	C

			Matt.c16_59	C Ἐλίαν

---

[27] In a footnote, Moo notes the use of the relative pronoun instead of the article, but does not offer any exegetical explanation, *Romans*, 837.

	S	cj	C	
Matt.c16_60 `c16_58`	ἕτεροι	δὲ		**C**
			Matt.c16_61	Ἰερεμίαν ἢ ἕνα τῶν προφητῶν

The first clause provides an opportunity to examine the ὁ δέ shorthand. Frequently in narrative, verbs of speaking are preceded by ὁ δέ and the name of the person speaking, as the following examples illustrate:

Matt 16:6, Mark 10:5, 38, 39, 12:17, ὁ δὲ Ἰησοῦς εἶπεν αὐτοῖς· *but Jesus said to them,*

Matt 19:4, Mark 8:29, 14:6, 62, Luke 8:46, ὁ δὲ Ἰησοῦς εἶπεν· *but Jesus said,*

Matt 19:23, ὁ δὲ Ἰησοῦς εἶπεν τοῖς μαθηταῖς αὐτοῦ· *but Jesus said to his disciples,*

Matt 26:50, Mark 10:18, ὁ δὲ Ἰησοῦς εἶπεν αὐτῷ· *but Jesus said to him,*

Matt 27:49, οἱ δὲ λοιποὶ ἔλεγον· *but the rest were saying,*

Mark 13:5, ὁ δὲ Ἰησοῦς ἤρξατο λέγειν αὐτοῖς· *but Jesus began to say to them,*

Mark 14:29, ὁ δὲ Πέτρος ἔφη αὐτῷ· *but Peter said to him,*

Mark 15:12, ὁ δὲ Πιλᾶτος πάλιν ἀποκριθεὶς ἔλεγεν αὐτοῖς· *but Pilate again answering was saying to them,*

Mark 15:14, ὁ δὲ Πιλᾶτος ἔλεγεν αὐτοῖς· *but Pilate was saying to them,*

Luke 5:34, ὁ δὲ Ἰησοῦς εἶπεν πρὸς αὐτούς· *but Jesus said to them,*

Luke 22:58, ὁ δὲ Πέτρος ἔφη· *but Peter said,*

Acts 4:19, ὁ δὲ Πέτρος καὶ Ἰωάννης ἀποκριθέντες εἶπον πρὸς αὐτούς· *but Peter and John answering said to them,*

Acts 22:28, ὁ δὲ Παῦλος ἔφη· *but Paul said,*

In other instances, we observe the same structure. However, instead of the name of the person speaking, the writer employs ὁ δὲ ἀποκριθείς:

Matt 15:24, 25, 17:11, 19:4, 21:29, 30, 26:23, Luke 10:27, ὁ δὲ ἀποκριθεὶς εἶπεν· *but the one answering said,*

Matt 16:2, 24:2, Mark 6:37, 10:33, ὁ δὲ ἀποκριθεὶς εἶπεν αὐτοῖς· *but the one answering said to them,*

Matt 26:66, Luke 9:19, οἱ δὲ ἀποκριθέντες εἶπαν, *but the ones answering said,*

Mark 9:19, ὁ δὲ ἀποκριθεὶς αὐτοῖς λέγει· *but the one answering says to them,*

Mark 15:2, ὁ δὲ ἀποκριθεὶς αὐτῷ λέγει· *but the one answering says to him,*

Luke 8:21, ὁ δὲ ἀποκριθεὶς εἶπεν πρὸς αὐτούς· *but the one answering said to them,*

Luke 13:8, ὁ δὲ ἀποκριθεὶς λέγει αὐτῷ· *but the one answering says to him,*

Though this is a long list of examples, they are but a fraction of the occurrences of the ὁ δὲ construction involving verbs of speaking. More could be provided that incorporate other kinds of verbs. In the examples that employ ὁ δὲ ἀποκριθεὶς, the article and the participle agree in case, number and gender, suggesting that they function together as head and modifier, *the one answering*. However, it is also possible that a different head term, such as a name, has been elided and the article has been elevated to the role of head term. In this case, the participle functions as an adjunct, for example: [*Jesus*], *answering, said to him*. In either case, in ὁ μὲν and ὁ δὲ structures that incorporate a verb of speaking, it is reasonable to suggest that when there is no head term, it has been elided (whether that head term be a name or some other noun, or even ἀποκριθεὶς), and the article has been elevated to the role of head term. The natural morphological and functional relationship between the relative pronoun and the article likely contributed to the ease Greek speakers felt in elevating the article to head in these circumstances. When we observe the numerous examples of ὁ δὲ εἶπεν, ἡ δὲ εἶπεν, and οἱ δὲ εἶπαν in the New Testament, it is not difficult to envision Greek speakers choosing to shorten a very common construction to something more concise, efficient, and easy to use. If the speaker or writer believes that the head term of the article is obvious, he or she may choose to simply omit it, confident that the ellipsis is apparent enough. This same use of ellipsis explains the article's use with the particle μέν.

Returning to the example of Matt 16:14, there are several candidates for the elided element in οἱ δὲ εἶπαν. Two are found in the preceding clauses in 16:13:

Ἐλθὼν δὲ ὁ Ἰησοῦς εἰς τὰ μέρη Καισαρείας τῆς Φιλίππου ἠρώτα τοὺς μαθητὰς αὐτοῦ λέγων· τίνα λέγουσιν οἱ ἄνθρωποι εἶναι τὸν υἱὸν τοῦ ἀνθρώπου;

But Jesus, coming into the region of Caesarea Philippi, asked his disciples saying, "Who are the people saying the son of man is?"

The structure οἱ δὲ εἶπαν in 16:14 leaves the reader with a sense of incompleteness; he or she expects the article to be followed by a head term.[28] In this instance it is not. If the article has been elevated to function as the

---

[28] As Halliday and Hasan wrote (cited above), "We can take as a general guide the notion that ellipsis occurs when something that is structurally necessary is left unsaid; there is a sense of incompleteness associated with it," *Cohesion*, 144.

head term, the elided element must agree in gender and number. One possibility is the plural form of the participle ἀποκριθείς. Based on agreement in number and gender, two other options would be τοὺς μαθητὰς or οἱ ἄνθρωποι. Logically, the only group that may speak in this instance are τοὺς μαθητὰς, since they are the ones to whom Jesus directs his question, and οἱ ἄνθρωποι are not actually present. If the writer concluded that μαθηταί may be presumed from what came before, he may have chosen to leave it out.[29] In this instance, this seems to be the best explanation for the present structure.

Moving on to οἱ μὲν ... in Matt 16:14, elision is not enough to explain the use of the article. Instead, its use is comparable to what was observed in ὅς μὲν ... ὅς δὲ structures above, where each of the three groups in the μὲν ... δὲ structure is a subset of οἱ ἄνθρωποι: *the ones ... but others ... but others*. The use of the article in this construction may be explained by the subsequent use of the adjectives ἄλλος and ἕτερος in the structure. The article is frequently used in attributive structures involving adjectives. It is also used to "substantivize" adjectives. The use of the article provides a sense of balance. In addition, the three parts of the structure are not fully realized clauses, but word groups. Since the article typically operates at the level of group or phrase, it is more natural to employ it in a group structure.

A structure similar to that in Matt 16:14 is found in John 7:12:

κat γογγυσμὸς περὶ αὐτοῦ ἦν πολὺς ἐν τοῖς ὄχλοις· οἱ μὲν ἔλεγον ὅτι ἀγαθός ἐστιν, ἄλλοι [δὲ] ἔλεγον· οὔ, ἀλλὰ πλανᾷ τὸν ὄχλον.

And there was much grumbling about him among the crowds. *Some were saying, "He is good," [but] others were saying, "No, but he is deceiving the crowd."*

| John.c7_38 | cj | S | | | P | C | A |
| ⌐c7_36 | καὶ | γογγυσμὸς περὶ αὐτοῦ | | | ἦν | πολὺς | ἐν τοῖς ὄχλοις |

| John.c7_39 | S | cj | P |
| ⌐c7_38 | οἱ | μὲν | ἔλεγον |

| John.c7_40 | cj | C | P |
| ⌐c7_39 | ὅτι | ἀγαθός | ἐστιν |

---

[29] Per Halliday, the use of ellipsis "makes it possible to leave out parts of a structure when they can be presumed from what has come before," *Functional Grammar*, 535.

John.c7_41	S	cj	P
↖c7_39	ἄλλοι	δὲ	ἔλεγον

John.c7_42	A
↖c7_41	οὔ

John.c7_43	cj	P	C
↖c7_42	ἀλλὰ	πλανᾷ	τὸν ὄχλον

The three groups identified in the μὲν ... δὲ structure are each a subset of τοῖς ὄχλοις. They represent certain competing elements of *the crowds* who are saying this or that about Jesus. Unlike the example from Matt 16:14 above, the article is the subject of an indicative verb in a clause structure. In addition, there is no obviously elided element. As demonstrated above, it is common to find ὁ μὲν and ὁ δὲ along with verbs of speaking. Thus, despite that absence of an obviously elided element, the author may have believed it was appropriate to use this kind of short hand in this situation.

Acts 14:4 provides an example of a standard ὁ μὲν ... ὁ δὲ structure:

> ἐσχίσθη δὲ τὸ πλῆθος τῆς πόλεως, καὶ οἱ μὲν ἦσαν σὺν τοῖς Ἰουδαίοις, οἱ δὲ σὺν τοῖς ἀποστόλοις.

> But the entire city was divided; *the ones* were with the Jews, *but the ones* with the apostles.

Act.c14_13	P	cj	S
↖c14_8	ἐσχίσθη	δὲ	τὸ πλῆθος τῆς πόλεως

Act.c14_14	cj	S	cj	P	A
↖c14_13	καὶ	οἱ	μὲν	ἦσαν	σὺν τοῖς Ἰουδαίοις

Act.c14_15	S	cj	A
↖c14_14	οἱ	δὲ	σὺν τοῖς ἀποστόλοις

In this instance, there is no grammatical concord between the two articles in the ὁ μὲν ... ὁ δὲ structure and any previous element. There is no evidence of ellipsis. Thus, the articles function independently in the same manner as a relative pronoun. As with previous examples, the two groups may be interpreted as subsets of the class τὸ πλῆθος.[30] The use of the masculine article was likely influenced by a logical, rather than grammatical, factor: as groups of people they should be identified by means of the masculine gender instead of the neuter. As with ό-items in general, though there is a sense of pointing back to a previous referent, it is not in a demonstrative sense. Instead, the article, like the relative pronoun, is used to introduce new participants whose identifying characteristics are provided by the writer. In a sense, the two groups could be viewed as providing further elaboration upon τὸ πλῆθος as does a non-defining relative clause.

The ὁ μὲν ... ὁ δὲ structure in Acts 28:24 is another example of the independent use of the article. As with the previous example, it functions like a relative pronoun:[31]

καὶ οἱ μὲν ἐπείθοντο τοῖς λεγομένοις, οἱ δὲ ἠπίστουν·

And *the ones* were persuaded by the things spoken, but *the ones* disbelieved.

Act.c28_106 ↖c28_101	cj καὶ	S οἱ	cj μὲν	P ἐπείθοντο	A	
					Act. c28_107	P τοῖς λεγομένοις

Act.c28_108 ↖c28_106	S οἱ	cj δὲ	P ἠπίστουν

Here, again, the ὁ μὲν ... ὁ δὲ structure is used to introduce subsets, though one must look back to 28:17 to find the class: τοὺς ὄντας τῶν Ἰουδαίων πρώτους. Like the relative pronoun, the article indicates that the referents are identified solely on the fact of their *being*; they are characterized merely as *the ones*.

In 1 Cor 7:7, Paul employs a ὁ μὲν ... ὁ δὲ structure to contrast the individualized nature of the gifts that God gives:

---

[30] This is Porter's conclusion, though he attributes this to the possibility of the article functioning as if it were a demonstrative or personal pronoun, *Idioms*, 112–13. Robertson also cites this instance as an example of the article's demonstrative force, *Grammar*, 695.

[31] Wallace cites this passage as an example of the use of the article as an alternative personal pronoun, *Greek Grammar*, 212–13. He says the same of the next example from 1 Cor. 7:7. As I have argued, it is more accurate to compare the Greek article to the alternate English WH- item (that is, relative pronoun) that uses a TH- item, than to a personal pronoun.

ἀλλὰ ἕκαστος ἴδιον ἔχει χάρισμα ἐκ θεοῦ, ὁ μὲν οὕτως, ὁ δὲ οὕτως.

But each has his own gift from God; *the one* thus, but *the one* thus.

1Cor.c7_21 ↖c7_19	cj ἀλλὰ	S ἕκαστος	C ἴδιον P ἔχει χάρισμα	A ἐκ θεοῦ

1Cor.c7_22 ↖c7_21	S ὁ	cj μὲν	A οὕτως

1Cor.c7_23 ↖c7_22	S ὁ	cj δὲ	A οὕτως

The participants in the ὁ μὲν... ὁ δὲ structure may be interpreted as subsets of the general class ἕκαστος, *each*. This is indicated by the agreement in gender. As seen in previous examples, the use of the article is likely motivated by the fact that the construction is a word group rather than clause. As will be seen below, the article is at times used to "substantivize" adverbs, which would explain its function here.

In Phil 1:16–17, the articles in the μὲν... δὲ structure perform the same function as in the previous example:

οἱ μὲν ἐξ ἀγάπης... οἱ δὲ ἐξ ἐριθείας.

The ones from love... but *the ones* from hostility.

Phil.c1_30 ↖c1_29	S οἱ	cj μὲν	A ἐξ ἀγάπης

Phil.c1_33 ↖c1_30	S οἱ	cj δὲ	A ἐξ ἐριθείας

Immediately preceding this, Paul writes, *some* [τινὲς μὲν] *preach Christ out of jealousy, but some* [τινὲς δὲ] *out of good will*. The agreement in gender between τινὲς and οἱ suggests a connection. However, rather than indicating subsets, the articles in this example are likely substantivizing the prepositional groups. The two groups in the two μὲν... δὲ structures stand in apposition to one another (though in reverse order).[32] In the example from 1:16–17, the article is used to indicate that the information provided by the writer in the form of the prepositional groups is to be used as the identifying characteristic of each group.

The μὲν ... δὲ structure in Heb 12:10 is quite similar to the previous example:

οἱ μὲν γὰρ πρὸς ὀλίγας ἡμέρας κατὰ τὸ δοκοῦν αὐτοῖς ἐπαίδευον, ὁ δὲ ἐπὶ τὸ συμφέρον εἰς τὸ μεταλαβεῖν τῆς ἁγιότητος αὐτοῦ.

The ones discipline for a little while based on what they consider appropriate; but *the one* for the common good to share his holiness.

Heb.c12_38 ↖c12_37	S oἱ	cj μὲν	cj γὰρ	A πρὸς ὀλίγας ἡμέρας	A			P ἐπαίδευον
					Heb. c12_39	P κατὰ τὸ δοκοῦν	C αὐτοῖς	

Heb.c12_40 ↖c12_38	S ὁ	cj δὲ	A ἐπὶ τὸ συμφέρον	A		
				Heb.c12_41	P εἰς τὸ μεταλαβεῖν	C τῆς ἁγιότητος αὐτοῦ

The two elements in the μὲν ... δὲ structure in 12:10 stand in apposition to *our fathers by the flesh*, τοὺς τῆς σαρκὸς ἡμῶν πατέρας, with *the father of spirits*, τῷ πατρὶ τῶν πνευμάτων, in 12:9, which also are elements of a μὲν ... δὲ structure.[33] Both contrast God and human fathers.[34] However, the article is not used in 12:10 in a demonstrative sense. Each introduces new information that is to be used for the purpose of identification. As in the previous example from Philippians, the articles in this μὲν ... δὲ construction indicate that the information provided by the writer in the prepositional phrases is to be used for the purpose of identification.

---

[32] Robertson uses the terms *Chiasm* or *Reverted Parallelism, Grammar*, 1200. See also Lightfoot, *Philippians*, 89; Fee, *Philippians*, 118-20; O'Brien, *Philippians*, 97, 100.

[33] It should be noted that the δέ in 12:9 is a textual variant, though it is well attested in the manuscript tradition. It is addressed in the apparatus of NA27, but not USB4.

[34] Ellingworth, *Hebrews*, 652–54. See also O'Brien, *Hebrews*, 466–68.

3. Independent ὁ μὲν and ὁ δὲ Structures

In addition to μὲν...δὲ structures, we also observe the article occurring without a head term in independently occurring ὁ μὲν and ὁ δὲ structures. In these structures, as argued above, the absence of a head term may be explained as a matter of ellipsis. For example, sometimes the head term is present, as is seen in the following two instances:

Acts 16:5, Αἱ μὲν οὖν ἐκκλησίαι ἐστερεοῦντο τῇ πίστει.

And so *the churches* were being strengthened in the faith.[35]

	S αἱ	P ἐστερεοῦντο	A τῇ πίστει
Act.c16_17 ⤢c16_14	cj μὲν cj οὖν ἐκκλησίαι		

Acts 23:31, Οἱ μὲν οὖν στρατιῶται...

And so *the soldiers*...

---

[35] The use of the English definite article in this and the following translations must be understood as a matter of English usage, not Greek. For example, in this instance, the sample text is taken from Acts 16, which begins with a narration of Paul's ministry activities in the cities of Derbe, Lystra and Iconium. Since it is established that there are Christian congregation in these cities, in English, we employ the definite article to signal to the recipient that he or she knows the identity of the referent. Likewise, in the example of Acts 23:31, the soldiers have been previously introduced to the discourse. Once again, the definite article signal to the reader, "you know the soldiers I am talking about." The incidence of the article in both the original language and the translation is not a matter of mere coincidence; each performs a function that does, to a small degree, overlap with the other (as will be demonstrated below, see chapter 6.1). However, it should not be interpreted as a one-to-one correspondence.

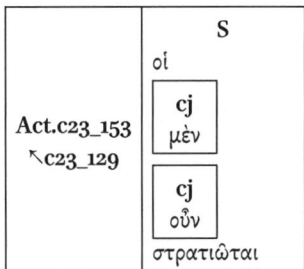

Act.c23_153 ⌐c23_129	S oἱ		
		cj μὲν	
		cj οὖν	
		στρατιῶται	

In some instances, it is difficult to determine if the head term has been elided and only the article is left, or if the article is modifying another element. Consider Acts 1:6:[36]

Οἱ μὲν οὖν συνελθόντες ἠρώτων αὐτον λέγοντες· κύριε,

And so, *the* [*apostles*], gathering together, were asking him saying, "Lord…"

Act.c1_20 ⌐c1_13	S oἱ	cj μὲν	cj οὖν	Act. c1_21	P συνελθόντες	P ἠρώτων	C αὐτὸν	A	
								Act. c1_22	P λέγοντες

The identity of *the ones* in this instance may be implied by means of ellipsis. In v. 2, *the apostles*, τοῖς ἀποστόλοις, receive instructions from Jesus. Reference to *the apostles* is continued through the use of relative and personal pronouns up to v. 6, which allows for the writer to employ elision, confident that the implied element is obvious to the reader(s). However, there is also agreement between the article and the participle συνελθόντες. Though the OpenText.org annotation does not reflect this, it is possible that the article is modifying the participle. Thus another possible translation would be, *therefore the ones gathered asked him, saying*. Either possibility is consistent with the article's use.

The possibility of an elided element is again observed in Acts 5:41:

Οἱ μὲν οὖν ἐπορεύοντο χαίροντες ἀπὸ προσώπου τοῦ συνεδρίου,

And *the* [*apostles*] were going from the Sanhedrin rejoicing.

---

[36] Robertson cites this as another example of the demonstrative use of the article, *Grammar*, 695.

Act. c5_173 ↖c5_172	S οἱ	cj μὲν	cj οὖν	P ἐπορεύοντο	A		A ἀπὸ προσώπου τοῦ συνεδρίου
					Act. c5_174	P χαίροντες	

There is no need to suggest that the article is functioning as a personal pronoun in this structure. The apostles, who are primary participants in the discourse and are explicitly identified in the previous verse, could possibly be the elided element since the article agrees in number and gender with τοὺς ἀποστόλους in the previous clause.

In Matt 8:32, there is also a question of whether the article marks an elided element or modifies a participle:

> οἱ δὲ ἐξελθόντες ἀπῆλθον εἰς τοὺς χοίρους.

> And *the* [*demons*], after being cast out, went into the pigs.

Mat.c8_145 ↖c8_143	S οἱ	cj δὲ	A		P ἀπῆλθον	A εἰς τοὺς χοίρους
			Mat. c8_146	P ἐξελθόντες		

In this instance, the OpenText.org annotation does not place the article and the participle together as a group. This structure is commonly seen in the expression ὁ δὲ ἀποκριθεὶς εἶπεν (Matt 12:48; 15:3, 13, 24, 26; 16:2; 17:11; 24:2; 25:12; 26:23; Mark 6:37; 7:38; 9:19; 10:3; Luke 8:21; 9:19; 10:27; 13:8; 15:29).

S ὁ	cj δὲ	A		P εἶπεν
		Matt.c 5_7	P ἀποκριθεὶς	

Were it not for the postpositive δὲ, the article would clearly be understood as modifying the participle. In the immediate co-text, we observe the article separated from its head term by δέ. In 8:31, the head term is a noun:

> οἱ δὲ δαίμονες παρεκάλουν αὐτὸν λέγοντες·

> But *the demons* plead with him, saying...

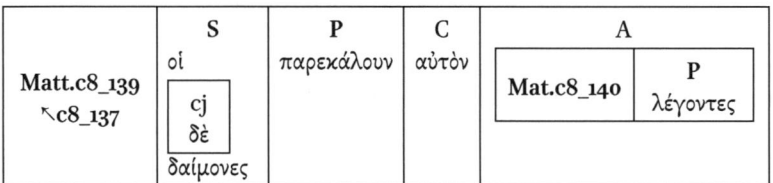

However, in 8:33 the head term is a participle:

οἱ δὲ βόσκοντες ἔφυγον,

But *the ones herding* ran away,

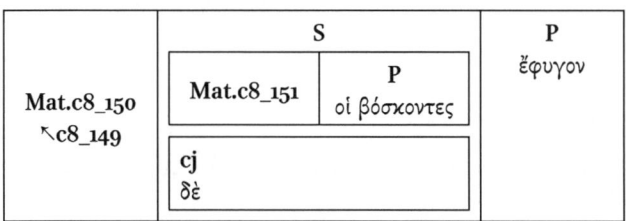

There are many other instances where the article and its participial head term are clearly separated by δέ:

Matt 15:38, οἱ δὲ ἐσθίοντες ἦσαν τετρακισχίλιοι ...

But the one who ate were four thousand ...

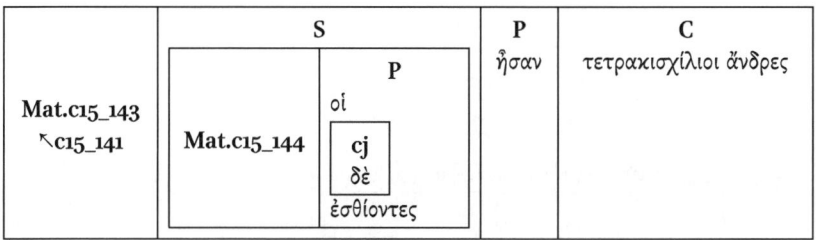

Acts 23:4, οἱ δὲ παρεστῶτες εἶπαν·

But *the ones present* said,

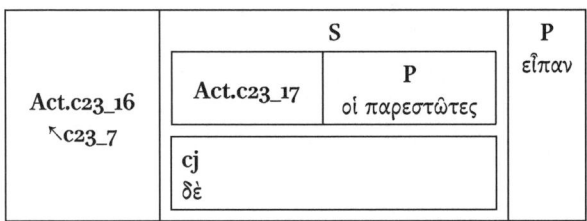

In all of these instances, the conjunction δέ separates the head term from the article. Therefore, we must entertain the possibility that this is the case in Matt. 8:32. In the end, it is most likely that δαίμονες has been elided and the article elevated to the role of head term. The writer concluded that it was sufficiently obvious, and so the head term was left out.

Ellipsis easily explains the ὁ δὲ in Mark 6:24:[37]

> καὶ ἐξελθοῦσα εἶπεν τῇ μητρὶ αὐτῆς· τί αἰτήσωμαι; ἡ δὲ εἶπεν· τὴν κεφαλὴν Ἰωάννου τοῦ βαπτίζοντος

> And going out she said to her mother, "what shall I ask?" And *her* [*mother*] said, "The head of John the Baptist."

Mar.c6_99 ⌐c6_96	cj καί	A		P εἶπεν	C τῇ μητρὶ αὐτῆς
		Mar.c6_100	P ἐξελθοῦσα		

Mar.c6_101 ⌐c6_99	C τί	P αἰτήσωμαι

Mar.c6_102 ⌐c6_99	S ἡ	cj δὲ	P εἶπεν

Mar.c6_103 ⌐c6_102	C
	τὴν κεφαλὴν Ἰωάννου
	Mar.c6_104 — P τοῦ βαπτίζοντος

---

[37] Wallace cites this passage as an example of the article functioning as a personal pronoun: *he, she, it.* He correctly notes that this occurs when "the subjects are speakers and the interchange is one of words, not actions." However, it is not "used to refer back to someone prior than the last-named subject," in the sense of a personal pronoun, *Greek Grammar*, 211–12. Ellipsis provided a more accurate description of the phenomenon.

The ὁ/ἡ δὲ εἶπεν, οἱ εἶπαν structure is exceedingly common in narrative text. In the example above, the exchange that takes place is between Herodias and her daughter. In the immediate co-text, the daughter is not identified by name, but by the pronoun reference, αὐτῆς, *of her*. Herodias is not mentioned by name, but by the titular reference, τῇ μητρὶ αὐτῆς, *the mother of her/her mother*. The feminine singular article could, theoretically, indicate that either participant is the elided element. However, in the logical unfolding of the exchange, one expects that the question posed by the daughter would be immediately followed by a response from the mother. Therefore, logically, the elided element must be τῇ μητρὶ αὐτῆς.

The identification of an elided element is difficult to determine in John 18:7:

πάλιν οὖν ἐπηρώτησεν αὐτούς· τίνα ζητεῖτε; οἱ δὲ εἶπαν· Ἰησοῦν τὸν Ναζωραῖον.

Again he asked them, "Whom do you seek?" And they said, "Jesus of Nazareth."

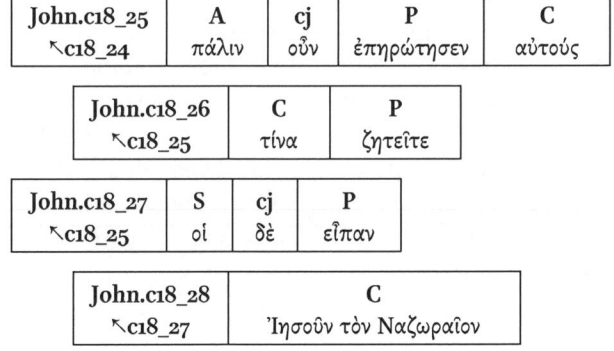

In this instance, an elided element is nowhere to be found in the preceding co-text. It is possible that the implied elements are ὁ Ἰούδας, *Judas*, τὴν σπεῖραν, *the band of soldiers*, or the ὑπηρέτας, *servants* from v. 3. The masculine plural article would then be used inclusively. It may not be possible to conclusively identify a specific elided element. However, the frequency of this structure in narrative discourse suggest that it had, by this time, become so common, so conventional, that it was no longer felt that the lack of an identifiable elided element was a stumbling block to understanding. The expression ὁ/ἡ δὲ εἶπεν and οἱ εἶπαν, along with other variants incorporating verbs of speaking, had become idiomatic.

4. Conclusion

The use of both the article and relative pronoun in μὲν ... δὲ structures, as well as in independent uses of μέν and δέ, provides further illustration of how the two elements are used to fill the same syntactical and functional slots. In these structures, their functional correspondence is not as exact as with relative clauses. However, it is demonstrable that they function in a manner that is similar and complementary. As in the preceding chapters, this reinforces the hypothesis that the two parts of speech should be viewed as members of a shared category.

It has also been argued that the categorization of ὁ-items as demonstrative and personal pronouns in these structures is an incorrect reading of the data. Historically, this categorization arose from the necessity of using these English pronouns in instances where Greek speakers employed ὁ-items. However, this necessity should not be employed to inform descriptions of Greek usage. Instead, these instances are better explained by descriptions that are consistent with the broad use of ὁ-items. In certain instances, ὁ-items are employed in a manner that is comparable with the alternate WH- form in English, *the one* or *the one who*. In other instances, the use of ellipsis provides a better and more grammatically consistent description of the function of the article than association with demonstrative or personal pronouns. In addition, it is arguable that the structure ὁ/ἡ δὲ εἶπεν, οἱ δὲ εἶπον, and its variants involving other verbs of speaking had become colloquialisms, a kind of narrative short hand. If this is true, it further eliminates the necessity of associating the article with the demonstrative or personal pronoun.

CHAPTER SIX

THE FUNCTION OF THE ARTICLE DEFINED

There is a certain irony regarding the "basic" function of the article. On the one hand, it is widely accepted that it primarily functions as a modifier, and that the modification it produces is essentially that of *substantivization*. On the other hand, this function is not recognized as the article's *defining* function. Under the category of the use of the article *As a Substantiver (With Certain Parts of Speech)* Wallace writes, "The article can turn almost any part of speech into a noun."[1] As true as this statement may be, in actual usage the article is used to modify nouns more than all other parts of speech combined.[2] To say that the article can turn almost any part of speech into a noun provides no insight into how if functions in the majority of instances in which it occurs.

In a sense, the answer has been hidden in plain sight. The so called *substantiving* function of the article, as Wallace puts it, is in fact its defining function. The problem lies in the fact that the language used to describe the article's function has created its own misunderstandings. The term *substantive* has often been treated as more or less synonymous with *noun*.[3] To say the article can turn any part of speech into a noun by substantiving it assumes that at least certain Greek nouns are already substantives, that their semantic condition as "something of substance" is an inherent quality apart from the presence or absence of the article. In the following chapters, it will be argued that this so-called "substantiving" function must be applied to nouns as well in order to understand how the article functions as a modifier. As a result, the reader may be tempted to

---

[1] Wallace, *Greek Grammar*, 231.

[2] In the OpenText.org Syntactically Analyzed Greek New Testament found in the Logos software, there are 19,861 instances of the Greek article (there are 19,844 instances in NA27/UBS4). Using a syntax search to identify instances of the article with a noun head term, the search yielded a result of 11,435 occurences. Statistically, 58% of all instances of the Greek article in the New Testament are in structures where a noun is the head term.

[3] In addition to Wallace, grammars often in some way address the use of the article *with Substantives*: Robertson, *Grammar*, 758; Porter, *Idioms*, 104, 107. In Turner's *Syntax*, the author addresses the "Substantival Article," 36, the "Substantival Pronoun," 37, as well as an entire chapter on "ATTRIBUTIVE RELATIONSHIP: SUBSTANTIVES," 206ff. In general, the term appears to be used to differentiate between lexical items that denote things that exist in a material sense from those that denote abstract ideas such as *faith, hope*, and *love*.

conclude that the following description is merely a statement of the obvious. This is, in one sense, true. Though what follows is not necessarily
revolutionary in its basic premise, it is quite so in application.

1. THE FUNCTION OF THE ARTICLE AS A 'Ο-ITEM

In the previous chapters, we made certain observations that are critical
for understanding the function of the article as a modifier. First and foremost was the fact that ό-items in general, and the article specifically, are
more analogous to English WH- items than they are to TH- items, including *the*. With regard to the Greek article, it is most closely associated with
the alternative WH- form that uses a TH- item as a relative: *the one that
I saw*.[4] In English, the definite article indicates that the speaker or writer
is saying to the recipient, "You know which one I'm talking about," that is,
"the subset in question is identifiable; but this will not tell you how
to identify it—the information is somewhere around, where you can
recover it."[5] If this information is not supplied by the speaker or writer,
"The subset in question will either be obvious from the situation, or else
will have been referred to already in the discourse."[6] In English, the definite article indicates that the information necessary to identify the referent is somehow available to the recipient, who is able to establish identity
based on the fact of his or her own "seeing" of this information, to use
Halliday's words.[7] In Greek, the article does not indicate this. Instead,
it is the means by which the speaker/writer indicates that the information necessary for identification is being provided to the recipient. Rather
than indicating, "You know which one I'm talking about," the Greek article
indicates to the recipient, "I'm telling you which one I'm talking about."
Rather than indicating, "the information is somewhere around, where you
can recover it," the Greek article indicates, "I am providing you with the

---

[4] Thus, in a very broad sense, the Greek article and the English definite article may be
classified together. In English, WH- elements are "part of a wider set embracing both WH-
and TH- forms, which taken together fulfill a *deictic* or 'pointing out' function," Halliday,
Functional Grammar, 86. However, traditional grammars have treated the Greek article
as analogous to English TH- elements. As stated above, the Greek article is, in fact, more
closely analogous to English WH- elements. Thus, the distance in classification between
the Greek article and English definite article is far greater than historically recognized.

[5] Halliday, *Functional Grammar*, 314.

[6] Halliday, *Functional Grammar*, 314.

[7] Halliday, *Functional Grammar*, 86.

information." We also observed that relative clauses and word groups that function as reduced relative clauses qualify the head term by providing additional information or characterization which further identifies the head term. The article is employed by the speaker/writer to indicate that the information inherent in the head is to be used for the purpose of identification. The speaker/writer presents this information to the recipient as something he or she has seen. The recipient must accept the speaker/writer's "seeing" for the purpose of identification, not his or her own. The Greek article does not direct the recipient to the information necessary for identification, nor does it indicate that this information is already possessed by the recipient. Instead, it indicates that the necessary information is being provided. Thus, the identity of the thing indicated by the article is based on the speaker or writer's "seeing," not the recipient's. Its orientation is to the speaker, not the recipient.

Second, whereas the article indicates that the thing to which it is attached is characterized as *concrete*, it is neither definite nor indefinite. Rather, it is non-definite, in that the status of the referent's definiteness is indeterminate from the point of view of the article; any indication of definiteness or indefiniteness is outside the scope of the article's function. This means that the quality of *concreteness* is not an either/or proposition. Instead, it must be viewed as a cline or scale. The identity of the referent may be that of an actual person, thing, or event; it may be presented as such a person, thing, or event that does exist without reference to any specific occurrence; or it may be presented as something hypothetical, merely held out for the recipient's consideration. In each case, it is something that is held out for examination; it is characterized as *concrete*. The degree to which it is concrete is indicated by additional co-textual elements such as qualifiers or phrases. By using these observations, we are able to construct a definition of the Greek article's function that grows organically from the Greek language, one that is not dependent upon, nor imposes, English categories of usage.

2. How the Article does not Function

Though exhaustive attempts have been made to describe the Greek article's function, these attempts have produced results that are problematic in that they do not account for the full range of occurrences in a comprehensive and uniform manner. This is due to a continued association of the Greek article with English TH- items. This is plainly illustrated in

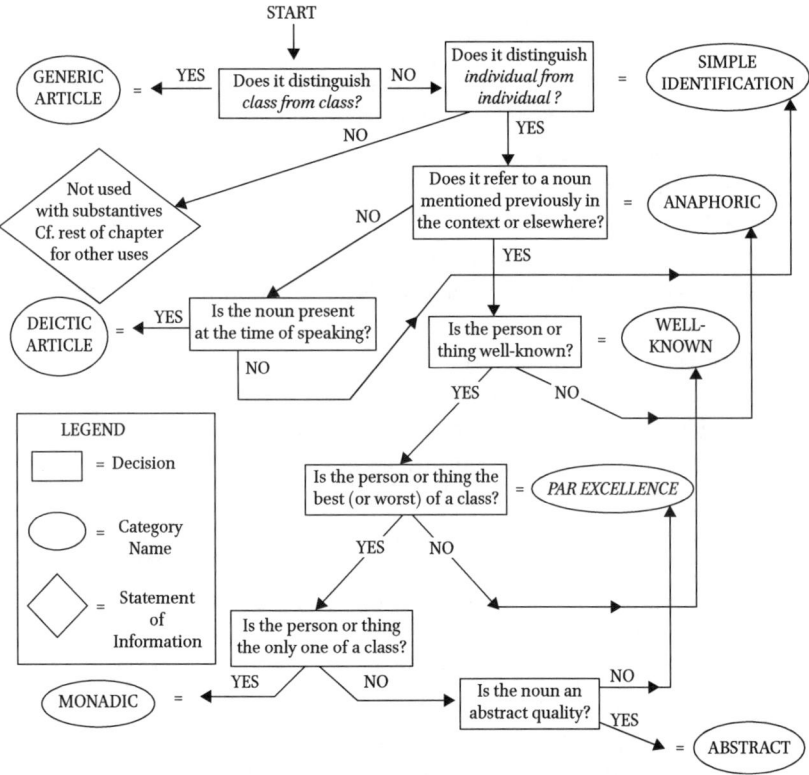

Chart 20   Flow Chart on the Article with Substantives

Wallace's *Grammar*. The flow chart he provides is meant to provide the translator or interpreter with a means to determine the article's function in any given instance. For our purposes, it illustrates the high degree of inconsistency, as well as unnecessary complication, associated with the treatment of the article. The result of this kind of arbitrary methodology is the formulation of categories and descriptions that are often disconnected and contradictory.

An examination of this flowchart reveals a number of inconsistencies. For example, a "substantive" that is modified by the article may, on the one hand, be abstract or generic. On the other hand, it may be monadic, well known, or even *par excellence.* Underlying these categories is the basic understanding that the Greek article functions in a manner consistent with English TH- items. For example, regarding the deixis of the article, Wallace states that it may be either anaphoric or kataphoric. He translates Acts 19:15, τὸν Παῦλον ἐπίσταμαι, as "*this* Paul I recognize," arguing that the article points back to a previous reference to the apostle.[8] The statement in 1 Tim. 1:15, πιστὸς ὁ λόγος, is interpreted as kataphoric, pointing ahead to a following quotation.[9] In both of these examples, Wallace interprets the article's function as directing the recipient toward the information necessary for identification. In other instances Wallace writes, "The article is occasionally used to point out an object or person which/ who is *present* at the moment of speaking. Thus, in Matt. 14:15, ἔρημός ἐστιν ὁ τόπος is interpreted as "*This* place is deserted," and John 19:15, ἰδοὺ ὁ ἄνθρωπος, "Behold, *the* man."[10] We have already argued that this cannot be the case. While it is inevitable that English idiom may on occasion require the English definite article in instances where the Greek article is used, this in no way indicates grammatical or functional correspondence. In the previous chapters, we demonstrated that ὁ-items are not analogous to TH- items in English, but WH- items. Because of this, we should not expect the Greek article to direct the reader/listener to the identity of the thing it modifies as demonstratives do, contra "*This* place is deserted." Nor should we expect it to signal "you know which one I am talking about," the way the English definite article does. Thus, Pilate does not say, "Behold, *the* man [you know which man I'm talking about]."[11] Yet this is the very assumption behind categories such as the "Individualizing Article" or the "Monadic Article," not to mention the "Well-Known" or "*Par Excellence*" categories. In place of these assumptions, one must approach the function of the Greek article in terms of identification based on an orientation to the speaker or writer, not the recipient. In this way, we may still say, with Wallace, that the article functions for the purpose of "simple identification," but identification based on the "seeing" of the speaker/writer, not the recipient.

Other descriptions draw near the mark, yet are either imprecise in their language or only partially accurate. For example, Wallace distinguishes between the *individualizing* article and the *generic* article by stating that the former "distinguishes or identifies a particular object belonging to a larger class," while the latter "distinguishes one class from another."[12] In the previous section, we observed that one of the functions of structures

---

[8] Wallace, *Greek Grammar*, 219.

[9] Wallace, *Greek Grammar*, 220.

[10] Wallace, *Greek Grammar*, 221, emphasis his.

[11] We cannot escape the use of the English definite article in the translation of this passage. An expanded translation might read, "Behold, the man [I am providing you with the identity of the man I'm talking about]."

[12] Wallace, *Greek Grammar*, 227.

that employed ό-items was to identify a thing as a subset of a class. We should expect this function to be consistent to some degree in every instance of ό-items. If this proves true, then Wallace's definition of the *individualizing* article is on the right track, but requires further specification, while the definition of the *generic* article must be essentially abandoned.

3. THE SEMANTIC FUNCTION OF THE ARTICLE

The following definition is presented to fulfill the deficiency noted by Bakker and Middleton's editor H.J. Rose. It will attempt to avoid the mistake of previous grammars which "present manifold rules for the use of the article, but do not supply a hierarchy for the application of these rules. In this way, there will be numerous instances where various rules are in conflict with each other."[13] It will not consist of "detached and unconnected rules," an approach that persists to this day, but will present a very refined theory, "professing, at least, to account for all the usages of the Article on one principle."[14]

The Greek article's function may be summarized by a single sentence, which certainly accounts for all of its usages on a single principle:

> The function of the Greek article is that of a modifier within a nominal group

The structure of a nominal group consists of a head term along with optional modifiers.[15] In Greek, one of the possible modifiers is the article. The head term indicates a particular class, while the modifiers indicate categorization within the class. Halliday identifies four functional elements that perform this task: Deictic, Numerative, Epithet and Classifier.[16] As observed in the previous sections, ό-items are deictic in function. However, the nature of the Greek article's deixis is different than that of the English TH- items. It orients the identification of the referent to the speaker. Unlike the English definite article, it does not indicate that the recipient possesses the information necessary for identification or that the information is recoverable or obvious in the discourse. Instead,

---

[13] Bakker, *The Noun Phrase*, 147.
[14] Middleton, *Doctrine*, vi.
[15] Halliday and Hasan, *Cohesion*, 147.
[16] Halliday, *Functional Grammar*, 312.

the Greek article indicates that this information is being provided by the speaker. Based on this, we may add an additional element to the definition:

> The function of the article is that of a deictic modifier within a nominal group.

The nature of the article's deixis must always be kept in mind. Because identification is based on an orientation to the speaker, the head term is not presented as proximate to the recipient, nor is it presented as recoverable from the text. This function does not rule out the possibility that the referent has been previously mentioned in the text, that somehow its identity may be recoverable from the discourse, or that it is obvious from the discourse. It means that the article gives no indication of this. The referent may indeed be known to the recipient. What is imperative to recognize is that the article does not indicate this. Rather, it indicates that the referent is known to the speaker, and the recipient must take this fact of knowing as the basis of identification. It orients the identification of the referent to the speaker, not this recipient.

Because the article is a modifier, it enters into a meaningful relationship with the head term. By this we mean that the article influences the meaning of the head term in some way. Another of the observations from the previous chapters is that ὁ-items indicate that something or someone is being held out as *concrete*. Based on this observation, we may make the following statement:

> The function of the Greek article is to characterize whatever part of speech it modifies as concrete.

Historically, this has been expressed in terms of a *substantiving* function, which in turn was understood as turning a part of speech into a noun. As noted, this does not explain the function of the article with nouns. Therefore, a description of the article's function must be articulated that is able to account for all uses. For this purpose, the term *concrete* is far more satisfactory than *substantive*.[17] Parts of speech that are presented as concrete name a real thing or class of things and are "characterized by or

---

[17] The term *substantive* and its cognates are satisfactory. However, to use them here invites the possibility of misunderstanding if readers associate them with usage in previous grammars. Therefore, it seems better to employ a term that is consistant with *substantive* but does not bring potential categorical baggage that is inconsistent with the description offered here.

belonging to immediate experience of actual things or events."[18] Often something that is characterized as concrete is associated with a specific instance. However, this is not universally the case. Based on these definitions, we may propose the following with regard to the article:

> The presence of the article indicates a speaker or writer's subjective characterization of the head term of a nominal group, which is presented as something concrete, in that it is characterized as belonging to immediate experience as an actual thing or event, or is associated with a specific instance.

Elements of this definition require comment. First, the use of the article represents the writer or speaker's *subjective* view. This means that articular structures must be understood from the point of view of the speaker or writer whose perspective may or may not reflect actual reality. Second, the presentation of the head term is a *characterization*. Thus, the referent will sometimes be an actual thing or something that is associated with a specific instance. However, the article alone will not indicate this. Sometimes it will present an item that is representative of *such a thing* or *instance*, without making a specific identification. In other instances, the referent is characterized as concrete so that it may be held out for the recipient's consideration, though it is in fact strictly hypothetical. In yet other instances, something that does not exist is deliberately characterized as concrete as a form of deception. In this way, *concreteness* is not an either/or proposition. Rather, it is a scale. In some instances, other discourse features will often play a role in determining whether or not the referent does exist, is such a thing that does exist, or is something that may or may not exist and is simply being held up for consideration for the sake of argument. In other instances, the speaker or writer will trust in the recipient's knowledge of the referent to make this determination for him or herself.

Because of the nature of the Greek article's deixis, it is necessary to include a statement regarding the orientation of the characterization of the head term.

> The characterization of the head term in a nominal group as concrete is based solely on the fact of the speaker or writer's "seeing" of the referent. It gives no indication to the recipient of how or where to locate the identity of the item so characterized, or that the identity is proximate in such a way as to be immediately recoverable.

---

[18] Webster's Collegiate Dictionary, "Concrete," 273.

As stated earlier, this in no way excludes the possibility that the thing is indeed identifiable to the recipient; it may well be. It only means that the article gives no indication of this one way or another. If the speaker or writer wishes to direct the recipient to the information necessary to identify the head term, additional grammatical elements will be employed to perform this function.

4. THE DISCOURSE FUNCTION OF THE ARTICLE

a. *Markedness and Prominence*

Within the field of biblical Greek language and linguistics, there is a growing interest in markedness theory. Porter has done considerable work in developing the theory with regard to the Greek New Testament. He divides markedness into five categories: material, implicational, distributional, positional, and cognitive.[19] Of the variety of ways markedness may be realized, the one that bears most directly upon the present investigation is that of *positional markedness*. Porter provides the following definition:

> Positional markedness defines markedness in relation to the position of an element within a given linguistic unit, for example, the position of a noun or verb group within a clause, or a word within a group. When elements are found in certain positions, they take on marked value in relation to the other units (e.g. pre-positional order).[20]

For our purpose, what is at issue is the position of a definer in relation to the head of a nominal group. Beginning Greek grammars generally point out to students that a definer may either precede the head term (first attributive) or follow the head term (second attributive). In either position, it will typically be modified by the article. However, what is not discussed is whether one of these positions represents an unmarked form, while the other a marked form. As Steven Runge writes, markedness theory seeks:

> to differentiate a set of similar items from one another based on the unique quality the each member brings to bear. The members are similar but not the same, so there must be something that sets each apart from the other.[21]

---

19 Porter, "Prominence: An Overview," 56.
20 Porter, "Prominence: An Overview," 56.
21 Runge, *Discourse Grammar*, 10.

In the classical expression of markedness theory, the existence of these two forms and the choice their existence forces upon the speaker or writer conforms to the basic notion of binary or polar opposition. When a speaker or writer wishes to define a head term, he or she must choose between two options: to place the definer before the head or after it. Though similar, the two structures are distinct. The question that lies before us has to do with what sets these two structures apart from one another and whether one represents a default or unmarked structure, while the other a marked structure.

b. *Grounding and Salience*

As a modifier, the function of the Greek article is to influence the meaning of the head term by characterizing it as concrete. By characterizing the head term thus, the article also performs a pragmatic function within the nominal group, which impacts the function of the group within discourse. This function may be understood in terms of *grounding*.

Stephen Wallace divides information conveyed in discourse into *foreground* and *background*. According to the theory he presents, certain elements in discourse will "stand out" as more salient than others. These are foregrounded elements, which usually are:

– More important events of a narrative
– More important steps of a procedure
– The central points of an exposition
– Main characters or entities involved in an episode

By contrast, backgrounded elements are:

– Events of lesser importance
– Subsidiary procedures
– Secondary points, descriptions, elaborations, digressions
– Minor characters or things[22]

Wallace suggests that the distinction between linguistic foreground and background may be understood in terms of "the universal perceptual distinction between figure and ground."[23] He goes on to say that certain

---

[22] Wallace, "Figure and Ground," 208.
[23] Wallace, "Figure and Ground," 213.

linguistic categories function "to differentiate linguistic figure from linguistic ground," in order to "structure an utterance (of one or more sentences) into more or less salient portions."[24] He then provides the following table which identifies the characteristics of figure and ground:[25]

FIGURE	GROUND
thing-like, solid discrete	unformed, diffuse, shapeless, continuous, unbroken
well-defined, tightly organized	less definite, unstructured, loosely organized
contoured, surrounded, bounded, enclosed	boundless
localized	unlocalized
with distinguishable parts	without distinguishable parts
small	large
near	far
above, in front	below, behind
more impressive color	less impressive color
greater contrast	lesser contrast
stable	unstable
symmetric	irregular
"meaningful," familiar	"meaningless," unfamiliar

The theory presented by Wallace is important for understanding and identifying the various methods speakers employ to highlight the elements of discourse they deem important.

The matter of prominence, with its roots in Wallace's theory of *figure and ground*, has been taken up with modification and applied by New Testament scholars working in the fields of linguistics and discourse analysis.[26] Foregrounding certain elements in a discourse gives such material *prominence* or indicates *salience*. Choice of lexis or representation may produce prominence: "Prominence always implies a contrast with the background, so that the more salient features will stand out in comparison with relatively less salient features."[27] Based on Wallace's

---

[24] Wallace, "Figure and Ground," 214.
[25] Wallace, "Figure and Ground," 214.
[26] See, for example, three chapters in Porter and O'Donnell, *The Linguist as Pedagogue*: Porter, "Prominence: A Theoretical Overview," Cynthia Long Westfall, "A Method for the Analysis of Prominence in Hellenistic Greek," Randall K. Tan, "Prominence in the Pauline Epistles."
[27] Westfall, "Analysis of Prominence," 91.

distinction between *figure* and *ground,* Reed produced the following chart that distinguishes between grades of salience:[28]

More Salient	Less Salient
human	non-human
animate	inanimate
concrete	abstract
thing-like, solid, discrete	unformed, diffuse, shapeless, unbroken
well-defined, tightly organized	less definite, unstructured, loosely organized
contoured, surrounded, bounded, enclosed	boundless
localized	unlocalized
with distinguishable parts	without distinguishable parts
near	far
above, in front	below, behind
greater contrast	lesser contrast
stable	unstable
symmetric	irregular

Whether it is Wallace's *Figure* or Reed's *More Salient,* many of the characteristics each writer identifies are consistent with the function of the article in terms of characterizing the head term. In narrative, for example, when a speaker or writer chooses to characterize a participant as concrete, it may be for the purpose of producing prominence or indicating salience. Since there are only two options available, articular or anarthrous, the two possibilities are foreground or background respectively.[29] The metaphor of a stage is often used to illustrate this function. In the case of the article, when a Greek speaker wishes to move a participant to the background of the stage, he or she may do so in part by characterizing the participant as abstract. Conversely, when a speaker wishes to bring a participant to the foreground of the stage, the participant will be characterized as concrete. Thus, even in a single episode, participants will move in and out, to the front and to the back, based on their immediate role. Another analogy

---

[28] Reed, *Philippians,* 113; also Westfall, "Analysis of Prominence," 91.

[29] The number of choices available to the speaker is important for understanding the potential layers of grounding. For example, Porter identifies three verbal aspects in NT Greek, giving the speaker a choice between three options. Therefore, grounding must be viewed in terms of three layers: background, foreground, and frontground, Porter, *Idioms,* 22–23.

is the shift of focus from one actor to another in a movie. At times, this is done simply to get the viewer to give attention to the actor who is currently speaker. However, sometimes the speaker is left out of focus because the director wants the viewer to give his or her attention to the reaction of the character who is listening. Even though the character who is out of focus is speaking, it is the character that is in focus that is most salient (at least to the director).[30] When this understanding is applied to the characterization of participants in discourse in the Greek New Testament, it will provide insight into the choices speakers make with regard to the use of the article. It will be seen that the use of the article is not a matter of individual style or personal idiom. Instead, it is the result of a conscious decision on the part of the speaker to characterize an element of the discourse in a way so as to perform a discourse function. This view will be particularly helpful in understanding the role of the article with proper nouns.

5. Conclusion

The following chapters will provide examples that illustrate the function of the Greek article. They will demonstrate that the article does indeed char- acterize the head term as *concrete*. By employing the article, the speaker or writer indicates to the recipient that the information grammaticalized by the element modified by the article is to be used for the purpose of identification. The article orients this information to the speaker or writer only. It gives no indication as to whether the recipient also possesses this information, or that it is recoverable by the recipient, nor does it direct the recipient to this information.

   The choice of characterization is based on the motives of the speaker or writer. In determining his or her motive, the analyst must take into con- sideration possible discourse functions, such as *grounding* and *salience*. Based on the work of Stephen Wallace and those who have followed him, we can expect that elements that are characterized as concrete will stand out as *figures* (generally foreground elements) in the discourse and will

---

[30] This illustrates why characterization must be viewed as subjective on the part of the speaker or writer. Movie viewers may identify secondary characters as their favorites, thus disagreeing with the director. However, as the one who has produced the movie, the director gives clues that are meant to help the audience see what he or she sees as the director. In the same way, a speaker or writer provides clues to help the recipient identify elements that are salient.

typically be more *salient*. In contrast, those elements that are characterized as *abstract* will be part of the grounding (generally background elements) of the discourse. This is consistent with Middleton's contention that the article is "the symbol of that which is uppermost in the speaker's mind."[31]

---

[31] Middleton, *Doctrine*, 25. See above, chapter 1.6, 63.

CHAPTER SEVEN

THE ARTICLE WITH INDIVIDUAL PARTS OF SPEECH

The definition proposed above will be tested by examining how the article is employed to characterize a wide variety of parts of speech, from individual lexical items to groups and phrases, as *concrete*. Historically, the function of the article with these various parts of speech has been defined in terms of converting them into a substantive; that is, something that is like a noun.[1] Thus, the terms "substantive" and "noun" have been used in a more or less synonymous manner.[2] This usage assumes that a noun is, in fact, a substantive apart from the presence of the article.[3] The description proposed in the previous chapter challenges this assumption. Since descriptions of the use of the article with "substantives," that is, nouns, display the greatest lack of consistency and uniformity, it seems best first to establish a general pattern of usage that is evidenced by the article's use with other parts of speech. Once established, the characteristics revealed by these patterns of usage will be applied to nouns. Therefore, the use of the article with nouns will be addressed last.

---

[1] One of Wallace's plethora of categories of usage is the article "*As a Substantiver*," for which he provides the following definition: "The article can turn almost any part of speech into a noun," *Greek Grammar*, 231.

[2] Thus, Robertson classifies one usage of the article as "With Substantives," *Grammar*, 758; Wallace can write of the use of the article "*With Substantives*," *Greek Grammar*, 216; as well as Porter: "The article may particularize a substantive," *Idioms*, 104. It is partly for this reason that I have chosen to use the term *concrete*. The term *substantive* has a long standing tradition of usage. I would agree that the function of the article could be described in terms of charactizing the head term as having *substance*, which is consistent with the sense of *concrete*. However, this would entail redefining the use of *substantive*. To avoid confusion, it seems best simply to employ a different term.

[3] This work has its origins in this observation and a single question that arose from it: if the article characterizes various parts of speech as "substantive," and if they are not substantive apart from its presence, isn't it possible that this is true of nouns as well? In order to test this theory, it has been necessary to challenge the assumptions about the nature of nouns and so-called "substantives." This gives rise to a further question: if a noun is truly only characterized as "substantive" when it is modified by the article, what is the nature of the characterization when it is not present? The description provided in the previous chapter is the direct product of this line of questioning.

1. The Article with Participles

This usage was explored at length in chapters 3 and 4. However, our focus was on how the structure functioned as a relative clause. Here, we will examine how the article functions as a modifier when the participial clause functions as subject or compliment. In this structure, the article indicates that the process grammaticalized by the participle is used for the purpose of identification. The referent is a class which, for the present purpose, is identified solely on the basis of this process. The referent so identified is characterized as concrete. Participles generally do not function as the head of a nominal group apart from modification by the article.[4] These instances illustrate most acutely the fact that the characterization is based on an orientation to the speaker, rather than the recipient. The speaker does not direct the recipient to the information necessary for identification, nor is there any indication that the recipient already possesses this information. Rather, this information is provided to the recipient by the speaker.

In Matt 13:3, the process of *sowing* is presented by the speaker as the identifying characteristic of the referent:

ἰδοὺ ἐξῆλθεν ὁ σπείρων τοῦ σπείρειν.

Behold, *the one who sows* went out to sow.

In this parable, the main participant is *the one who sows*, or perhaps more "literally," *the one sowing*. The speaker uses the process of *sowing* for the purpose of identification. This information is not known to the recipient; it is provided by the speaker. Thus, the article does not indicate to the recipients, "You know who I am talking about." Rather, it indicates, "I am telling you about someone else." In order for the story to work, this person must be characterized as *an actual person*, that is, as *concrete*. However,

---

[4] In his chapter on participles, Porter includes the sub-category of the substantive use of the participle. He makes the same general observation regarding the use of the article in these instances: "One of the distinguishing characteristics of the substantival uses of the participle is the frequent syntactical accompaniment of the article (absence of the article does not guarantee that it is not substantival, however)." He cites Luke 3:14 as an example of this usage: "ἐπηρώτων... αὐτὸν καὶ στρατευόμενοι... (those serving as soldiers asked him...)," *Idioms*, 183. The OpenText.org clause annotation agrees with this interpretation, identifying the participle as the subject of the clause. Based on the present description of the article's function and the numerous examples cited to support it, it would be expected that one could state unequivocally that a participle is not characterized as a substantive apart from modification by the article. Admittedly, an explanation for the usage in Luke 3:14 remains elusive.

there is no indication that this person does indeed exist, that he is a specific individual who could be identified by name and face. He is merely held out as such a person who does exist. There is nothing in the deixis that indicates where the identity of this individual may be recovered, or that the information regarding his identity is somewhere around where the recipients can recover it.[5] Because the speaker is "telling them about someone else," the audience must accept the fact of the speaker's "seeing" for the purpose of identification. Thus, the orientation is to the speaker. He is the one who provides the information necessary for identification to the recipients.

The process of *feeding* is the sole identifying characteristic of a group of participants in Mark 5:14:

Καὶ οἱ βόσκοντες αὐτοὺς ἔφυγον καὶ ἀπήγγειλαν εἰς τὴν πόλιν καὶ εἰς τοὺς ἀγρούς.

And *the ones feeding them* fled and told [what had happened] in the city and in the countryside.

This marks the entrance of these participants into the discourse for the first time. The article does not indicate that the audience knows the identity of these individuals. Instead, it identifies them by their activity of feeding the swine. This activity is known by the speaker, not the recipients. Therefore, since this information is provided by the speaker and is not recoverable to the audience, they must accept this identification based on his knowledge of the activity taking place. Since the story is presented as an account of an actual event, not a parable, it is arguable that these individuals do exist, and are not presented as "such individuals that exist." However, the fact of their existence is something that is obvious in the discourse; it is not indicated by the article.

Jesus identifies a particular group solely on the basis of the fact that they engage in *killing* in Luke 12:4:

μὴ φοβηθῆτε ἀπὸ τῶν ἀποκτεινόντων τὸ σῶμα.

Do not fear *the ones who kill the body*.

In the immediately preceding text, Jesus has spoken out against the Jewish religious leaders. Therefore, it is reasonable to suppose that he has them in view as *the ones who kill the body*. However, this association is not made explicit. The article does not direct the recipient back into the text

---

[5] Halliday, *Functional Grammar*, 314.

to make this association, nor is Jesus saying, "The ones who kill the body (you know who I'm talking about)." The reader or listener may make this associative leap, but is not directed to do so by the article. Jesus' presentation merely holds these people out as such persons who exist, without comment on specifically who they may be.

Rom 1:25, ἐλάτρευσαν τῇ κτίσει παρὰ τὸν κτίσαντα.

They served the created thing instead of *the one who created*.

The one who created is characterized by Paul as someone concrete, as belonging to experience as an actual person. Based on the theological understanding of God as the creator that Paul and his readers share, Paul expects the readers to identify this person as God by means of *inference*.[6] Indeed, God is the topic of Paul's discourse here at the beginning of Romans, and has already been named several times. Therefore, when Paul introduces *the one who created*, he has in view the same God he has been talking about. However, the function of the article in the clause *the one who created* is not to direct the reader to make this identification. It does not indicate that the recipients already possess the information necessary to make this identification, that it is available so that the recipients can recover it in terms of the immediate discourse. The article does not direct the reader to the previous references to God in a deictic manner. Instead, by employing the article, Paul indicates that he is providing this information, which the readers, in turn, will use so that they will think

---

[6] Regarding *inference*, John Sinclair writes, "There are always a number of inferences to be drawn from the timing and placing and wording of the utterance in relation to the unique set of circumstances that constitute the context of the utterance. An adequate listener/reader will convert these inferences, again by a process that we cannot describe, into additional features of the message," *Trust the Text*, 157. Brown and Yule define *inferrables* as "entities which the speaker assumes the hearer can infer from a discourse entity which has already been introduced," *Discourse Analysis*, 182 (see also 33–35, 239, 256–70). Thus, while deixis is a deliberate directive action on the part of the speaker or writer, inference is an association or connection made by the recipient that is not necessarily at the direction of the speaker or writer: "there is a wide range of possible inferences made by readers in interpreting discourse and it is not always easy to determine which were intended by the text-producer and which were not," Brown and Yule, *Discourse Analysis*, 225. Among various kinds of reference, Martin and Rose identify *homophoric reference*, which "involves information which is to be found in the cultural knowledge that writer and reader share," *Working with Discourse*, 170. When a speaker or writer is able to assume shared cultural knowledge, he or she may reasonably expect the recipient to engage in inference. Thus, inference "is used to describe that process which the reader (hearer) must go through to get from the literal meaning of what is written (or said) to what the writer (speaker) intended to convey," Brown and Yule, *Discourse Analysis*, 256.

about God's identity specifically in terms of his creative activity. Having done so, he is then able to make the distinction between worshiping the creator and worshiping created things. In addition, it produces cohesion within the immediate discourse, with its general emphasis on creation and the created order.

In 1 John 2:10–11, the author contrasts two individuals whose identities are based on opposite activities:

ὁ ἀγαπῶν τὸν ἀδελφὸν αὐτοῦ ... ὁ δὲ μισῶν τὸν ἀδελφὸν αὐτοῦ

The one who loves his brother ... the one who hates his brother.

Both of these individuals are characterized as concrete. However, there is no further indication regarding whether or not they are real people. Both are presented as concrete so that they may be held out for the audience's consideration as such a person who may exist. Something that is concrete is something that may be examined. There is no indication that the information necessary for their identification is somewhere around or is obvious from the context. The audience must accept the information provided by author as the sole basis of identification. Though characterized as concrete, they are neither specific nor definite.

The use of the article with participles illustrates how a speaker or writer employs the article for the purpose of identification. The information necessary for identification is provided by the speaker or writer and is based on his or her "seeing" of the process or state, not that of the recipient.

2. THE ARTICLE WITH ADJECTIVES

When a participle functions as the head of a nominal group and is modified by the article, the speaker/writer is indicating that the process grammaticalized by the participle is to be used for the purpose of identification. In the same way, when an adjective functions as the head of the group and is modified by the article, it indicates that the quality grammaticalized by the adjective is to be used for the purpose of identification. The article and adjective combine to indicate that the referent is a class whose identity is based solely on the quality expressed by the adjective.

In Matt 5:3, the quality *poor* is the identifying characteristic of a particular class:

Μακάριοι οἱ πτωχοὶ τῷ πνεύματι,

Happy are *the poor in spirit,*

The more pedantic translation *the ones who are poor* helps us capture the sense of the article's function as something analogous to the alternate WH- form. Typically, the adjective πτωχός is used to modify the head of a nominal group by classifying it according to the condition of poverty. When this adjective is used as the head term and is modified by the article, this classification alone functions as the means of identification, which the speaker/writer presents to the recipients. The recipients must accept the information so provided as the basis of identification. The class that is in view is defined by a single quality: poverty. In this instance, *the poor* are characterized as something concrete so that they may be examined by the recipients; they are characterized as belonging to experience of an actual thing. However, the identification of *the poor* with a specific, definite group is not indicated or obvious from the situation. This class is held out simply as *such a class*.

Two contrasting qualities are used in Matt 20:16 as the identifying characteristics of two groups of people:

ἔσονται οἱ ἔσχατοι πρῶτοι καὶ οἱ πρῶτοι ἔσχατοι.

The last will be first and *the first*, last.

Though each group is characterized as concrete, as belonging to experience as actual people, there is no indication that individuals who could be identified by name and face are in view. They are such people, who are so characterized in this manner so that they may be examined by the recipients. Once again, the speaker provides the recipients with the information necessary for identification, which they must accept.

As seen in Luke 4:1, ἔρημος is frequently used as the identifying characteristic of certain regions or places:

καὶ ἤγετο ἐν τῷ πνεύματι ἐν τῇ ἐρήμῳ.

And he was led by the Spirit to *the desert*.

The adjective ἔρημος expresses the quality of a wilderness or deserted place. When used as a modifier, it classifies the referent as belonging to a subset identified by this quality. When functioning as the head term and modified by the article, the referent is identified solely on the basis of this quality. By itself, the use of article indicates that this place is characterized as concrete, as an actual place. The fact that it occurs in narrative purporting to relate an actual event indicates it is presented as a real place, and is not hypothetical or *such a place*. In this respect, we may say that it is more concrete than the previous example because the characterization is of an actual place. However, this identification is not grammatical but situational. In addition, there is nothing to suggest this place is definite, that it is a region that may be identified by name or associated with a specific location. While it could have been, this information has not been provided.

Unlike the previous example, where a region is characterized by a certain quality, in John 3:12 two classes are identified solely on the basis of their region:

εἰ τὰ ἐπίγεια εἶπον ὑμῖν καὶ οὐ πιστεύετε, πῶς ἐὰν εἴπω ὑμῖν τὰ ἐπουράνια πιστυέσετε;

If I speak *earthly things* to you and you do not believe, how will you believe if I speak *heavenly things* to you?

The two classes of *things* to which Jesus refers are identified solely on the basis of the fact that each possesses a certain quality that designates a region or domain. The first class is characterized as *earthly*; the second as *heavenly*. Both are presented as concrete, but not in the sense that we have been most accustomed. Most of the examples we have examined have characterizations of people, places, or other material things. In this instance, the referent is more conceptual than actual. Such things are often considered abstract rather than concrete. However, ideas and concepts may be narrowly classified as specific ideas and concepts. Hope is abstract, but "hope" may refer to a specific instance of hope, like hope in the resurrection. This is more concrete. Hence our definition of the article's function that the head term is characterized as concrete, that it is *associated with a specific instance*. τὰ ἐπίγεια, *the earthlies* or *earthly things*, is characterized as concrete, as a specific instance of something. Likewise τὰ ἐπουράνια is also characterized as concrete. However, both are non-definite. While they are characterized as associated with a specific instance, neither is definitely associated with a specific instance. They are *such things*.

Paul uses the quality of *goodness* as the identifying characteristic of a class in Rom 7:13:

Τὸ οὖν ἀγαθὸν ἐμοὶ ἐγένετο θάνατος;

Did *the good thing* become death to me?

The quality of *goodness* is the identifying quality of the referent. It is presented by Paul to the recipients, who must accept the information provided by the apostle for the purpose of identification. Apart from Paul

providing this information, they would not know the identity of this referent. Whatever it is, it is a class that is identified solely on the basis of this
quality. It is held out as concrete, as something that may be examined by
the recipients. It is not the abstract quality of goodness, but something
that is characterized by the fact that it possesses the quality of goodness:
a good thing. Based on the content of the immediate discourse, this *good
thing* may be identified with the previously mentioned *law* and *commandment.* However, this identification is logical, not grammatical. The article
does not point the recipients to this identification, nor does it suggest that
it is known to the recipients. With regard to the referent, Paul is merely
saying, "you must accept its identity based on this information I am providing: it is a good thing." Any additional identification is up to the reader.
It may be obvious from co-text, but the article does not direct him or her
to it.

In the New Testament, believers are often identified as those who possess the quality of *holiness*, as is seen in 1 Cor 6:2:

ἢ οὐκ οἴδατε ὅτι οἱ ἅγιοι τὸν κόσμον κρινοῦσιν;

Or don't you know that *the holy ones* will judge the world?

This designation for believers was commonly used by Paul. The quality
of holiness is used as the sole means of identification. As always, Paul
presents this information to the recipients for them to use as the basis
of identification; it is not information they possess. In this instance, this
group is characterized as concrete; in the future such people as these will
engage in the activity of judgment. The future indicative form grammaticalizes the expectation that this activity will actually take place, which
lends a sense of definiteness in a very broad sense to the class. Other elements may also produce a sense of definiteness to this class. For example,
Paul addresses Philippians "to all the holy ones in Christ Jesus who are
in Philippi," πᾶσιν τοῖς ἁγίοις ἐν Χριστῷ Ἰησοῦ τοῖς οὖσιν ἐν Φιλίπποις. The
phrase τοῖς οὖσιν ἐν Φιλίπποις associates this group with a specific, known
city. While the article does not indicate definiteness, the information provided by this phrase does.

A temporal quality is used for the purpose of identification in Heb 7:3:

μένει ἱερεὺς εἰς τὸ διηνεκές.

He remains a priest into *the forever.*

In this instance, the function of the article is to characterize the abstract
notion of *forever* as something concrete. *Forever* is presented as an actual

instance, of a period of time that will actually occur. By characterizing *forever* as something concrete, it may be held out for examination and consideration by the recipients. However, they must accept this identification based on the writer's provision of the necessary information.

While there are instances when an adjective is specifically employed as the head of a nominal group, there are other instances when this structure may be the result of ellipsis. Consider, for example, Matt 6:3:

σοῦ δὲ ποιοῦντος ἐλεημοσύνην μὴ γνώτω ἡ ἀριστερά σου τί ποιεῖ ἡ δεξιά σου,

But when you are performing your acts of charity, do not let your *left [hand]* know what your *right [hand]* is doing.

In this instance, the elided element is not present in the co-text. However, it is possible that the speaker believes that it is sufficiently obvious. First, the kind of processes associated with the verb ποιέω frequently (though certainly not exclusively) involve the hands. Second, both adjectives are feminine, which agrees with the Greek χείρ, *hand*. While the article indicates that these things are concrete, the use of the genitive σοῦ indicates that they are presented as definite, something possessed by the recipient: *your left hand/your right hand*.

A more obvious case of elision is found in Matt 10:23:

Ὅταν δὲ διώκωσιν ὑμᾶς ἐν τῇ πόλει ταύτῃ, φεύγετε εἰς τὴν ἑτέραν·

But whenever they persecute you in this city, flee to *another*.

The elided element, πόλις, is clearly recoverable from the co-text, and is indicated by the feminine τὴν ἑτέραν.

The same may be said of 1 Pet 2:18:

Οἱ οἰκέται ὑποτασσόμενοι ἐν παντὶ φόβῳ τοῖς δεσπόταις, οὐ μόνον τοῖς ἀγαθοῖς καὶ ἐπιεικέσιν ἀλλὰ καὶ τοῖς σκολιοῖς.

Servants submitting to masters in all fear, not only *to the good* and *gentle*, but also *to the corrupt*.

In this instance, the elided element is τοῖς δεσπόταις, which is indicated by the gender and number agreement. In its absence, the adjectives ἀγαθοῖς and σκολιοῖς have been upgraded to head terms.

3. THE ARTICLE WITH ADVERBS

Greek speakers often employed the article in ways that seem quite unusual to English speakers. Among these is the use of the article with adverbs.[7] As with participles and adjectives, when the article is used to modify an adverb, the adverbial idea is used as the identifying character-istic of the referent. Concurrently, the referent is characterized as some-thing concrete, as belonging to the realm of the experience of an actual thing or event.

In John 8:23, the author identifies specific regions through the use of adverbs that indicate spatial locations:

> ὑμεῖς ἐκ τῶν κάτω ἐστέ ἐγὼ ἐκ τῶν ἄνω εἰμί· ὑμεῖς ἐκ τούτου τοῦ κόσμου ἐστέ, ἐγὼ οὐκ εἰμὶ ἐκ τοῦ κόσμου τούτου.
>
> You are from *below*, I am from *above*; you are from this world, I am not from this world.

The use of the plural article suggests that the identification may be some-thing to the effect of *the regions below* and *the regions above*. *Above* and *below* are characterized as concrete places. The recipients must accept the fact that Jesus has provided the information necessary for the pur-pose of identification. Based on Jesus' next statement, *the regions below* are in some way associated with *this world*.[8] However, this is a matter of inference; the article does not direct the recipients to this identifica-tion. The lack of concord between the plural article and the singular τοῦ κόσμου confirms this observation. Conversely, while the article charac-terizes κόσμου as something concrete, the use of the deictic τούτου, *this*, directs the recipients to the information necessary to identify τοῦ κόσμου. *The world* is something in proximity to the recipients; it is recoverable, something that they may "see." The addition of this deictic element indi-cates that the identity of the referent is based on information that both

---

[7] In his section on *Adverbs Treated as Substantives*, Robertson notes that this is typically true "of words of place and time," *Grammar*, 547. Contrary to the argrument presented here, he writes: "It is not merely when the adverb has the article that it is treated as sub-stantive," *Grammar*, 547. This is one of the many reasons I have chosen not to use the term *substantive*. As is often the case, Robertson is using the term as essentially synonymous with *noun*. The description of the article's function here focuses on the function of the article in terms of *characterization*: speakers use the article to *characterize* the head term as *concrete*. Robertson, by contrast, concludes that the head term is *treated as* a substan-tive, that is, a noun, irrespective of the article's presence or absence.

[8] This is in contrast to Wallace, who writes: "The articles indicate more than a mere general sentiment as to origins; heaven and hell are implied," *Greek Grammar*, 232. Carson agrees with my basic conclusion: "They are *from below*, which does not mean 'from Hell' or 'from the underworld' or the like, but *of this world*, this fallen moral order in conscious rebellion against its creator," *John*, 342 (though I might not read as much into *from below*). See also Westcott, *John*, 130–31; Brown, *John I–XII*, 347; Beasley-Murry, *John*, 130; Keener, *John, Vol. 1*, 743–44.

the speaker and recipients share. They are not solely dependent on the speaker to provide the information necessary for identification. He has indicated that it is available to them as well.

Paul employs the article to characterize a point in time as something concrete in Phil 1:5:

> ἀπὸ τῆς πρώτης ἡμέρας ἄχρι τοῦ νῦν.

> From the first day until *now*.

The article characterizes the adverb νῦν as something concrete, as belonging to experience as an actual event, or more specifically, an actual place in time. However, apart from its situation, this would not be any more definite. In this instance, Paul is relating actual events and times. Because of this, the co-textual situation indicates a sense of definiteness. While the article characterizes the adverb as something concrete, the situation provides the sense of definiteness.

The apostle's usage in Col 3:1–2 is similar to that observed in John 8:23:

> τὰ ἄνω ζητεῖτε... τὰ ἄνω φρονεῖτε, μὴ τὰ ἐπὶ τῆς γῆς.

> Seek *the things from above*... Think about *the things from above*, not the things on the earth.

In the two instances of τὰ ἄνω, the locative quality expressed by the adverb is used for the purpose of identification. By employing the neuter plural article, the writer indicates that the identifying characteristic of a certain class of things is their location, expressed by the adverbial quality *above*. Apart from this, they have no other identifying features or characteristics. The recipients have only this information, provided by the writer, to use for the purpose of identification. In the same manner, the article characterizes the prepositional phrase *on the earth* as something concrete: *the things on the earth*. These things are presented in contrast with *the things above*. The information necessary to identify either of these groups is not recoverable from the text, nor is it obvious. The writer has characterized them as concrete so that they may be held out for the audience's examination.

In some instances, what at first glance appears to be the use of the article with an adverb is in fact an instance of ellipsis. Consider 2 Cor 4:16:

> ἀλλ' εἰ καὶ ὁ ἔξω ἡμῶν ἄνθρωπος διαφθείρεται, ἀλλ' ὁ ἔσω ἡμῶν ἀνακαινοῦται ἡμέρᾳ καὶ ἡμέρᾳ.

> But if our outer person is wasting away, our inner [person] is being restored day by day.

In the instance of ὁ ἔσω ἡμῶν, the elided element is ἄνθρωπος.[9] Based on the co-text, the elided element is sufficiently obvious. Thus, the adverb has been upgraded to the head term.

4. The Article with Numerals

It is not uncommon to see numerals used as the head term and modified by the article, though sometimes this is a matter of ellipsis. When functioning as the head term and modified by the article, the speaker or writer indicates that this numeric quality is the identifying characteristic of the referent.

In Matt 20:24, a group or class is identified by their number:

οἱ δέκα ἠγανάκτησαν περὶ τῶν δύο ἀδελφῶν.

The ten were angry with the two brothers.

The article characterizes the numeral as something concrete; in this instance the ten apostles who are angry at the request made by James and John. The English translation, *the ten*, the appropriate in its own right, creates a different sense of identity than the Greek. In English, this indicates "you know which ten I am talking about, the information is somewhere around where you can recover it or is obvious from the situation." In fact, this is true for the English reader, who does indeed know who the ten are. However, this must not be read back into the Greek usage. In this instance, the author provides the number *ten* to the recipients so that they will use for the purpose of identification. In Greek, association of this group with the twelve apostles isn't a matter of deixis, but inference. Based on their shared knowledge, the author may reasonably trust the recipients to make this inference.

In both 1 Cor 6:16 and Eph 5:31, Paul uses the same expression, in which he employs a numeral as the identifying characteristic of a particular class:

ἔσονται οἱ δύο εἰς σάρκα μίαν.

The two will be into one flesh.

---

[9] Robertson agrees, *Grammar*, 766. See also Harris, *The Second Epistle to the Corinthians*, 359–60. Harris does not state explicity that ἄνθρωπος has been elided, but does place it in brackets. The assumption of this elided element is also observed in Furnish, *II Corinthians*, 289; Barnett, *The Second Epistle to the Corinthians*, 246.

This is a verbatim quotation of Gen 2:24 from the LXX. In both the original context of Gen 2 and Paul's usage, *the two* are characterized as something concrete, as such people who exist, without further identification with specific individuals. As with the previous example, the English translation gives the sense of identity that is obvious from the situation, which is true in both the Greek original and English translation. However, it is not the function of the Greek article to indicate this.

Paul employs a similar expression in Phil 1:23:

συνέχομαι δὲ ἐκ τῶν δύο.

I am torn between *the two.*

In this instance, association of *the two* with the aforementioned options of life and death for Paul is a matter of inference. The recipients will certainly make this connection, but it is not the function of the article to direct them to this. It simply characterizes *the two* as something concrete, a specific instance of *two.* While Paul expects the recipients to make this association, it is semantic, not grammatical. Paul merely provides the recipients with the information necessary for identifying the referent and indicates this by means of the article.

As with adverbs, sometimes what appears at first glance to be an article with a numeral may in fact be an instance of ellipsis.

In Matt 18:12, the speaker may have assumed that an element was sufficiently obvious and so chose to leave it out:

οὐχὶ ἀφήσει τὰ ἐνενήκοντα ἐννέα...

Will he not leave *the ninety-nine...*

While it is possible that the article is being used to characterize the numerals as concrete, it is more likely that the word πρόβατα, mentioned earlier, has been elided and the numeral has been upgraded to head. Since the identity is proximate and recoverable from the co-text, this is the more probable explanation.

The same may be said of Matt 22:28:

ἐν τῇ ἀναστάσει οὖν τίνος τῶν ἑπτὰ ἔσται γυνή;

In the resurrection, *of the seven,* whose wife will she be?

In verse 25, the participants are introduced as ἑπτὰ ἀδελφοί. As in the previous example, this could be interpreted as the article modifying the numeral, but is more likely an instance of ellipsis.

5. THE ARTICLE WITH PARTICLES

Another unusual use of the article (for English speakers) is with particles. While rare, this usage is consistent with the article's function of characterizing the head term as concrete.

In 2 Cor 1:17, Paul uses the article to characterize two particles as concrete:[10]

> ἵνα ᾖ παρ' ἐμοὶ τὸ ναὶ ναὶ καὶ τὸ οὒ οὔ;
>
> So that with me *"yes"* may be "yes" and *"no,"* "no?"

In contrast to the translation provided here, both modern translations and commentators interpret each particle as a double "yes, yes," and "no, no."[11] However, in a similar construction in James 5:12, the articular particle is treated as subject, while the anarthrous particle is complement, as seen in the OpenText.org clause annotation:

> ἤτω δὲ ὑμῶν τὸ ναὶ ναὶ καὶ τὸ οὒ οὔ,
>
> Your *"yes"* must be "yes," and *"no,"* "no."

Jam.c5_44 ↖c5_43	P ἤτω	cj δὲ	S ὑμῶν τὸ ναὶ	C ναὶ

Jam.c5_45 ↖c5_44	cj καὶ	S τὸ οὒ	C οὔ	

As a general rule, the element that has the article is understood to be the subject of a linking verb.[12] In the treatment of Jas 5:12, this is clearly the understanding. In light of this, it is reasonable at least to consider the possibility that the articular particles in 2 Cor 1:17 should be understood

---

[10] Robertson places this instance under the category of usage with adverbs, *Grammar*, 765.

[11] Harris sees this as a doubling of the particles and so translates the clause, "So that with me it is first 'Yes, yes', and then 'No, no'?" *The Second Epistle to the Corinthians*, 197. He makes no mention of the article, suggesting he does not afford any significance to its presence. Barnett notes its presence but places it before each particle as a double, ναὶ ναὶ and οὒ οὔ. *The Second Epislte to the Corinthians*, 102, footnote 20.

[12] Porter, *Idioms*, 109.

as subjects and the anarthrous particles as complements as well.[13] In both of these examples, the articular particles are characterized as specific instances of *yes* and *no* respectively. In 2 Cor 1:17, they are characterized as Paul's words; in Jas 5:12, they are the words of the recipients. For each, their specific use of the words *yes* and *no* are characterized as conforming to the abstract quality of *yes* and *no*, though depending upon how Paul's words are interpreted, this may be in question. Admittedly, the Greek of 2 Cor 1:17 is more challenging than that of Jas 5:12. However, it is reasonable and consistent to interpret the articular particles in both examples as grammatical subjects. With regard to the present discussion, the function of the article with the particle is to characterize it as a specific instance, in contrast to an abstract notion. It is noteworthy that Paul employs the anarthrous ναί and οὔ in 1:18–19, where neither is characterized as a specific instance, but refers to *yes* and *no* in the abstract. In 1:20, the apostle returns to the articular ναί, while also adding articular ἀμήν. Both are, again, characterized as specific instances of *yes* and *amen.*

6. The Article with Infinitives

Infinitives are often described as verbal nouns because, like verbs, they grammaticalize aspect (or tense) and voice, and like nouns they are often modified by the article which indicates gender and case.[14] Robertson writes: "Originally ... the infinitive was a substantive, but a verbal substantive."[15] Turner agrees: "the infin. is probably in origin a noun."[16] Moulton argues that the articular infinitive is "the most characteristic feature of the Greek infinitive in post-Homeric language."[17] He concluded that, "the articular infinitive is almost entirely a development of Attic literature, especially oratory, from which it passed into the daily speech of the least cultured people in the later Hellenistic world."[18]

---

[13] Robertson seems to reflect this understanding. In his citation of this passage, he does not include the two doublets, but lists them simply as "τὸ ναί and τὸ οὔ," though this is, admittedly, not certain, *Grammar*, 765. Wallace's translation also reflects this understanding: "the 'yes' should be 'yes' and the 'no' [should be] 'no' with me," *Greek Grammar*, 237.

[14] Porter, *Idioms*, 194.

[15] Robertson, *Grammar*, 1056.

[16] Turner, *Syntax*, 140.

[17] Moulton, *Prolegomena*, 213.

[18] Moulton, *Prolegomena*, 215.

Historically, the presence of the article has not been viewed as having a significant effect on the meaning of the infinitive. Regarding anarthrous and articular constructions, Robertson writes: "There is no essential difference in idea, and the mere presence or absence of the article is not to be pressed too far."[19] Turner argues that, "the function of an article with an infin. is the same as with a noun since the infin. is probably in origin a noun, except that with the infin. the article often appears for no reason except to supply the case-ending which is lacking."[20] Porter observes that this understanding still prevails: "Most scholars are agreed that the difference between the two structures does not warrant a major distinction in meaning."[21] Wallace writes: "The *neuter* article really has no other significance than a formal attachment."[22] As noted above, this is also the position of Burk, who concludes that "it is unhelpful to say that the article is used with the infinitive in exactly the same way that it is used with other nouns."[23] Such conclusions rest on the premise that the Greek article is a determiner, which we have argued is incorrect. If the premise is false, the conclusions must be called into question. It is, in fact, demonstrable that the article does exert a semantic influence on infinitives, which is observable once one is correctly oriented to the nature of that influence. Since we have argued at length that there is a correlation between choice and meaning, the choice to use or not use the article with an infinitive cannot be viewed meaningless or arbitrary. It is a meaningful choice, and even if we might agree with Robertson that this choice must not be pressed too far, we cannot ignore it.

On the positive side, Porter writes: "The articular infinitive is marked by the article either establishing a syntactical relation (such as case) or emphasizing the infinitive's substantival characteristics."[24] While grammarians agree regarding the case marking function of the article with infinitives, they have little or nothing to say regarding a function that emphasizes the infinitive's substantival characteristics. Based on our observations, this function likely plays a greater role than previously recognized. Clearly, there is a danger in oversimplifying the situation. There

---

[19] Robertson, *Grammar*, 1063.

[20] Turner, *Syntax*, 140.

[21] Porter, *Idioms*, 194.

[22] Wallace, *Grammar*, 589.

[23] Burk, *Articular Infinitives*, 46.

[24] Porter, *Idioms*, 194. Conversely, Robertson asserts, "The article did not make a substantive of the infinitive," *Grammar*, 371.

is no question that formulating a description of the article's function with infinitives presents a challenge. However, while acknowledging this challenge, there is every reason to believe that a general theory of the article's function does indeed inform this structure as well.

When the article modifies a participle, the verbal element of the participle is used as the identifying feature of a class. With an infinitive, this is also true. However, with participles a person or thing is identified by its engagement in the verbal process or state. With an infinitive, the process is the only thing that is identified. As with other parts of speech, the process or state by itself can be a simple abstraction, such as *run*. When modified by the article, the process is characterized as something concrete, as belonging to experience of an actual process. This may explain why infinitives are articular when they are the object of a preposition. As an object, Greek speakers naturally felt the need to emphasize the substantive, or nominal, aspect of the infinitive.

By contrast, it is arguable that when an infinitive does not have the article, the verbal quality is in view. For example, infinitives are often used in catenative constructions, where a main verb such as δεῖ, δύναμαι, θέλω, or μέλλω and the infinitive combine to form a single syntactical unit.[25] In these constructions, the verbal quality of the infinitive takes priority, so it is anarthrous. Thus, though Wallace asserts that anarthrous infinitives may function substantivally,[26] it is more likely that in these instances the speaker or writer is indicating an emphasis on the verbal force of the infinitive. For example, he cites Mark 9:5, ῥαββι, καλόν ἐστιν ἡμᾶς ὧδε εἶναι, *Rabbi, it is good for us to be here*, as an instance of a substantival anarthrous infinitive.[27] Instead, it is more likely that the state of *being here* is being emphasized by the speaker.

When an articular infinitive stands alone, the emphasis is on its nominal or substantive quality. Thus, it is characterized as concrete. This is observed in Rom 7:18:[28]

---

[25] Porter, *Idioms*, 197.

[26] Wallace, *Gramar*, 234.

[27] Wallace, *Gramar*, 600.

[28] It is of note that, by an overwhelming margin, the majority of instances of articular infinitives in Paul follow a preposition; and the majority of these follow εἰς.

τὸ γὰρ θέλειν παράκειταί μοι, τὸ δὲ κατεργάζεσθαι τὸ καλὸν οὔ·

For *desire* is present in me, but *to successfully perform* the good thing is not.[29]

Paul characterizes *desire* and *successful performance* as concrete things. It is not a person or thing that is identified by these processes, but the process itself that is so characterized. Both infinitives are the subject of the main verb (in the second instance, the verb is elided). By characterizing them as concrete, Paul places greater emphasis on the fact that these items are classes of such things that can *exist*. He holds each item out as something that can be examined by the recipients. The article indicates that the writer is providing the information necessary for the identification of each class. The recipients must accept this information that is provided to them as the basis of identification.

This same kind of usage is observed in 1 Cor 14:39:

ζηλοῦτε τὸ προφητεύειν καὶ τὸ λαλεῖν μὴ κωλύετε γλώσσαις·

Desire *prophecy* and do not prevent *speaking in tongues.*

In this instance, Paul employs the article to characterize the processes of *prophecy* and *speaking in tongues* as specific instances of these activities. Thus, the activity of *prophesying* is characterized as concrete, as belonging to experience of an actual things that may be desired. Likewise, the activity of *speaking in tongues* is also characterized as concrete, as something that ought not to be prevented. As always, though they are characterized in this way, there is no indication that Paul has definite processes in view. Specific instances that can be located in space and time are not indicated, only that such processes as these that do indeed occur. The same can be said of the following example from Phil 1:21:

Ἐμοὶ γὰρ τὸ ζῆν Χριστὸς καὶ τὸ ἀποθανεῖν κέρδος.

For to me *to live* is Christ and *to die* is profit.

Both *to live* and *to die* are characterized as a class of thing. They are not processes, in the general sense of verbs. Instead, the processes are characterized as a thing that has a material existence (though obviously, not in

---

[29] Wallace's translation, "*the* willing is present with me, but *the* doing [of] the good is not," is an example of continued over dependence upon the English definite article, *Greek Grammar*, 234.

a literal sense). Thus, they are subjectively characterized as *concrete*. Even a state of being may be so characterized, as seen in Phil 2:6:

οὐχ ἁρπαγμὸν ἡγήσατο τὸ εἶναι ἴσα θεῷ,

He did not consider *being equal* with God something to be held tightly.

In this instance, the verbal state grammaticalized by the infinitive, *to be*, is completed by ἴσα θεῷ, *equal to God*.

Articular infinitives that stand alone (that is, that are not the object of a preposition) are exceedingly rare in the General Epistles. Where they do appear, they conform to the same general description presented above. This is observed in Heb 10:31:

φοβερὸν τὸ ἐμπεσεῖν εἰς χεῖρας θεοῦ ζῶντος.

It is a terrible thing *to fall* into the hands of the living God.

	C φοβερὸν	S		
Heb.c10_98 ↖c10_96		Heb.c10_99	P τὸ ἐμπεσεῖν	A εἰς χεῖρας θεοῦ
				Heb.c10_100 | P ζῶντος

The infinitive is part of a larger group structure, *to fall into the hands of the living God*. The process *to fall* is characterized as concrete, as belonging to experience of an actual thing. The emphasis is on the nominal quality of the infinitive, which is something that can be predicated by the elided *to be* verb.

7. CONCLUSION

The examples provided above reflect a consistent usage of the article in conformity to the description provided in chapter 6. This may be summarized by the following points. First, no matter what part of speech is employed, when it is modified by the article, the speaker or writer indicates that the particular quality grammaticalized by that part of speech is to be used as the identifying characteristic of a class. This class may be an individual person or a group of people; an individual thing or a group of things. Second, in accordance with the description proposed in chapter 6, the class is characterized as concrete; that is, it is characterized as belonging to experience as an actual thing or a specific instance. Third, this characterization is subjective, in that the identification of the referent is oriented to the speaker or writer, who provides the recipients with the information necessary for identification. The article does not indicate that this information is available to the recipients, though it does not rule out the possibility either. Fourth, the article alone does not indicate that the referent is an actual person or thing. Such identification is indicated by other elements of the discourse. In conclusion, the use of the article is not a matter of individual idiom, nor is it determined by the demands of syntax. Instead, its use is motivated by a conscious decision on the part of the speaker for the purpose of characterization, which is used to indicate the identifying characteristic of a class.

CHAPTER EIGHT

THE ARTICLE WITH GROUPS

In addition to individual lexical items, the article is often employed to modify larger structures such as word groups. As with individual lexical items, the information provided by the word group is used as the identifying feature of a class that is identified by the article. The word group is characterized as concrete. In these instances, the structure functions similar to a relative clause as subject or object, even though it does not incorporate a verb form such as a participle.

1. The Article with a Genitive Group

Occasionally, a speaker or writer will employ the article to characterize a word group in the genitive case as concrete. We noted above that *restriction* is "the essential semantic feature of the genitive case."[1] When a word group in the genitive case is modified by the article, the restricting activity of the word group is held out as the identifying feature of the class. As always, this information is presented by the speaker or writer to the recipients to be used for the purpose of identification.

In Mark 8:33, Jesus distinguishes between two classes by means of a general association with God and humanity:[2]

οὐ φρονεῖς τὰ τοῦ θεοῦ ἀλλὰ τὰ τῶν ἀνθρώπων.

You do not have in mind *the things of God* but *the things of humanity.*

The neuter plural article indicates that the referent is a class of things whose sole identifying characteristic is defined by its association with an individual or group: the first class of things is the associated with God; the second class of things is associated with mankind or humanity.[3] Beyond

---

[1] Porter, *Idioms*, 93.

[2] The genitive case restricts the head term in terms of a *quality, definition, or description*, Porter, *Idioms*, 92.

[3] As a distinct category of usage, Robertson addresses the article *With Genitive Alone.* With regard to the neuter plural article, "[It] is common for the notion of 'affairs' or 'things,'" *Grammar*, 767.

this, neither of these classes may be further identified; they are characterized in the most generic manner. In this way, the speaker makes a very
sweeping criticism of the recipient. Peter's rebuke of Jesus is a single error.
However, it is indicative of, and thus the result of, a general pattern of
thinking that is based on human priorities, which stand in contrast to
those of God.[4] Jesus makes a similar distinction in Luke 20:25. Once again,
two classes are distinguished from each other by a single identifying characteristic. In this instance, the things that compromise each class belong
to a different owner:

> τοίνυν ἀπόδοτε τὰ καίσαρος καίσαρι καὶ τὰ τοῦ θεοῦ τῷ θεῷ.

> Therefore, give *the things of Caesar* to Caesar and *the things of God* to God.

The neuter plural article is employed to indicate that the two classes of
things are to be identified solely on the basis of the fact that they belong
to Caesar and to God respectively.[5] Though presented as something concrete, *such things*, no further specification is made. Each is characterized
as belonging to experience of actual things: Caesar and God do indeed
have possessions that should rightfully be rendered back to them. However, there is nothing to indicate definiteness, such as *these* possessions
specifically.

In Rom 8:5, Paul employs the article to characterize both genitive word
groups and prepositional groups, as well as a participial clause:

> οἱ γὰρ κατὰ σάρκα ὄντες τὰ τῆς σαρκὸς φρονοῦσιν, οἱ δὲ κατὰ πνεῦμα τὰ τοῦ
> πνεύματος.

> For the ones who are according to the flesh think about *the things of the
> flesh*, but the ones according to the Spirit *the things of the Spirit*.

---

[4] "The characterization of Peter's ideas as τὰ τῶν ἀνθρώπων as opposed to τὰ τοῦ θεοῦ
sums up the problem which we have seen in considering the call to secrecy in v. 30. The
divine purpose revealed in v. 31 makes no sense in human terms... The problem lies not
at the level of competing loyalties... but at that of incompatible ideologies, of a human
perspective which cannot grasp the divine purpose," France, *Mark*, 339.

[5] Marshall interprets this construction somewhat differently: "τὰ τοῦ Καίσαρος goes
beyond the payment of taxes and refers to rendering to the ruler whatever he may lawfully
prescribe. The saying affirms the general principle of submission to political authority,"
Luke, 736. Though I would affirm the general principle, I disagree that this is the point of
this saying. Jesus' point is that the coin bears Caesar's image and name, "In all probability,
the denarius in question in this scene bore the image of Tiberius and the inscription, 'Tiberius Caesar, son of the divine Augustus,'" Green, *Luke*, 715. Thus, it is Caesar's possession.
As such this and anything else that belongs to him, τὰ τοῦ Καίσαρος, should be given back
to him if he so demands.

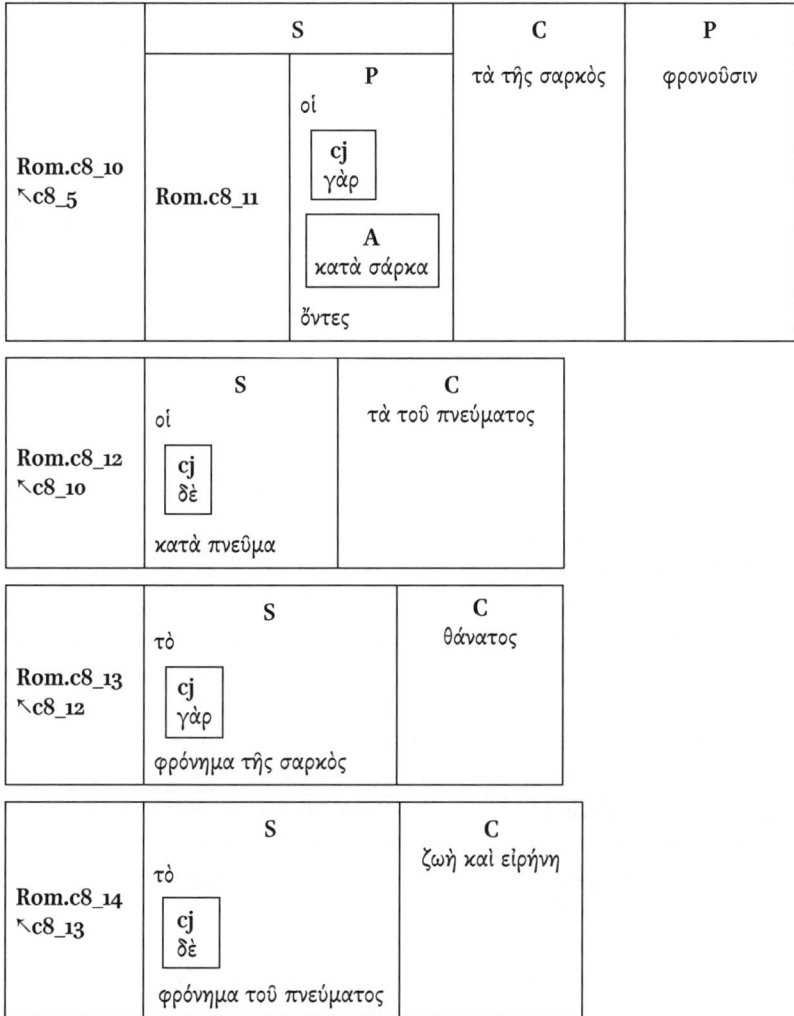

This example begins with an articular participial clause that functions as a relative clause: *the ones being* (that is, *who are*) *according to the flesh*. As seen above, this kind of clause fills the same slot, and performs the same function, as a relative clause that functions as subject. This particular class of people is identified by a single characteristic: they are *according to the flesh*. The nature of their being is defined by this quality.[6] By employing

---

[6] "The expression he uses here perhaps conveys a hint at what these people are rather than what they do, but we should not press this," Morris, *Romans,* 305. Cranfield expresses

the article, the writer indicates that he is providing the information necessary for identification. At the same time, he uses the article to characterize the class as concrete, as belonging to experience as an actual group of people.

Next, the writer employs a neuter plural article to modify a word group in the genitive case: τῆς σαρκὸς, *of the flesh*. The essential function of the genitive case is that of *restriction*.[7] The word or group in the genitive case qualifies the head term by restricting it in some way. In this instance, the class is identified by the restriction grammaticalized by the genitive group: it is *the things of the flesh*. This information is provided by the speaker. Once again, the article also characterizes the referent as concrete, as belonging to experience of an actual thing.

The following clause has elided the participle ὄντες, *the ones [who are] according to the Spirit*.[8] This clause performs the same function as the previous articular participial clause and is characterized in like manner. The identity of the final class is indicated by a neuter plural article. The identifying characteristic of this class is established by the restriction of the genitive τοῦ πνεύματος; it is *the things of the Spirit*. This group is part of a clause that also has an elided element: φρονοῦσιν. Like *the things of the flesh, the things of the Spirit* are characterized as concrete. While this is not necessarily in the material sense, they are concrete in the sense of characterization as belonging to experience of actual things. Both are held out as something that may be examined by the recipients. In all of the occurrences, the article indicates that the information necessary for identification is provided by the writer. The recipients are dependent upon him for this information and must accept it for identification.

---

a similar sentiment, *Romans 1–8*, 385. It is not necessary for them to hedge. The participial phrase is rightly understood as a characterization, as indicated by the use of the article. Cranfield believes that Paul "simply used οἱ κατὰ σάρκα ὄντες as synonymous with οἱ κατὰ σάρκα περιπατοῦντες," *Romans 1–8*, 385. Conversely, Moo does not think that "being according to the flesh/Spirit" is the same as "walking according to the flesh/Spirit" in v. 4b in the sense of "lifestyle" or "daily conduct." Rather, it is the same as "being in the flesh," Moo, *Romans*, 486. I would argue that Paul's characterization is more ontological than locative. The construction indicates that such persons' very being is defined as κατὰ σάρκά, *according to flesh*. Dunn writes, "The οἱ κατὰ ... ὄντες should not be taken as an ontological classification, as though Paul envisaged two classes of humankind, created differently and forever locked into a particular character and destiny." Instead, he argues that this class is a "variant or at least complement of οἱ κατὰ σάρκα περιπατοῦντες," *Romans 1–8*, 425. This is an unnecessary overstatement. To say that this quality defines their being is not to suggest that they were created thus and forever locked into it. Paul clearly articulates a belief that an individual's nature can be transformed by Christ (2 Cor. 5:17).

[7] Porter, *Idioms*, 92.

[8] Morris, *Romans*, 305, footnote 24.

In Gal 5:24, belonging to Christ is the identifying characteristic of a group:[9]

οἱ δὲ τοῦ Χριστοῦ ['Ιησοῦ] τὴν σάρκα ἐσταύρωσαν.

But *the ones of Christ [Jesus]* crucified the flesh.

In this instance, the class indicated by the article is restricted based on their relationship with Christ. They are *the ones of Christ*, that is, those who belong to him or stand in relationship to him.[10] This restriction is employed as the sole identifying feature of this class. As the subject of the finite verb, they are characterized as concrete, as such people who may engage in the process of crucifying the flesh. They are characterized thus so that they may be held out for the recipients' examination. However, though characterized as concrete, there is nothing to indicate anything more definite.

The usage in Phil 2:21 is of the same sort as observed in Mark 8:33 and Luke 20:25:

οἱ πάντες γὰρ τὰ ἑαυτῶν ζητοῦσιν, οὐ τὰ 'Ιησοῦ Χριστοῦ.

For all seek *the things of themselves*, not *the things of Jesus Christ*.

The class οἱ πάντες is identified based on the quality grammaticalized by the adjective: *all*. This class is characterized as concrete, as belonging to experience of actual people who may engage in the process of *seeking*. However, they are characterized as *such people* who do this, without further identification with any known or specific group. The things that are sought are also characterized as concrete and are identified by the restricting function of the genitive. In addition, the deictic function of the pronoun anaphorically directs the reader back to οἱ πάντες. Whatever these things are, the only identifying characteristic the author provides is that they belong to the class οἱ πάντες. Though not necessarily material things, they are characterized as actual things that may be sought. These things stand in contrast to τὰ 'Ιησοῦ Χριστοῦ, *the things of Jesus Christ*, which are identified solely on the basis of their being the possession of Jesus Christ.

---

[9] For οἱ τοῦ Χριστοῦ, see also 1 Cor. 15:23.

[10] Robertson suggests that μαθηταί should be supplied, *Grammar*, 767. Bruce translates the construction as, "The people of Christ [Jesus]," *Galatians*, 256. Fung's translation interprets the genitive as indicating possession: "Those who belong to Christ Jesus," *Galatians*, 274.

1 John 4:3, the article modifies a genitive word group and functions much like a relative clause as complement:

τοῦτό ἐστιν τὸ τοῦ ἀντιχρίστου.

This is *the thing of the anti-Christ.*[11]

The identity of this class is defined by the restricting function of the genitive τοῦ ἀντιχρίστου. The sole defining quality of this class is its being restricted by anti-Christ, thus *of anti-Christ.*[12] The neuter demonstrative pronoun anaphoricaly directs the recipients back to the previous statement regarding each spirit (πᾶν πνεῦμα) that does not confess, "Jesus is from God." This adds a sense of definiteness that would not otherwise have been indicated.

In some of these instances above, this structure suggests that an element has been elided. One that is commonly observed indicates some type of kinship. This particular ellipsis is likely a form of shorthand that has become idiomatic.

Matt 1:6, Δαυὶδ δὲ ἐγέννησεν Σολομῶνα ἐκ τῆς τοῦ Οὐρίου,
David begat Solomon from *the [wife] of Uriah,*
John 19:25, Μαρία ἡ τοῦ Κλωπᾶ...
Mary *the [wife] of Clopas...*

The feminine article suggests that the elided element is likely γυνή.

Matt 4:21, Ἰάκωβον τὸν τοῦ Ζεβεδαίου
James *the [son] of Zebedee*

---

[11] Brown translates this construction, "*It is rather of the Antichrist,*" *The Epistles of John,* 496. His translation of the passage reflects a significant interpretive leap: "Everyone who negates the importance of Jesus reflects a Spirit which does not belong to God. It is rather of the Antichrist," 485. Kruse translates the construction, "This is the spirit of antichrist," *The Letters of John,* 147. This would require the neuter article to function either as a demonstrative, anaphorically referring back to πνεῦμα, or as the head as a result of ellipsis of πνεῦμα. The first option is not consistent with the function of the article as a ὁ-item. The second option is at least possible, and I will argue below that this is indeed the case in certain instances. However, one must question whether πνεῦμα is sufficiently obvious to justify being elided, which is one of the primary criteria. Westcott opts for the latter: "The omission of πνεῦμα in the phase τὸ τοῦ ἀντιχρίστου gives greater breadth to the thought," *The Epistles of St. John,* 143. Unfortunately, there is no decisive evidence either for or against ellipsis. I simply question if an elided element is sufficiently obvious (an admittedly subjective conclusion at best).
[12] The translation *anti-Christ* is here preferred to *Antichrist* based on the understanding that the term refers broadly to any identification of Christ/Messiah that runs counter to that of the author. Such is a Christ *in place of* the Christ he teaches. This is in contrast to the popular notion of the Antichrist as an end-times figure associated with the Beast of Revelation.

Mark 2:14, Λευὶν τὸν τοῦ Ἀλφαίου
Levi *the [son] of Alphaeus*
John 21:2, οἱ τοῦ Ζεβεδαίου
The [sons] of Zebedee
Acts 13:22, Δαυὶδ τὸν τοῦ Ἰεσσαί
David *the [son] of Jesse*

The masculine article suggests that the elided element is υἱός.

In other instances, the elided element is recoverable from the co-text.

Luke 5:33, οἱ μαθηταὶ Ἰωάννου νηστεύουσιν πυκνὰ καὶ δεήσεις ποιοῦνται ὁμοίως καὶ οἱ τῶν Φαρισαίων,

The disciples of John often fast and pray as also *the [disciples] of the Pharisees,*

The elided element μαθηταὶ is clearly recoverable from the co-text.

Heb 7:27, ὃς οὐκ ἔχει καθ' ἡμέραν ἀνάγκην, ὥσπερ οἱ ἀρχιερεῖς, πρότερον ὑπὲρ τῶν ἰδίων ἁμαρτιῶν θυσίας ἀναφέρειν ἔπειτα τῶν τοῦ λαοῦ·

Who does not have a daily obligation, such as the high priests, first to bear sacrifices on behalf of their own sins, then *the ones of the people.*

The word ἁμαρτιῶν has been elided from the group τῶν τοῦ λαοῦ.

In instances of ellipsis, as outlined in chapter 4, there is "something left unsaid." However, what is left unsaid is "understood nevertheless." It is an element that "goes without saying." Therefore, in order to argue for ellipsis, it must be demonstrable, within reason, that these criteria have been fulfilled. The elided element must be sufficiently obvious to the recipient. In the examples cited above, a pattern of routine elision of regularly occurring elements is observed. However, elision will not always be a matter of an observable pattern. In these instances, it must be admitted that "sufficiently obvious" will at times be a subjective interpretation.

2. THE ARTICLE WITH PREPOSITIONAL GROUPS

It common to observe the article with a prepositional group that is functioning as the head term. Prepositions generally serve to indicate a relation in terms of "being situated in, moving toward or moving away from a location," in either a literal or metaphorical sense.[13] When modified by the article, the relation grammaticalized by the prepositional phrase is

---

[13] Porter, *Idioms*, 142.

employed as the defining characteristic of the class. The first example of this construction is found in Mark 2:25:

Δαυὶδ ὅτε χρείαν ἔσχεν καὶ ἐπείνασεν αὐτὸς καὶ οἱ μετ' αὐτοῦ,

David, when he had need and was hungry, he along with *the ones with him*,

In this episode, Jesus gives justification for the actions of his disciples based on an appeal to the actions of David in the Old Testament, which establish a precedent. In addition, he also makes it clear that David was not alone; *the ones with him* joined David in his actions. As participants in the discourse, their function is to illustrate that, in a time of need, David's men joined him in doing *that which was not lawful*.[14] Therefore, these individuals are identified by a single characteristic: they were *the ones with him*. They are not identified in any other way because this manner of identification is sufficient for the requirements of the discourse: one group's actions are justified by the precedent set by another group's actions. Because this class is a participant in the narrative, it is characterized as concrete, as belonging to experience as an actual thing. As a participant in narrative discourse, and because their identity is based on association with David by means of anaphoric reference (αὐτοῦ), the class has a sense of definiteness. They are not merely *such people*; they are actual people.

In Rom 3:19, Paul identifies a class based on its relation to the law:

οἴδαμεν δὲ ὅτι ὅσα ὁ νόμος λέγει τοῖς ἐν τῷ νόμῳ λαλεῖ,

But we know that as much as the law says, it speaks *to those in the law*.

The metaphorical sense of being situated *in the law* is used to identify the class. In accordance with its regular function, the article indicates that the information provided by the writer is to be used for the purpose of identification. In this instance, the information is ἐν τῷ νόμῳ, *in the law*. This group, or class, is characterized as concrete, as *such a group of people*, without going so far as to identify them with an actual group in a real

---

[14] France interprets the inclusion of David's companions as providing "a precedent for the principle that the disciples' action (to which objection has been made in the first place) is covered by the personal authority of the leader," *Mark*, 146. In 2:23, only Jesus' disciples are identified as the ones plucking wheat. In order to associate Jesus with David, the narrative would need to indicate that he was engaged in the activity along with his disciples. It seems better to explain the association of the disciples of Jesus with David and his men as a simple matter of identifying one group (Jesus' disciples) with another group (David and his men) rather than with an individual (David alone).

sense; people identifiable by name and face. The writer does not indicate, "You know which ones I am talking about," as would be the case with the English definite article. Instead, he indicates, "I am talking about something else." He provides the information necessary for identification. He does not direct the recipients to it or indicate that they already possess it.

In Rom 16:10–11, Paul provides interesting examples that illustrate the article's wide range of uses:

> ἀσπάσασθε τοὺς ἐκ τῶν Ἀριστοβούλου … ἀσπάσασθε τοὺς ἐκ τῶν Ναρκίσσου τοὺς ὄντας ἐν κυρίῳ.

> Greet *the ones from the household of Aristobulus* … Greet *the ones from the household of Narcissus who are in the Lord.*

First, we observe him employing a genitive plural article with the genitive singular Ἀριστοβούλου and Ναρκίσσου. The plural articles in these instances each indicate a class of people whose identity is based on their association with these individuals. This is most commonly employed in instances that indicate a familial relationship (as seen above), though the plural suggests something other than elision of an element such as υἱός. This would lead us to conclude that it indicates a broader, yet unspecified, familial relationship: *the relatives of Aristobulus … the relatives of Narcissus.* This may even be extended further to encompass the members of their households in general, not just family members.[15] Next are the articles modifying the prepositional groups. These articles indicate identification of a class based on the familial relationship: *the ones from the relatives of Aristobulus … the ones from the relatives of Narcissus.* The imperative, "Greet," produces the sense that this group that is characterized as concrete by the article is also definite. They are not *such a class*, but a group of specific individuals identifiable by name and face who may actually be greeted.

Paul identifies a group he opposes by means of a relationship in Gal 2:12:

> φοβούμενος τοὺς ἐκ περιτομῆς.

> Fearing *the ones from circumcision.*

---

[15] Turner suggests, "The possession of slaves by a family may be indicated by this construction," referencing these examples specifically, *Syntax*, 169. Moo places emphasis on non-family membership, "'Those who are of Aristobulus' are probably members, especially slaves, of the household of a man named Aristobulus … As in v. 10, the people Paul greets will have been the members of Narcissus' household," *Romans*, 925. For similar opinions, see also Morris, *Romans*, 535–36; Dunn, *Romans 9–16*, 896.

The prepositional phrase, *from circumcision*, provides the information by which this class is identified. They are held out as concrete, as belonging to experience of an actual group who may be feared. Beyond this, they are not characterized as definite, such as *the circumcision party*.[16] However, as participants in narrative discourse, they are understood as actual people with whom Peter could interact, producing *fear* on his part. The article indicates they are a class whose defining characteristic is their relationship to the practice of circumcision. The co-textual features of the narrative indicate that actual people are in view; individuals who could, potentially, be identified by name and face.

In Gal 3:7, a class is identified based on their relationship to *faith*:

γινώσκετε ἄρα ὅτι οἱ ἐκ πίστεως, οὗτοι υἱοί εἰσιν Ἀβραάμ.

Therefore you know that *the ones from faith*, these are sons of Abraham.

This class is identified based solely on the fact of a single relation: they are *from faith*. In this instance, *faith* is characterized in a general, abstract sense. It is not necessarily faith in a specifically Christian sense or faith directed toward some goal or object. Thus, this class of individuals is identified by the fact that they have a relationship to *faith*; they are *of faith* or *from faith*. This information is presented to the recipients by Paul for the purpose of identification. By characterizing this class as concrete, Paul holds them out for examination by the recipients; they are *such a class of people*. Specific believers, identifiable by name and face, are not indicated. Whereas the article does not direct the recipients to the information necessary for identification, the pronoun οὗτοι does. Its deixis is anaphoric, directing the recipient back to οἱ ἐκ πίστεως.

Paul identifies two classes of things based on their relationships to contrasting regions in Eph 1:10:

ἀνακεφαλαιώσασθαι τὰ πάντα ἐν τῷ Χριστῷ, τὰ ἐπὶ τοῖς οὐρανοῖς καὶ τὰ ἐπὶ τῆς γῆς ἐν αὐτῷ.

...to bring together all things in Christ, *the things on the heavens* and *the things on the earth* in him.

---

[16] Wallace translates this as "those of the circumcision [party]," *Greek Grammar*, 236. The use of "those" is incorrect. Demonstrative usage is inconsistent with the function of ὁ-items. As to "the circumcision [party]," for reasons that will be made clear in the next chapter, this kind of definite connotation is also incorrect. Instead, περιτομῆς is used in an abstract sense, simply *circumcision*. Association with a specific *circumcision party* is not indicated. Bruce also favors "the circumcision party," *Galatians*, 128, 131. Lightfoot suggests, "not 'Jews' but converts *from* Judaism', for this seems to be the force of the preposition," *Galatians*, 112. Fung prefers "advocates of circumcision," *Galatians*, 108.

Before introducing two contrasting classes, Paul identifies another broad class that encompasses these two. He employs the adjective πάντα and modifies it with a plural neuter article. The adjective functions as the head term and indicates that the class is identified by this quality: *all things*. As a result, the head term is characterized as concrete, as belonging to experience of an actual thing. The class *all things* refers[17] to all that exists. Next, Paul introduces two more classes, each identified by its location. The first is located *among the heavens*. This, then, is the identifying feature of this class. The second is located *on the earth*. Both function in a manner similar to a non-defining relative clause in that they provide further elaboration or specification of the class *all things*. This is consistent with the general function of ό-items, which is to indicate that the speaker or writer is providing information to the recipients. In this instance, it is additional information about *all things*.

In Heb 7:5, the author identifies a class based on a familial relationship:

οἱ μὲν ἐκ τῶν υἱῶν Λευὶ.

The ones from the sons of Levi.

The prepositional group is employed to provide the identifying characteristic of this class, which is based on their relationship to *the sons of Levi*.[18] The writer likely has in mind the priests who served in the tabernacle and later in the temple, as evidenced by the following participial group, τὴν ἱερατείαν λαμβάνοντες, *receiving the priesthood*. Because this is an actual group of people, they are characterized as concrete. Any sense of definiteness is based on the implicit sense that this group actually existed at one time in the past; that they could be identified by name and face. However, this would be a matter of *inference* based on a body of knowledge the author and recipients share. This is not a function of the article. Even though this group was likely known to the recipients, with regard to the role they play in the discourse, the writer provides the information necessary for identifying this class. He does not indicate to the recipients, "You know which ones I am talking about." The Greek article does not indicate that information that the recipients *never* knew is being introduced.

---

[17] O'Brien, *Ephesians*, 112.

[18] Regarding the identity of this group, commentators are generally more interested in the meaning of the preposition ἐκ, while passing over the article without comment. See Westcott, *Hebrews*, 175–6; Lane, *Hebrews 1–8*, 168; O'Brien, *Hebrews*, 251; Ellingworth, *Hebrews*, 362.

Rather, it indicates that the speaker or writer is introducing information into the discourse without comment on whether or not the recipients may make the identification for themselves.

John identifies Jesus using a uniquely Johannine expression in 1 John 2:13 (repeated again in 2:14):[19]

ἐγνώκατε τὸν ἀπ᾽ ἀρχῆς

You know *the one from the beginning.*

The identity of the class, in this instance a class made up of a single individual, is established based on a temporal relation: *from the beginning.* Specific association with Jesus is a matter of inference, not deixis. John does not direct the reader to this identification, but can reasonably assume it based on the common body of knowledge he and the readers share. This allows him the freedom to characterize Jesus in a way that makes a theological statement about his preexistence.[20]

Later, in 1 John 4:4, the author contrasts two individuals based by identifying them with reference to their location:

μείζων ἐστὶν ὁ ἐν ὑμῖν ἢ ὁ ἐν τῷ κόσμῳ.

Greater is *the one in you* than *the one in the world.*

The writer employs spatial relations as the identifying characteristic of these two individuals. One is characterized as *in you,* while the other is characterized as *in the world.*

Certain instances of this construction, like many examined above, may be the result of ellipsis. This is demonstrable in Rom 1:26:

μετήλλαξαν τὴν φυσικὴν χρῆσιν εἰς τὴν παρὰ φύσιν,

They exchanged natural sexual desire for *the one contrary to nature.*

---

[19] Robertson cites this as an example of τόν as a demonstrative, *Grammar,* 694. Wallace translates the phrase, "*the* [one who was] from the beginning," *Greek Grammar,* 236. As seen many times, this illustrates an over dependence upon analogy with the English definite article.

[20] Contra Brown, who interprets the prepositional phrase as a reference to "the beginning of Jesus' self-revelation to his disciples in the ministry," *The Epistles of John,* 303. So also Kruse, "[the author] is referring not to the beginning of time, but to the time when the Word of life was incarnate in Jesus Christ," *The Letters of John,* 90. It is difficult not to believe that John's frequent use of ἀρχή is to some degree a deliberate attempt to recall Gen. 1:1 LXX. See also Westcott, *The Epistles of St. John,* 60; Bruce, *The Epistles of John,* 59; Marshall, *The Epistles of John,* 139.

The feminine article suggests that the elided element is χρῆσιν. This would meet the criteria of an element that "goes without saying" and is sufficiently obvious.

3. CONCLUSION

The use of the article with word groups conforms to the definition and the description outlined above. When employed in these structures, it is used to indicate that the information necessary for identifying the referent is being supplied by the speaker or writer. The article indicates that the relationship grammaticalized by the group is the identifying characteristic of the referent. The recipients must accept this information for the purpose of identification. The word group so modified is used as the head term. The article characterizes the head term as concrete, as belonging to experience as an actual person or thing. If the referent is indeed an actual person or thing, this will be indicated by additional elements or the context of the discourse.

CHAPTER NINE

THE ARTICLE WITH NOUNS

1. Description of the Article's Function

Nowhere is there a more urgent need for a uniform theory of the article's function than in regard to nouns. By an overwhelming majority, nouns are the most common elements to be modified by the article.[1] Yet it is in regard to nouns that, historically, the function of the article has been treated in a most un-uniform and even contradictory manner. For this reason it is necessary to articulate a theory that describes how nouns are characterized based on both the article's presence and absence. To accomplish this task, it is essential that we once and for all abandon classical notions regarding the function of the article. The Greek article has not "detached itself for special functions answering generally to those of our own *the*."[2] It is not "associated with gesture and aids in pointing out like an index finger."[3] Such views associate the Greek article with English TH- items. As argued above, it is more closely analogous to English WH-items. Even the gloss *the* too often leads to false conclusions. While English idiom will require us to use the definite article in certain structures, it should be approached with caution as a matter of *translation*.

As noted above, historically, attempts to define the function of the article have created their own complications. By stating that the article can turn any part of speech into a noun, one does nothing to define its function *with* nouns. The reason for leaving the treatment of nouns until this point has been to comprehensively demonstrate certain fundamental functions of ό-items in general and the article in particular. First, the Greek article indicates that the speaker or writer is providing information that is necessary for identifying a referent. There is no indication that this information is recoverable or obvious in the discourse. This is the primary characteristic that distinguishes the Greek article from the English definite article. Second, the function of the Greek article is to characterize

---

[1] See chapter 6.
[2] Moulton and Howard, *Accidence*, 117.
[3] Robertson, *Grammar*, 756.

the head term as *concrete*, as *belonging to experience of an actual thing or event*. If this is true when other parts of speech are modified by the article, it is reasonable to conclude that this is its function with nouns as well. Based on this, we will restate the function of the article in terms specific to nouns:

> The presence of the article indicates the speaker or writer's subjective presentation of a noun, which is presented as something concrete, in that it is characterized as belonging to immediate experience as an actual thing or event, or is associated with a specific instance.

In addition:

> The characterization of a noun as concrete is based solely on the fact of the speaker or writer's provision of the information necessary for identification. It gives no indication to the listener or reader of how or where to locate the identity of the noun, or that the identity is proximate in such a way as to be immediately recoverable. The Greek article orients the identification of the head term to the speaker or writer, not the recipient.

Using these observations regarding the characterization of nouns that are modified by the article, a description of how nouns are characterized when they are not modified by the article may also be formulated. In contrast to being characterized as *concrete* when modified by the article, nouns are characterized as *abstract* when not modified by the article. Thus:

> The absence of the article indicates the speaker or writer's subjective characterization of a noun, which is presented as abstract, in that it is characterized as not belonging to immediate experience as an actual thing or event, or is not associated with a specific instance. The noun has no referent in terms of a class whose identifying characteristic is grammaticalized by the noun. It is an abstraction.

Using these working definitions, we will examine various examples of articular and anarthrous nouns in the New Testament. Ultimately, it will be demonstrated that the use of the article was not a matter of personal idiom or style, nor was its presence or absence a matter of structural considerations.[4] Instead, it will be demonstrated that Greek speakers employed

---

[4] In the next chapter, it will be demonstrated that the article was creatively used to realize various group structures that perform a variety of discourse functions. However, its use in such structures presumes that it was present first as a necessary modifier, deliberately employed by the speaker or writer for the purpose of characterization. Thus, its use as a modifier is its primary function, while its use as a structural element is secondary and subordinate to the primary function. The article cannot be used as a structural element unless it is *already* present as a modifier. A lack of recognition of this functional hierarchy

the article because it entered into a meaningful relationship with the head term, which was a necessary function for establishing meaning.

One of the difficulties we will encounter will be determining the factors that govern a speaker or writer's choice to characterize the head term as concrete or abstract. In some instances, this will be fairly obvious from the discourse. In other instances where this is not the case, we will be required to theorize about such motives in a manner that is consistent with what is observable in the discourse. Though challenging, by using the definitions proposed here, this exercise may yield results that provide insights that have exegetical value.

While we may expect many positive results, it is also true that some interpretations will have to be overturned. For example, Wallace translates Jas 2:14, μὴ δύναται ἡ πίστις σῶσαι αὐτόν; "This [kind of] faith is not able to save him, is it?"[5] The underlying assumption is that the article functions like a TH- item and "points back to a certain kind of faith as defined by the author and is used to particularize an abstract noun."[6] The first part of this interpretation of the article's function is most certainly incorrect. Because the article does not function as a demonstrative, it does not point back in this way. The second part is nearly correct, but can be improved. Rather than say the article particularizes an abstract noun, it is more accurate to say it characterizes the noun as concrete, as pertaining to a particular instance of faith. While this particular instance may be the aforementioned faith, the article does not direct the reader to make this connection. Instead, the identification of *faith* is based on an orientation to the author; he provides the information necessary for identification to the recipients, who must accept this information for the purpose of identification. The translation *this faith* indicates that the author is directing the recipients to the information necessary for identification. Such an interpretation of the article's function misinterprets the deixis of the article. This is not to say that Wallace's rendering is inappropriate; it may be fine as far as idiomatic English is concerned. However, this rendering does not reflect the Greek usage. Instead, it becomes the basis to read English usage into Greek. Likewise the so-called *Par Excellence* translation of John 1:21, ὁ προφήτης εἶ σύ; "Are you the prophet?"[7] assumes that the Greek article

---

has been the "Achilles heel" of many grammars, which have attempted to explain the presence and absence of the article primarily on the basis of syntax.

[5] Wallace, *Greek Grammar*, 219, emphasis his.

[6] Wallace, *Greek Grammar*, 219.

[7] Wallace, *Greek Grammar*, 222, emphasis his.

indicates "you know which prophet I'm talking about." Again, we have argued that the Greek article does not function in this way and therefore this interpretation, as well as this category, must be rejected.

In an analysis of the function of the article, one must take into account that the choice of characterization is often motivated by discourse considerations. In chapter 6.4, the discourse function of the article was defined in terms of *grounding* or *salience*. In some instances, the characterization of the head term is an end unto itself. The decision to characterize the head term as *concrete* or *abstract* is a reflection of the speaker or writer's subjective perspective of the substance or nature of the referent. The function of the characterization is limited to the nominal group. However, in other instances, the characterization will perform a function above that of the nominal group at the level of the overall discourse. At times, a speaker or writer will use the article to characterize the head term as concrete in order to foreground that element or give it greater salience. By doing so, the articular element is understood as a *figure* in the discourse. Conversely, the speaker or writer may choose not to employ the article, thus characterizing the head term as abstract. By doing so, this element is moved to the background of the discourse or identified as less salient. In this way, its function is to establish the *grounding* of the discourse; it provides the backdrop against which a *figure* or *figures* are seen. By taking into consideration the discourse function of speaker or writer's choice of characterization, we will be able to produce a detailed, comprehensive description of the article's function.

It must be stated at the beginning that space does not allow for an examination of each of the thousands of nouns in the New Testament individually. Examples will be chosen that allow us to observe both articular and anarthrous structures in such a way that illustrates how each is characterized differently. In this way, the implications for translation and exegesis will be plainly demonstrated.

2. The Article with Nouns

Matt 3:4 includes both articular and anarthrous elements. The choice of characterization may be interpreted as an indication of the function of the elements.

αὐτὸς δὲ ὁ Ἰωάννης εἶχεν τὸ ἔνδυμα αὐτοῦ ἀπὸ τριχῶν καμήλου καὶ ζώνην δερματίνην περὶ τὴν ὀσφὺν αὐτοῦ, ἡ δὲ τροφὴ ἦν αὐτοῦ ἀκρίδες καὶ μέλι ἄγριον.

> But John himself had clothes of camel hair and a leather belt around his
> waist, and his food was locust and wild honey.

To understand the use and non-use of the article, one must always keep
in mind that either choice represents a *subjective* characterization on
the part of the speaker or writer. The use or non-use of the article indicates how the speaker or writer wishes to characterize the head terms.
This choice of characterization is a meaningful choice and must not be
ignored. Understanding this characterization is crucial for both the translator and interpreter.

We first observe that John's clothes, τὸ ἔνδυμα αὐτοῦ, are articular and
thus characterized as concrete, as belonging to experience of an actual
thing.[8] Conversely, the materials he used to make his clothing, τριχῶν
καμήλου καὶ ζώνην δερματίνην, are anarthrous, thus characterized as
abstract. These choices give insight into the discourse function of each
element. On the one hand, John's clothes are more salient, while the
material of his clothes is less salient. For the purpose of the discourse, the
function of the material is to say something about the nature of John's
clothes; they are not salient themselves, they function as elements that
ground the discourse. Thus, the author employs this characterization to
communicate the nature of John's wardrobe, rather than its precise composition. Matthew is not interested in communicating the exact material
composition of John's wardrobe. Instead, he is more interested in what
John's clothes do or say about him. Clothing of this nature would cause
John to stand out from the people around him, as well as convey a sense
of poverty. John is different than everyone else. The interpreter may even
surmise that, while John had clothing made of such materials, this was not
his entire wardrobe. Thus, John's actual clothes are more salient than the
material of which they are made, which only function to communicate
something more abstract such as physical distinction or poverty, which in
turn may serve to identify him as a prophet or even a Nazirite.

Next, with regard to John's diet, we observe the same pattern of characterization. On the one hand his food, ἡ τροφὴ αὐτοῦ, is articular, thus
characterized as concrete, just as his clothes are. However, the specific
dietary items, ἀκρίδες καὶ μέλι ἄγριον, are characterized as abstract, just
like the material of his clothes. As before, John's food is more salient,
while the specific things that he ate are less salient. For the purpose of

---

[8] Regarding ὁ Ἰωάννης, the function of the article with proper nouns will be treated
below.

the discourse, the specific items of his diet only function to say something about the nature of his *food*. They provide the *ground* against which the *figure, food*, is seen. Like his clothing, this kind of diet both sets him apart from the general population and communicates a state of poverty, which may again identify him as a prophet or Nazirite. With this understanding of the function of the various elements of the discourse in mind, the interpreter should focus less on the material of John's clothing and the elements of his diet, and more on what they represent.[9]

The articular and anarthrous elements of Mark 3:31–35 also provide an excellent sample to analyze characterization and discourse function.

Καὶ ἔρχεται ἡ μήτηρ αὐτοῦ καὶ οἱ ἀδελφοὶ αὐτοῦ καὶ ἔξω στήκοντες ἀπέστειλαν πρὸς αὐτὸν καλοῦντες αὐτόν. καὶ ἐκάθητο περὶ αὐτὸν ὄχλος, καὶ λέγουσιν αὐτῷ· ἰδοὺ ἡ μήτηρ σου καὶ οἱ ἀδελφοί σου [καὶ αἱ ἀδελφαί σου] ἔξω ζητοῦσίν σε. καὶ ἀποκριθεὶς αὐτοῖς λέγει· Τίς ἐστιν ἡ μήτηρ μου καὶ οἱ ἀδελφοί [μου]; καὶ περιβλεψάμενος τοὺς περὶ αὐτὸν κύκλῳ καθημένους λέγει· ἴδε ἡ μήτηρ μου καὶ οἱ ἀδελφοί μου. ὃς [γὰρ] ἂν ποιήσῃ τὸ θέλημα τοῦ θεοῦ, οὗτος ἀδελφός μου καὶ ἀδελφὴ καὶ μήτηρ ἐστίν.

And his mother and his brothers came and standing outside they sent to him calling him. And a crowd was standing around him saying to him, "Behold, your mother and brothers [and sisters] are outside seeking you." And answering he said to them, "Who are my mother and my brothers?" And looking around at the ones standing around him in a circle he says, "Behold my mother and my brothers. The one who does the will of God, this one is my brother and my sister and my mother."

This section is a continuation of a larger unit of discourse. In 3:20, the reader is informed that Jesus ἔρχεται εἰς οἶκον, *went into a house*. At the point that we take up the narrative, Jesus is apparently still in the house. It is noteworthy that, in this statement, οἶκον is anarthrous. Based on the definition proposed above, οἶκον is characterized as *abstract*, that is, it is not

---

[9] By contrast, commentaries generally devote considerable space to the elements themselves. See for example Nolland, *Matthew*, 138–40. Though a commentary on the Greek text, he makes no mention of the presence or absence of the article. France devotes equal space to both the elements themselves and what they represent, *Matthew*, 105–7. In fairness, commentaries do address the significance of John's wardrobe and diet. With regard to his attire, they frequently observe a connection with Elijah. This is not meant to be a harsh criticism, but an observation that sometimes significant emphasis is placed on details that the author intended to be secondary. An analysis of this nature enables the interpreter to focus on the elements that the author himself indicates are most important. Those who do indeed see significance in John's attire could use this data to reinforce their interpretation. See also Davies and Allison, *Matthew*, 295–97; Hagner, *Matthew 1–13*, 48–9; Keener, *Matthew, IVPNTC*, 77–8; *Matthew*, 118–19; Luz, *Matthew 1–7*, 135–36; Turner, *Matthew*, 109.

characterized as belonging to experience as an actual thing or a specific instance. At first, this may seem odd, since its role in the narrative is that of a real house. However, the choice of characterization is motivated by other discourse considerations that may be explained in terms of *grounding*. At this point, οἶκον, *house*, functions as a part of the backdrop of the narrative. Its role is to set the scene. To use Stephen Wallace's terminology, it is not a *figure* in the discourse, but a part of the *ground*, that is, the background.[10] The writer mentions the *house* for no other reason but to set up what comes next. Therefore, he characterizes it in such a way as to position it in the background of the discourse.

The current section begins by introducing Jesus' mother and brothers into the discourse: ἡ μήτηρ αὐτοῦ καὶ οἱ ἀδελφοὶ αὐτοῦ. These participants are standing outside the house where Jesus currently is, apparently trying to get him to come out so that they may talk to him. Both are articular; they are characterized as concrete, as belonging to experience as actual things. Logically, this is to be expected. Jesus' mother and brothers are actual people; therefore, one would expect them to be characterized as concrete. However, as observed above, these kinds of expectations are not always consistent with the way a speaker or writer choses to characterize a participant. With regard to Jesus' mother and brothers, their function in the discourse must also be considered when explaining their characterization. To again employ Stephen Wallace's terminology, the choice of characterization indicates that these participants are not used for the purpose of *grounding*, but function as *figures* in the narrative. One may also employ Reed's terminology. These participants are characterized as *more salient* to the discourse. The purpose of the discourse is to challenge and redefine familial relationships. Jesus' mother and brothers play a key role in illustrating the point Jesus will make.

Next, we observe that ὄχλος is not modified by the article, and is thus characterized as abstract. As with οἶκον, this is not what might one might expect at first glance. Since this group is a participant in the discourse, and is physically present with Jesus, the reader might expect it to be characterized as concrete, as belonging to experience as an actual thing. However, the characterization serves a discourse function. Like οἶκον, the choice of characterization is a matter of *grounding*. At this point, the *crowd* functions as a part of the backdrop of the narrative. Its role is to set the scene. It is not a *figure* in the discourse, but a part of the *ground*, that is, the

---

10 Wallace, "Figure and Ground," 214.

background. Thus, it is less *salient*. The question that they ask sets up Jesus' response, which is the point of the discourse. In fact, the question is more important than the ones asking it. Mark's characterization situates the *crowd* in the background of the discourse.

The crowd informs Jesus that ἡ μήτηρ, οἱ ἀδελφοί, and αἱ ἀδελφαί are seeking him. Once again, these participants are articular, and thus characterized as concrete. In terms of simple logic, this may be explained by the fact that they are individuals who may be specifically identified by name and face. Jesus' mother, brothers and sisters are real people who belong to experience of actual things. Since this is the crowd speaking to Jesus, it makes sense that they would characterize his mother, brothers, and sisters as concrete individuals who are *seeking* Jesus. From the perspective of the crowd, Jesus' family members are salient, and are therefore characterized in such a way as to indicate that they are figures. *They* are seeking Jesus.

In response, Jesus asks the question, *who are my mother and brothers* [ἡ μήτηρ μου καὶ οἱ ἀδελφοί]? For the third time, these participants are articular. In English, there are a number of ways to track participants in a discourse.[11] One of these ways is through the use of the article. Participants are often introduced as indefinite, while subsequent references are definite, employing *the*.[12] The definite article presumes that participants either have been introduced and their identities are either recoverable or that they are obvious in the discourse. Once a participant has been introduced, the speaker and recipient share in common the information necessary for identification. The definite article tracks participants only after they have been introduced.[13] It indicates, "You know which one I am talking about." In this manner, the definite article produces cohesion in the text.[14] Conversely, the Greek article is not used to track participants the way the English definite article does. Instead, by characterizing participants as *concrete* or *abstract*, it positions them in the discourse by situating them in the background or foreground, or by moving them forward and backward as needed.

---

[11] For an overview of tracking participants, see Martin and Rose, *Working with Discourse*, 155–85.

[12] Martin and Rose, *Working with Discourse*, 158, 163.

[13] Martin and Rose, *Working with Discourse*, 160–61. Sometimes participants are introduced with the definite article if their identity may be presumed without their being introduced. This would be the case if, for example, their identity was obvious or expected in the discourse.

[14] Halldiay and Hasan, *Cohesion in English*, 3, 70–74.

Interestingly, while ὄχλος is characterized as abstract, τοὺς περὶ αὐτόν, *the ones around him*, are characterized as concrete. The use of a participial clause is also noteworthy. The author could have simply said the Jesus spoke to *the crowd*, τῷ ὄχλῳ. Instead, he employs a significantly more complex structure. This has the effect of bringing the element to the foreground, drawing the attention of the reader to it. The reason for this is clear. Jesus is about to direct the attention of his audience to this group. Therefore, the writer prepares the reader for this by drawing his or her attention to this element by foregrounding it. In addition, this kind of characterization gives the impression of a significant number of people, enough to *stand around Jesus in a circle*. The noun κύκλῳ is characterized as abstract because the author is only interested in the quality of *circle*, not *circle* as something concrete.

When Jesus says, "Behold my mother and my brothers," *mother* and *brothers* are characterized as concrete. This is likely based on a number of motivating factors. Jesus calls them *my mother and my brothers*, ἡ μήτηρ μου καὶ οἱ ἀδελφοί μου. The genitive pronoun restricts the head terms by indicating possession. This pronoun in combination with the article characterizes the head terms as belonging to experience as actual people. The people to whom Jesus is referring are not *mothers* and *brothers* in an abstract sense. Jesus characterizes them as actual family members. Jesus directs the attention of the encircling crowd through the use of ἴδε. He wants them to look at the individuals around them. Therefore, he characterizes the objects that the crowd must take notice of as concrete, as belonging to experience of actual things. They are individuals who may in fact be seen.

We next observe a relative clause functioning as head: *the one who does the will of God.* This clause could have been worded using an alternate *Ho-* form such as ὁ ποιῶν. This, too, is a meaningful choice since both options are available to the speaker. The use of a relative clause, which is structurally more involved, rather than a participial clause, represents the use of a marked form.[15] This may indicate that the speaker wishes to highlight, or to foreground, this element. Intuitively, the reader will recognize

---

[15] Earlier, in chapter 2.2, under *Markedness and Prominence*, one of the recurring qualifications of a marked form was structural complexity. In Greek, as demonstrated above, the speaker often had the choice to employ structures that filled the same slot and performed the same function, but operated at different levels of rank: participial phrase or relative clause. The combined characteristics of structural complexity and higher rank suggest that, in instances where both options were available, the relative clause represents a marked form.

this as the peak of the discourse; this is the point that Jesus, as well as the author, wants to make. The use of a marked form confirms this.

Both θέλημα and θεοῦ are characterized as concrete. Though *will* is traditionally classified as an abstract noun, it is here characterized as something concrete. The speaker is not concerned with the abstract notion of *will*, but with a specific instance of will, that is *the will of God*. The use of the article with θεοῦ is more complex due to the question of whether θεός is used as a noun or a proper name.[16] It will be argued below that the characterization function of the article with proper nouns is the same as with any other part of speech, but is motivated primarily by discourse considerations.

Lastly, we observe that ἀδελφός, ἀδελφή and μήτηρ are characterized as abstract. This is because Jesus is not speaking of an individual or groups who represent a specific instance of a *mother, brothers*, or *sisters*. One might say that Jesus is not speaking of *mother, brother*, or *sister* in a "literal" sense, as actual blood relatives. Rather, he is now speaking in terms of the abstract qualities of *mother, brother*, and *sister*. Familial relations are now to be understood in this much broader, redefined way. In terms of discourse function, *the one who does the will of God*, as argued above, is the most prominent element. This characteristic of obedience, more than blood relationship, defines membership in the family of God. The pronoun οὗτος anaphorically directs the reader back to this element. In light of this, the elements ἀδελφός, ἀδελφή and μήτηρ are now moved to the background as material that supports the peak of the discourse as expressed in the relative clause; they are now less salient.

This type of analysis and the results it produces should provide translators with substantive data with which to make decisions regarding form of expression in a target language. While the Greek idiom may not translate one for one, understanding the speaker or writer's choice of characterization should direct the translator to an option or set of options that not only captures the meaning of the Greek words. In addition, if possible, the translator should strive to employ forms and structures in the target language that perform the same functions in terms of markedness, prominence, grounding, and salience. It must be admitted that this may not

---

[16] For example, this question lies at the heart of one of the chief points of dispute in the application of the Granville Sharp Rule. See Wallace, *Granville Sharp*, 251–255; *Greek Grammar*, 276. For a critique of Wallace, specifically with regard to the issue of proper names, see Porter, Review of *Granville Sharp's Canon*, 830–32.

always be possible. Therefore, it is incumbent upon the exegete to ensure that an explanation of the text reflects recognition of these elements.[17]

Luke 4:21 provides an example of how Greek speakers indicated deixis with regard to articular nouns:

σήμερον πεπλήρωται ἡ γραφὴ αὕτη ἐν τοῖς ὠσὶν ὑμῶν.

Today this scripture has been fulfilled in your ears.

As noted above, grammarians have argued that the article sometimes performs a deictic, or pointing, function.[18] The theory presented here has argued that this is not the case. In addition to the fact that this misunderstands the article's function, when Greek speakers wanted to perform this task, other parts of speech were employed. As with English TH- items, the function of the near demonstrative οὗτος was to direct the recipient to the information necessary for identification.

In the example above, both nouns in this clause, γραφή and ὠσίν, are characterized as concrete. With regard to γραφή, Jesus is referring to something that he wishes to characterize not only as concrete, but also as definite. Therefore, he directs the recipients to the information necessary for identification by employing the demonstrative αὕτη. By employing the article, he characterizes scripture as something concrete, as belonging to experience of an actual thing or a specific instance. By employing the demonstrative αὕτη, he directs the recipients to the information necessary for a definite identification. This is information that the speaker and recipients share in common, and is therefore available to the recipients and recoverable. Identification is not based on the speaker's seeing only. As a result, on the one hand the article characterizes the head term as

---

[17] In another instance of emphasis on less salient features, commentaries generally devote considerable space to matters such as the inclusion or non-inclusion of *sister*, the fact that there is no mention of *father*, or general conversations about familial relationships. Such matters are indeed germane to a discussion of the text. As noted above, the writer himself characterizes them as *more salient*. However, the amount of attention they receive is disproportional to that given to the element of the text that the speaker/writer indicates is most salient: *the one who does the will of God*. If the speaker/writer deliberately draws the attention of the recipient to this element, so should the commentator. See for example Marcus, *Mark 1–8*, 276–77, 285–87; Guelich, *Mark*, 182–86; Edwards, *Mark*, 124–26; France, *Mark*, 179–80. Collins does, in fact, draw more acute attention to the relative clause, but does not give justification: "The Markan scene, then, functions not primarily to record an incident in the life of Jesus but to make the point that doing the will of God is more important than one's relationships with mothers, brothers, and sisters," *Mark*, 236. However, like the others, she devotes a disproportionate amount of space to a discussion of family relationships.

[18] See Wallace, *Greek Grammar*, 217–21.

something whose identity is based on an orientation to the speaker. On the other hand, by employing the demonstrative, he is saying to the recipients, "You can see this as well." This structure is used to characterize the head term as both concrete and definite, with each element contributing in a different, unique way.

Just as the demonstrative pronoun creates a sense of definiteness, so does the personal pronoun. In the group τοῖς ὠσὶν ὑμῶν, *ears* is characterized as concrete, as belonging to the experience of actual things. The genitive pronoun indicates that this class is being restricted by the fact that it is the possession of the recipients. This is what provides the sense of definiteness. Thus, *ears* are both concrete and definite. Once again, both elements, the article and the pronoun, function differently through their unique contributions to the group, yet combine to produce a single sense.

John 1:1 involves one of the most debated non-uses of the article in the New Testament:

Ἐν ἀρχῇ ἦν ὁ λόγος, καὶ ὁ λόγος ἦν πρὸς τὸν θεόν, καὶ θεὸς ἦν ὁ λόγος.

In the beginning was the Word, and the Word was with God, and the Word was God.

It is an apt metaphor to say that a sea of ink that has been spilled analyzing the opening statement of the Fourth Gospel. Historically, Colwell's assertion that definite pre-verbal predicate nominatives generally do not have the article has, more than anything else, shaped the debate of the grammatical interpretation of the passage. However, as Porter notes, "this still begs the question of what a definite noun is."[19] The present theory of the article's function has consistently maintained that definiteness in Greek is indicated by discourse features other than the article and the head term; it is not an inherent or assumed quality of the head term. The definitions of articular and anarthrous constructions presented here will be applied to the question of how this important passage is to be interpreted.

John begins his Gospel with the words Ἐν ἀρχῇ, which are generally believed to be a conscious allusion to Gen. 1:1 (LXX).[20] If this is the case, then the characterization of ἀρχῇ is not that of the author of John, but the translator(s) of Genesis. This introduces questions of translation from

---

[19] Porter, *Idioms*, 109, footnote 2.
[20] Westcott, *John*, 2; Brown, *John*, 4; Carson, *John*, 113–14; Beasley-Murray, *John*, 10; Keener, *John. Vol. 1*, 365.

Hebrew to Greek that are beyond the scope of this work. However, we may suggest that abstract characterization in both Gen. 1:1 and John 1:1 serves the discourse function of grounding. The function of Ἐν ἀρχῇ is not to direct the recipient to a specific point in time in an absolute sense. Rather, it establishes a general point of reference that provides the background for what follows. The translation *in the beginning*, with the use of the definite article, must be viewed as accommodation to English. Any notion of definiteness must not be read back into the Greek.[21]

The nominal group ὁ λόγος occurs three times. In all three instances, it is characterized as concrete, as belonging to experience as an actual thing. While λόγος, *word*, alone is an abstract notion, the article characterizes λόγος as concrete, as someone or something associated with a specific instance (ultimately identified as Jesus). Of course, there is more to this characterization. ὁ λόγος also is a characterization of God's revelation, embodied in the human form of Jesus. It is not God's revealed word in a general or abstract sense, but in the sense of a specific instance. In terms of the discourse, ὁ λόγος is a *figure* in the discourse, and as such is a *more salient* element or participant. In the staging of the discourse, this participant plays a more prominent role.

Of the two instances of θεός, the first is articular, while the second is not. The introduction of this participant with the article, and the subsequent anarthrous reference, illustrates the previous assertion that the Greek article is not used for participant tracking the way the English article is. As stated earlier, one of the difficulties in treating θεός is the question of whether or not it is being used as a proper name. Robertson argues that θεός, "like proper names, may use the article where we do not need it in English."[22] Despite this, the structure of the two clauses suggests that the shift from articular to anarthrous θεός represents a conscious, deliberate move on the part of the writer. As always, each of these characterizations represents a meaningful choice. In the first instance, θεός is characterized as concrete, as belonging to experience of an actual person. This may be motivated in part because the author has in mind God the person, the God of Israel and the creator of all things. For the purpose of the discourse, both ὁ λόγος and ὁ θεός are *figures*. Both are salient participants and stand in the foreground. The writer situates ὁ λόγος in terms of a

---

[21] Contra Robertson, *Grammar*, 791; Wallace, *Greek Grammar*, 247. Characterization as *abstract* is not compatible with a sense of definiteness.

[22] Robertson, *Grammar*, 758.

spatial relationship with ὁ θεός; *the Word was with God.* This relationship is foundational for the recurring theme in the Fourth Gospel that the Word is the only one who has seen God (1:18; 3:31–32; 5:19; 6:46; 8:38; 17:5).

Conversely, in the next instance θεός is characterized as abstract, as not belonging to experience of an actual person. Because of this, we must reject Colwell's assumption that θεός is definite. It is neither definite nor concrete. This is because θεός now performs a different function in the discourse. In the first instance, the writer identified ὁ λόγος in terms of location. Now he makes a declaration regarding the nature of ὁ λόγος. Without the article, θεός must be interpreted in the abstract sense: god, deity, pertaining to divine. Many modern interpreters understand the author's statement as an affirmation of Jesus' divinity, so that θεός is interpreted in a *qualitative* sense; ὁ λόγος possessed the qualities of θεός. This is essentially correct, because the absence of the article indicates that the author has characterized θεός as abstract, not definite or indefinite.[23] However, many take exception to this interpretation. Carson writes:

> A long string of writers has argued that because *theos*, 'God', here has no article, John is not referring to God as a specific being, but to mere qualities of 'God-ness'. The Word, they say, was not God, but divine. This will not do. There is a perfectly serviceable word in Greek for 'divine' (namely *theios*).[24]

On the one hand, Carson's critique is correct in that "divine" is too weak.[25] However, it does not take into account the author's love of word play, as well as the significance of using θεός specifically.[26] For John, θεῖος will not do. By choosing the wording he does, the author makes a statement about the divinity of ὁ λόγος in a qualitative sense, while also making a connection in the personal sense with the God who created all things in Gen. 1:1. The previous use of the articular θεός, along with the allusion to Gen. 1:1 by means of Ἐν ἀρχῇ, sets up this word play. In addition, the choice of characterization moves the anarthrous θεός into the background of the discourse. θεός is no longer a figure but is now part of the ground. The interpretation of *abstract* characterization and *backgrounding* reinforce one another and so reveal the function of the distinct yet complementary articular and anarthrous constructions. In this way, the author

---

[23] Keener rejects the "weaker sense of merely 'divine,'" but affirms that "the nuance must be slightly different from 'God' elsewhere in this verse... However, the distinction is clearer from context than from grammar," *John, Vol. 1*, 373–74.

[24] Carson, *John*, 117. See also Beasley-Murray, *John*, 10–11.

[25] So also Brown, *John*, 5.

[26] Consider, for example, John's use of πνεῦμα as both *wind* and *spirit* in 3:8.

does not ask the reader to choose between *God* and *divine*. Rather, he reinforces both. As is often the case with John, the limitations of the English
language prevent us from fully capturing the word play.[27] To capitalize
God is essentially to use it as a proper name, while lower-case *god* better captures the notion of *deity* in the more abstract sense. While John's
purpose is likely *both/and* rather than *either/or*, the limitations of English
expression do not allow the translator to render this in a manner that fully
corresponds to the author's characterization.

To illustrate further this emphasis on abstract quality, we observe that
σάρξ does not have the article in John 1:14, Καὶ ὁ λόγος σάρξ ἐγένετο. Just
as θεός earlier, σάρξ is characterized as abstract, rather than concrete. This
is not to argue that the Word did not take on literal flesh, that he did is
another of the author's theses. Rather, he has simply chosen to characterize σάρξ as an abstract quality just as he chose to characterize θεός as an
abstraction in 1:1.

Rom 8:24 provides another opportunity to examine the shift from articular to anarthrous with regard to a single element:

τῇ γὰρ ἐλπίδι ἐσώθημεν· ἐλπὶς δὲ βλεπομένη οὐκ ἔστιν ἐλπίς

... for in hope we were saved, but hope being seen is not hope

Paul uses the word ἐλπίς, *hope*, three times in this passage. In the first
instance, it is articular. The second and third are anarthrous. In the first
instance, hope is characterized as concrete, as belonging to experience of
an actual thing or specific instance. This is because the hope Paul is identifying is the concrete, specific hope that Christians have in their future
eternal salvation that will be realized when all of creation is redeemed,
which he mentions in the previous clause.[28] Therefore, he modifies ἐλπίς
with the article, since it is something concrete. As always, though this
characterization is based on association with the aforementioned resurrection, the article does not direct the recipient to this identification; it is
a matter of inference.[29] The second and third instances do not have this

---

[27] As with ἄνωθεν in 3:3.

[28] Fitzmyer, *Romans*, 514–15; Schreiner, *Romans*, 439–40; Byrne, *Romans*, 263–65; Moo,
Romans, 521–22; Dunn, *Romans 1–8*; 475–76. Commentators are generally more interested
in the case of τῇ ἐλπίδι than the presence of the article.

[29] Jewett writes, "The expression with a definite article, τῇ γὰρ ἐλπίδι ('for in the hope'),
refers to the hope just mentioned in the preceding verse, thus justifying the translation 'in
this hope,' that is, the hope of fulfilled adoption as children of God and the final redemption of the creation," *Romans*. 520. Jewett is correct, but not for the reason he implies.
The use of the article does not "refer" the reader back to the aforementioned redemption

hope in view. They are not characterized as concrete because they are not tied to a specific instance. Rather, Paul has shifted to the idea of hope as a simple abstraction. *Hope*, in its abstract sense, is not *hope* if it is able to see its object. Thus, both are anarthrous. From a discourse perspective, *hope* in the specifically Christian sense that is based on anticipation of the resurrection is more salient. Conversely, *hope* in the abstract sense is less salient. It is a part of the grounding of the discourse. To employ a metaphor from photography, it is a part of the less focused background that draws attention to the element that is in focus, causing it to "pop out." In this instance, the element that "pops out" is the articular *hope*. Once again, we observe the use of the article to position elements in the discourse in terms of grounding. The implications of these observations cannot be understated, and will be further illustrated and expanded below. For the moment, one important implication must be made explicit. Previous grammarians have spoken of the article *with* substantives. The article is not attached to substantives; it, in a sense, "creates" substantives by characterizing the head term as concrete. The choice of this categorization not only says something about the element itself, but also performs a function at the level of discourse.

The complementary functions of characterization and discourse role are evidenced in 1 Cor 7:1–4, where the same items appear as both anarthrous and articular:

Περὶ δὲ ὧν ἐγράψατε, καλὸν ἀνθρώπῳ γυναικὸς μὴ ἅπτεσθαι· διὰ δὲ τὰς πορνείας ἕκαστος τὴν ἑαυτοῦ γυναῖκα ἐχέτω καὶ ἑκάστη τὸν ἴδιον ἄνδρα ἐχέτω. τῇ γυναικὶ ὁ ἀνὴρ τὴν ὀφειλὴν ἀποδιδότω, ὁμοίως δὲ καὶ ἡ γυνὴ τῷ ἀνδρί. ἡ γυνὴ τοῦ ἰδίου σώματος οὐκ ἐξουσιάζει ἀλλὰ ὁ ἀνήρ, ὁμοίως δὲ καὶ ὁ ἀνὴρ τοῦ ἰδίου σώματος οὐκ ἐξουσιάζει ἀλλὰ ἡ γυνή.

But concerning such things you wrote, "It is good for a person not to touch a woman." But because of sexual immorality each (man) must have his woman and each (woman) her own man. The man must give the duty to the woman, likewise the woman also to the man. The woman does not exercise authority over her own body, but the man. Likewise, the man does not exercise authority over his own body, but the woman.[30]

---

of creation; it is not anaphoric. Instead, Paul assumes a shared body of knowledge with his readers that allows him to reasonably expect them to draw an inferential connection between τῇ γὰρ ἐλπίδι and what came before. The translation *in this hope* makes explicit what Paul implies.

[30] The translation provided above is admittedly pedantic. Its purpose is simply to render the Greek in a "literal" manner for the purpose of discussion.

The opening statement of this section, Περὶ δὲ ὧν ἐγράψατε, *but concerning such things you wrote*, is generally recognized as marking a transition point in the letter. Paul moves from a discussion of matters that have been reported to him to questions contained in a letter sent to him from the Corinthian church.[31] This is followed by what many believe is Paul's quotation of a Corinthians slogan, καλὸν ἀνθρώπῳ γυναικὸς μὴ ἅπτεσθαι, "*It is good for a person not to touch a woman.*"[32] As such, the characterization is not that of the writer. He is passing the saying on in the form in which he received it. Nevertheless, the question of characterization may still be analyzed.

In this statement, both ἄνθρωπος and γυνή are anarthrous. Neither is characterized as concrete, as belonging to experience of actual things or as a specific instance. Instead, they are presented as abstract. This type of characterization is consistent with use in a slogan or aphorism. The elements *man* and *woman* are presented in the most general of terms; there is no indication that the referents belong to experience as actual people or specific instances. This may also explain the use of the more general ἄνθρωπος as opposed to ἀνήρ. Thus, the translation *it is good for man not to touch woman*, despite sounding archaic, more accurately captures the abstract sense of the Greek characterization. Since *touch a woman* is a euphemism for sexual intercourse, we might use an English euphemism to produce the same effect: *it is good for man not to sleep with woman*. However, while this may capture the sense of the Greek, it is too jarring for an English speaker. For this reason, one might employ the familiar English euphemism and translate the slogan as *it is good for a man not to sleep with a woman*.

The reason Paul disagrees with the Corinthians position is διὰ δὲ τὰς πορνείας, *because of illicit sexual behaviors*. The apostle characterizes this item as concrete. This characterization, along with the use of the plural,

---

[31] Barrett, *First Corinthians*, 153–54; Fee, *First Corinthians*, 266–67; Thiselton, *First Corinthians*, 483–84; Garland, *1 Corinthians*, 242. Ciampa and Rosner treat 4:18–7:40 as a single unit that addresses matters of sexual immorality and purity, *First Corinthians*, 189–92.

[32] Fee, *First Corinthians*, 272–77. For a full discussion of the pros and cons of this view, see: Thiselton, *First Corinthians*, 487–500; Smith, "Slogans in 1 Corinthians." The translation and analysis above proceeds from the view that the slogan is a general euphemism for sexual intercourse as opposed to marriage, Fee, *First Corinthians*, 274; Thiselton, *First Corinthians*, 500. Ciampa and Rosner present an interpretation that is in general agreement but more nuanced, *First Corinthians*, 273–78; also Roy E. Ciampa, "Revisiting the Euphemism in 1 Corinthians 7.1."

may be interpreted as indicating that actual, specific instances of this behavior are in view. This is the view taken by Thiselton:

> Indeed, the definite article τάς, while technically it may qualify any abstract noun, here seems likely to imply a specific allusion to the cases of irregular physical intimacy which he has identified in 5:1–5, 6:12–20, and possibly indirectly in 6:9–10.[33]

However, the function of the article, as defined above, is not to characterize the head term as an actual thing or specific instance in an absolute sense. Rather, specific instances are instances of *such things* that do happen in time and space, without indication that actual occurrences are in view. If the referent is an actual thing or specific instance in a real or absolute sense, there must be additional discourse elements to indicate this. Thiselton's argument seems to grow out of a view of the article's function that is similar to Wallace's: that the deixis of the article directs the recipient backward into the text. We have already argued that this is not the case, nor is it necessary. Immoral and deviant sexual behavior (from a Judeo/Christian point of view) was commonplace, and to a greater or lesser degree acceptable and expected, in Greco/Roman culture.[34] For Gentile Christians in particular, monogamy would represent a fundamental shift in moral priorities. While deviant behaviors previously mentioned in the letter would be included in this class, and the author may indeed have had them in mind, it is not the function of the article to direct the readers to this identification. As is always the case with the article, the information necessary for identification is oriented to the writer. It is he who provides this information to the recipients, who must accept his seeing as the basis of identification. The characterization of the head term also indicates greater saliency. It is διὰ δὲ τὰς πορνείας, *because of illicit sexual behaviors*, that Paul gives the instruction that follows.

There are four instances of both ἡ γυνή and ὁ ἀνήρ in 7:2–4; every instance is articular. While these items are characterized as concrete, there is no indication that Paul has specific individuals in view, individuals who could be identified by name and face; they are simply *such a woman* and *such a man*. Their identity is oriented to the writer. Paul does not indicate, "You know who I am talking about." Instead, at each instance he indicates,

---

[33] Thiselton, *First Corinthians*, 501, emphasis his. See also Ciampa and Rosner, *First Corinthians*, 276, though they do not argue from the presence of the article.

[34] Ciampa and Rosner, *First Corinthians*, 275–76. See also Ferguson, *Backgrounds of Early Christianity*, 63–64, 70–71.

"I am talking about someone else." Thus, the writer supplies the information necessary for identifying these two participants, which the audience must accept. The characterization allows the apostle to hold out ἡ γυνή and ὁ ἀνήρ for the recipients' examination as such things that exist. In this respect, they are figures in the discourse and therefore more salient.

The noun ὀφειλή is generally classified as an abstract noun. Apart from modification by the article, it would be interpreted in this abstract sense as simply *obligation* or *duty*. By employing the article, the writer characterizes it as concrete, as a specific instance of *obligation* or *duty*. In this case, it is the obligation of conjugal rights that, according to Paul, husbands and wives should reasonably be willing to render to one another.[35] This, too, is salient in the discourse.

Lastly, Paul twice employs the articular τοῦ ἰδίου σώματος in reference to both the wife and the husband's body. As with previous examples, Paul is not referring to *body* in the abstract sense, but the concrete sense. Husbands and wives have bodies and each spouse exercises authority over the other's body. Like ἡ γυνή and ὁ ἀνήρ, Paul is not referring to a specific, identifiable *body* in the real world, but *such a body*. Again, like ἡ γυνή and ὁ ἀνήρ, the characterization presents the referent in such a way that it may be, in effect, looked at and examined by the recipients. *The woman's own body* and *the man's own body* are both salient elements of the discourse.

1 Tim 4:12–13 provides an opportunity to compare and contrast elements that are anarthrous with others that are articular:

> Μηδείς σου τῆς νεότητος καταφρονείτω, ἀλλὰ τύπος γίνου τῶν πιστῶν ἐν λόγῳ, ἐν ἀναστροφῇ, ἐν ἀγάπῃ, ἐν πίστει, ἐν ἁγνείᾳ. ἕως ἔρχομαι πρόσεχε τῇ ἀναγνώσει, τῇ παρακλήσει, τῇ διδασκαλίᾳ.

> No one must look down upon your youth, but become an example of the faithful in word, in conduct, in love, in faith, in purity. Until I come, devote yourself to reading, to encouragement, to teaching.

Paul begins by stating that no one must look down upon σου τῆς νεότητος, *your youth*. Timothy's youth is characterized as concrete. This choice of characterization does not appear to be motivated by a desire or need associated with the sense of *youth* itself. Timothy's age could have been characterized in the abstract: *your youthfulness*. The choice of characterization may reflect the discourse function of σου τῆς νεότητος. Timothy's youthful-

---

[35] Fee, *First Corinthians*, 279–80.

ness is not a part of the ground of the discourse; it does not merely set the scene. It is a salient element of the discourse.

Paul next exhorts Timothy to become a τύπος, *an example*. This is characterized as abstract, as are the following qualities that Timothy is instructed to exemplify. Admittedly, this presents a challenge to the matter of discourse *grounding* and *salience*. To argue that these elements are a part of the background and are less salient might appear to run counter to the importance the reader instinctively places on them. After all, one might argue, instructions on moral and spiritual character must be more salient, not less. However, in light of the co-text, interpreting these elements as part of the grounding of the discourse makes sense. In v. 11, Paul instructs Timothy to Παράγγελλε ταῦτα καὶ δίδασκε, *command these things and teach.* Both of these injunctions address matters of the corporate service in which Timothy will engage. Scorn of his youth will compromise his ability to engage in this activity. In the following clause, Paul instructs Timothy to commit himself to devote himself *to reading, to encouragement, to teaching,* τῇ ἀναγνώσει, τῇ παρακλήσει, τῇ διδασκαλίᾳ. These three items are also matters of corporate service. Note that all three are articular. The interpreter should not conclude that matters of moral and spiritual discipline are unimportant to Paul *in general.* Instead, when read in terms of grounding and salience, the text reveals that Paul's main concern is with matters of corporate worship and Timothy's effectiveness as a minister in these situations.[36] For the purposes of this specific discourse, moral and spiritual discipline, which is necessary for effective ministry, is the ground upon which Timothy's own effectiveness as a young minister is based. Such matters are not unimportant *in principle,* but with regard to the present discourse, they are less salient. They are the supporting material that provides the backdrop of a discourse on the various duties that Timothy, a young man, must effectively perform. Paul's emphasis on moral and spiritual discipline is not merely for Timothy's personal benefit, but for the sake of effective ministry. The choice of characterization by means of the use and non-use of the article is instructive in terms of the grounding of the discourse and salience.[37]

---

[36] See also v. 14 where the gift Timothy received when the elders laid hands on him is articular: τοῦ ἐν σοὶ χαρίσματος. This is also a reference to a ministry element.

[37] It should be noted that the absence and presence of the article in the two lists respectively is generally passed by without acknowledgement in commentaries. Knight, by contrast, notes that "λόγος is used here without the article in the sense of 'speech,'" *The Pastoral Epistles,* 206. This is his only reference to the article in reference to either of the two lists.

The characterization of τῶν πιστῶν has been addressed in chapter 7.2. *The Article with Adjectives.*[38] By employing the article, the writer indicates that the quality of *faithfulness* is the identifying characteristic of this class. He indicates that he is providing the recipients with this information for them to use for the purpose of identifying this group of people. With regard to its discourse function, these participants are not a part of the ground, but function as figures. This is consistent with the salient elements of the discourse. The presence and involvement of τῶν πιστῶν is implicit in Paul's focus on corporate service.

In the discourse on faith and works found in Jas 2:18, we observe that the writer characterizes *faith* and *works* first as abstract, then as concrete:

σὺ πίστιν ἔχεις, κἀγὼ ἔργα ἔχω· δεῖξόν μοι τὴν πίστιν σου χωρὶς τῶν ἔργων, κἀγώ σοι δείξω ἐκ τῶν ἔργων μου τὴν πίστιν.

You have faith, and I have works. Show me your faith apart from works, and I will show you my faith from works.

As the seen in the text, James shifts from anarthrous to articular constructions in his characterization of πίστις and ἔργον. In the first instance of each of these items, James is speaking of the two classes, *faith* and *works*, as abstract ideas. Neither is associated with a specific instance, so James does not characterize them as concrete. This characterization performs the discourse function of setting the scene for what follows. As abstract notions of *faith* and *works*, these two elements ground the discourse and serve as the background for what follows.

In the succeeding clauses both *faith* and *works* are characterized as concrete. This is because each is associated with something that is identified specifically with the writer and with the hypothetical interlocutor. In the first instance of the articular πίστις, *faith*, it is not faith as an abstraction, but a specific instance of faith that is the "possession" of the interlocutor: *your faith*. The same is true of *works*. James is not speaking of the abstract notion of works, but works that are, by implication, a specific instance of works that should have been, but are not being, performed by the interlocutor. In the second instance of articular πίστις, it is again a specific

---

[38] Knight notes the use of the article in this instance: "With the definite [*sic*] article (τῶν) it designates the specific believers among whom Timothy lives," *The Pastoral Epistles*, 205. This conclusion is unlikely. To limit the class to those "among whom Timothy lives" is beyond the scope of the article's function. If Paul wanted to identify the believers with this level of specificity, he would have included other elements that would have performed that function.

instance of *faith*. This time, it is the faith that James possesses. *Works* also
are a specific instance: they are the works that James does indeed perform. Each of these instances of *faith* and *works* is presented as a salient
element of the discourse.

As is always the case, the function of the article is to characterize the
head terms as belonging to experience of actual things. This does not
mean that actual instances in a definite sense are in view. If the author
wished to indicate to the recipients that definite examples of faith and
works were in view, additional elements would be necessary to indicate
such further specification.

James follows this in verse 19, stating:

> σὺ πιστεύεις ὅτι εἷς ἐστιν ὁ θεός, καλῶς ποιεῖς· καὶ τὰ δαιμόνια πιστεύουσιν καὶ
> φρίσσουσιν.
>
> You believe that God is one, you do well. The demons also believe and they
> shudder.

James informs his interlocutor that he does well to believe that God is
one. However, simple belief is not enough. Even demons do this. The
item, *demons*, is also articular: τὰ δαιμόνια. From a discourse perspective,
it is not absolutely necessary to characterize a participant as concrete.
Demons could be characterized as abstract and still be presented as something that *believes* and *shudders*. However, by characterizing them as concrete, as belonging to experience of actual things, they function as figures
in the discourse; they are salient. The reader must perform a self-examination and determine if his or her faith is merely the faith of demons. As
Davids writes, "A faith which cannot go beyond this level is worse than
useless."[39]

3. The Article with Proper Nouns

The use of the article with names is arguably the most unusual for English
speakers. Beginning Greek students often can only shake their heads when
they are forced to translate a name as *the Jesus* or *the John*. While such
pedantic translations may make one smile, the darker side of the issue lies
in the fact that it has proven to be the most notoriously difficult usage to
comprehensively define. As with attempts to define the article's function

---

[39] Davids, *James*, 126.

in general, treatments of this feature have focused exclusively on matters of syntax, with varying results. Scholars are forced to acknowledge that there are too many exceptions and variations in patterns for any single theory to account for every instance. For example, one oft cited function of the article is to indicate the case of indeclinable names.[40] Yet examples abound of anarthrous indeclinable names whose case must be implied. To date, no comprehensive theory of the article's usage with names has yet to be offered.

Even within the framework of the theory here proposed, this usage seems, at first, unnecessary. A name is not an abstraction; it is associated with a specific instance, that being the individual so named. Speaking in English terms, each instance is definite, in that it identifies an actual individual. It is arguable that a name does not need to be characterized as belonging to experience of an actual thing because names, by their nature, name actual things. To use the article is superfluous.

One important aspect of the article's function may help to solve this riddle. The function of the article is to *characterize* the head. It is not used to present something as an actual condition of reality, but to *characterize* it as such. When this characterization is understood in terms of *grounding* and *salience*, the characterization may be understood as a function of the discourse. Porter suggests that one of the article's functions with names is to call attention to the name.[41] Based on the theory outlined above, this seems like the most likely answer. It is noteworthy that in both direct speech (including letters) and reported speech, when a speaker or writer addresses a person by name, he or she does not use the article. The same is true of self-reference (for example, Tertius does not use the article to name himself in Rom. 16:22).

This proposed function runs counter to the previous work of Heimerdinger and Levinsohn, and later Speilmann, who argue that the absence of the article with proper names represents a marked form and indicates salience. It is worthwhile to revisit their theory. Heimerdinger and Levinsohn write: "The unmarked way of mentioning a person by name is with the article. The omission of the article indicates that attention is being drawn to the person being named."[42] By arguing that the anarthrous construction represents the marked form, they argue that this form,

---

[40] Robertson, *Grammar*, 760; Moulton and Turner, *Syntax*, 167–68; Wallace, *Greek Grammar*, 240–41; Porter, *Idioms*, 107.

[41] Porter, *Idioms*, 107.

[42] Heimerdinger and Levinsohn, "The Use of the Definite Article," 17–18.

... draws particular attention to the person in question at that point in the narrative. The purpose of omitting the article frequently is to distinguish the person from other participants or even other possible participants and so the implication is that the person being named is "that one rather than some other".[43]

They believe that this rule explains why a participant's name is anarthrous when first mentioned and is then articular in subsequent occurrences:

> When a participant is first introduced into a story, the author almost always spotlights his initial appearance on stage so that his presence is clearly registered by the audience ... Subsequently, once the participant has entered into the story, he can be referred to as a known factor with the other possibilities already ruled out, and the article is therefore retained.[44]

In conjunction with this usage, the author's argue that the presence or absence of the article performs the discourse function of marking *salience*, which they define as, "attention being drawn to a specific participant."[45] They argue that the article is dropped in order to highlight certain characters: "Highlighting, however, occurs when one character or another becomes salient at various other points in the story, too,"[46] not just when they first enter.

The function of the article proposed in the current work argues essentially the opposite of Heimerdinger and Levinsohn's proposal. We would expect the article to indicate that the name so modified is more salient, not less. However, this may explain Heimerdinger and Levinsohn's observation that participants are often first introduced with an articular form. First, as noted many times above, when a speaker or writer employs the article, he or she indicates to the recipient "I am telling you about something else." The article is employed to indicate that the speaker or writer is providing the information necessary for identification. When a participant is introduced into the discourse, the speaker or writer employs the article to signal to the reader, "I am providing information for identification. I'm telling you about someone else." An additional actor is brought onto the stage. Second, at the point at which an articular participant is introduced into the discourse, he or she is salient. The speaker or writer, at least for the moment, draws attention to that participant. He or she is characterized as a figure. From this point on, the participant will move

---

43 Heimerdinger and Levinsohn, "The Use of the Definite Article," 18.
44 Heimerdinger and Levinsohn, "The Use of the Definite Article," 18.
45 Heimerdinger and Levinsohn, "The Use of the Definite Article," 20.
46 Heimerdinger and Levinsohn, "The Use of the Definite Article," 20.

from foreground to background as the needs and designs of the discourse dictate. This is based on the subjective characterization of the speaker or writer.

In terms of figure and ground, the participant identified by an articular proper name is a figure in the discourse. He or she stands in the foreground, at the front of the stage, as it were. By contrast, participants who are identified by anarthrous names are a part of the ground or background. They stand at the back of the stage. Participants identified with articular names are more salient; those identified by anarthrous names are less salient. However, these are not static conditions. The ebb and flow of a discourse will necessitate that certain participants be moved from front to back. Foregrounding and salience are a matter of individual moments in the discourse. Participants are not prominent or salient in discourse in a static sense; they are prominent or salient at various points in the discourse. The speaker or writer moves them forward or backward at his or her discretion based on subjective discourse priorities.

The best way to illustrate this usage is to analyze a substantial portion of discourse in which the grounding of participants may be illustrated. First, consider a portion of the transfiguration of Jesus in Matt 17:1–4:

> Καὶ μεθ᾽ ἡμέρας ἓξ παραλαμβάνει ὁ Ἰησοῦς τὸν Πέτρον καὶ Ἰάκωβον καὶ Ἰωάννην τὸν ἀδελφὸν αὐτοῦ καὶ ἀναφέρει αὐτοὺς εἰς ὄρος ὑψηλὸν κατ᾽ ἰδίαν. καὶ μετεμορφώθη ἔμπροσθεν αὐτῶν, καὶ ἔλαμψεν τὸ πρόσωπον αὐτοῦ ὡς ὁ ἥλιος, τὰ δὲ ἱμάτια αὐτοῦ ἐγένετο λευκὰ ὡς τὸ φῶς. Καὶ ἰδοὺ ὤφθη αὐτοῖς Μωϋσῆς καὶ Ἠλίας συλλαλοῦντες μετ᾽ αὐτοῦ. ἀποκριθεὶς δὲ ὁ Πέτρος εἶπεν τῷ Ἰησοῦ· κύριε, καλόν ἐστιν ἡμᾶς ὧδε εἶναι· εἰ θέλεις, ποιήσω ὧδε τρεῖς σκηνάς, σοὶ μίαν καὶ Μωϋσεῖ μίαν καὶ Ἠλίᾳ μίαν.

> And after six days Jesus took Peter and James and John his brother and led them into a high mountain alone. And he was transformed in front of them, and his face shone like the sun, and his garments become bright as light. And behold, they saw Moses and Elijah speaking with him! Then Peter said to Jesus, "Lord, it is good for us to be here. If you want, I will make three tents here, one for you, one for Moses, and one for Elijah."

In this instance, the grounding of the participants is relatively easy to explain. Only Jesus and Peter are identified with the article.[47] They are

---

[47] Nolland notes the absence of the article with James and John, as well as its presence with Peter. He argues that this "is likely to highlight the continuing role of Peter from the preceding chapter; it also prepares for his distinct role later in the account," *Matthew*, 698. This type of anaphoric and kataphoric interpretation is not consistent with the article's function.

the most salient participants; they essentially stand at the front of the stage. In this instance, they are also the only two who speak. The other participants, James, John, Moses, and Elijah, are part of the grounding of the scene. Their function is to provide the backdrop to Jesus and Peter and set the scene for their interaction.

In the parallel account in Mark 9:2–8, Peter, James, and John are all identified with the article. In the parallel in Luke 9:28–36, the three lack the article until later in the narrative. Beginning in v. 32, Luke records:

> ὁ δὲ Πέτρος καὶ οἱ σὺν αὐτῷ ἦσαν βεβαρημένοι ὕπνῳ· διαγρηγορήσαντες δὲ εἶδον τὴν δόξαν αὐτοῦ καὶ τοὺς δύο ἄνδρας τοὺς συνεστῶτας αὐτῷ. καὶ ἐγένετο ἐν τῷ διαχωρίζεσθαι αὐτοὺς ἀπ᾽ αὐτοῦ εἶπεν ὁ Πέτρος πρὸς τὸν Ἰησοῦν· ἐπιστάτα, καλόν ἐστιν ἡμᾶς ὧδε εἶναι,

> Peter and the ones with him were in a deep sleep. And waking up they saw his glory and the two men standing with him. And when they departed from him, Peter said, "Master, it is good to be here,"

Each author's use of the article may be explained in terms of his subjective choice regarding the staging of the participants. For Mark, James and John are not a part of the grounding of the discourse. He chooses to include them at the front of the stage with Peter and Jesus. In his subjective interpretation of the scene, even though they have no dialogue, they are still salient. One might hypothesize that, for Mark, the fact of their apostleship, as well as their singular presence for this formative event, justifies their more prominent role.

For Luke, Peter enters the scene in the background. Along with James and John, his initial function is to ground or set the scene. As the narrative progresses, Peter is moved from the background to the foreground, at which time he delivers his lines. To continue the stage metaphor, each writer is like the director of a play. Each has his own priorities and sense of staging. One may differ from the other in his subjective view of which participants are more or less salient, or when they should be positioned in the foreground or background of the scene.[48]

---

[48] This use of the article is the closest that speakers or writers come to an "idiomatic" usage, such as Funk and others have argued. However, it is not in the sense that he suggests. Greek speakers understood that the article modified the head term in a meaningful way, and that the characterization it produced performed a pragmatic function in discourse. Thus, subjectivity on the part of the speaker or writer was a matter of subjective *characterization through the use of the article*. It was more than mere personal preference in terms of expression or style, such that the actual presence or absence of the article could be viewed immaterial for indicating the characterization of the head term.

4. CONCLUSION

The function of the Greek article is understood best when it is considered in terms of both characterization and discourse function. Each of these functions informs the other. On the one hand, as proposed in the definition of its function, the article is used to characterize the head term as concrete, as belonging to experience of an actual thing or person, or a specific instance. With regard to nouns, the non-use of the article characterizes the head term as abstract, as not belonging to experience of an actual thing or person, or a specific instance. This categorization is subjective, and orients the identity of the referent to the speaker or writer. There is no indication that the speaker and the recipients share in common the information that is necessary for identifying the referent. On the contrary, by employing the article the speaker indicates that he or she is providing this information, upon which the recipient is dependent for identification.

The motivation for this characterization is often a matter of grounding or indicating salience. Anarthrous elements are employed to establish the ground of the discourse, against which the articular elements or figures are seen. Thus, articular elements are generally more salient than anarthrous elements. However, the matter of salience is not absolute, as if one element is not salient, while another is salient. It is a scale or cline of salience, with certain elements being more salient than others. Likewise, grounding is not an absolute state in discourse. Elements may be moved forward and backward in terms of grounding as the needs of the discourse and the subjective priorities of the speaker or writer demand.

The problem of the article with proper names has been, historically, the most perplexing of all articular structures. Attempts to describe its usage based on syntactical considerations have not produced consistent results. As with all other uses of the article, a functional view that addresses the meaningful effect the article has on the head is the best approach. It must first be recognized that the function of the article is for the purpose of characterization, even with proper names. When this characterization is understood as a function of grounding and salience in discourse, specific instances may be explained by a single, comprehensive description that accounts for all occurrences.

CHAPTER TEN

THE ARTICLE AS A STRUCTURAL ELEMENT

As stated earlier, the function of the article is as a deictic modifier within a nominal group. In addition to this, the flexibility of the Greek language allows for a great deal of variety in the composition of group structures and the article often plays a key role in their construction. The choices made by Greek speakers in the construction of these structures are not arbitrary, but meaningful. Recognizing the patterns of these structures will be helpful in understanding how Greek speakers organize and highlight information. This, in turn, will prove useful in both translation and exegesis.

Earlier, we briefly discussed Halliday's three metafunctions of language.[1] The textual metafunction is concerned with how the elements of language are used to "build up sequences of discourse, organizing the discursive flow and creating cohesion and continuity as it moves along."[2] An examination of how the article is employed to produce various structures belongs to the domain of the textual metafunction. However, this is not the end of its significance. These structures function in different ways in the communicative process. The concern of the ideational metafunction is the way language construes human experience.[3] Different structures construe experience in different ways which are significant and meaningful. Understanding how different structures function and their significance provides insight into meaning. At the same time language is construing human experience, it is also enacting personal and social relationships.[4] This is the domain of the interpersonal metafunction. A speaker or writer's choice of a particular structure expresses his or her appraisal of and attitude toward whoever is being addressed and the matter being talked about.[5] With regard to the article, understanding how it is used to produce distinctive structures and their significance is a tool for understanding how a speaker or writer is using language as both a means

---

[1] See chapter 2.1.
[2] Halliday, *Functional Grammar*, 30.
[3] Halliday, *Functional Grammar*, 29.
[4] Halliday, *Functional Grammar*, 29.
[5] Halliday, *Functional Grammar*, 29.

to construe human experience (the ideational metafunction) and enact personal relationships (the interpersonal metafunction).

When the article is employed within the nominal group, the most common structure is for the article to immediately precede the head term: ὁ λόγος. However, it is not uncommon for speakers and writers to insert other elements between the article and the head term. In these structures, the article and head term often delimit the boundaries of the nominal group. In some of these situations, elements that typically follow the head are moved forward, which may serve to draw greater attention to them. In other instances, these structures may function as marked forms that serve to give prominence to the group as a whole. With regard to the metafunctions of language, speakers or writers employ these structures to "build up sequences of discourse," which is the *textual* function; the structures name things and "construe them into categories," which is the *ideational* function; and they express an attitude toward the recipients and what is being said, which is the *interpersonal* function.[6] If, for example, a particular structure is associated with the higher rhetorical or literary style, it will impact the recipients' perception of the writer/speaker and the information grammaticalized in the text. This may in turn affect the potential that this information will be positively received and implemented by the recipients.

The following is an examination of various structures in which the article plays a critical role. Each structure will be analyzed to determine how information is organized and how this organization is used by the speaker or writers to highlight specific elements or groups.

1. Definers and Group Structures

Articular attributive structures have been traditionally defined solely on the basis of the position of the definer. In the so-called first attributive structure, the ordering of the elements is Article-Definer-Head.[7] In the

---

[6] Halliday, *Functional Grammar*, 29.

[7] For a discussion of attributive structure, see Porter, *Idioms*, 116–18. I have adapted the terminology for the purpose of the present work. For example, the terms used to describe the first attributive structure are generally article-adjective-noun (Wallace, *Greek Grammar*, 306) or article-adjective-substantive (Porter, *Idioms*, 117). However, other parts of speech may be employed to fill the adjective slot. While nouns are typically the head term, other parts of speech may fill this slot as well. The terminology I have employed indicates a functional element rather than a part of speech. Head = head term. A *definer* is "a modifier that attributes features or further defines the word it modifies. Common examples of

second attributive structure, the ordering of the elements is Article-Head-Article-Definer. While grammars take note of this distinction, there has been no significant treatment of how the choice of one structure over the other functions in discourse. As noted before, if choice and meaning are bound together, then this must be viewed as a meaningful choice.

In the production of text, a common function of the article is, in conjunction with the head term, to delimit the boundaries of a nominal group. As defined earlier, a nominal group is comprised of a head term and related modifiers. In the simplest form of the first attributive position, the head is modified by the article and a single definer, which may be an adjective, participle, or adverb. However, speakers and writers frequently separate the article from its head in order to bracket additional modifiers within the group, as seen in the following examples.

In Matt 12:35, the element in the definer position is an adjective:

> ὁ ἀγαθὸς ἄνθρωπος ἐκ τοῦ ἀγαθοῦ θησαυροῦ ἐκβάλλει ἀγαθά, καὶ ὁ πονηρὸς ἄνθρωπος ἐκ τοῦ πονηροῦ θησαυροῦ ἐκβάλλει πονηρά.
>
> *The good person* brings out good from *the good treasure*, and *the evil person* brings out evil from *the evil treasure*.

In this example, the article and the head delimit the boundaries of the nominal group. The two items bracket adjectives, which further define each head term, indicating that the referent is a subcategory of the class indicated by the head term.

In Rom 3:26, the element in the definer position is an adverb:

> τὴν ἔνδειξιν τῆς δικαιοσύνης αὐτοῦ ἐν τῷ νῦν καιρῷ[8]
>
> the evidence of his righteousness in *the present age*

In the second example, the article and head term bracket an adverb, which is also used to indicate that the referent is a subcategory of the class indicated by the head term. The item καιρῷ, when modified by the article, is characterized as something that belongs to experience of an actual thing, as a *time* or *age* that belongs to the reality of time and space. The adverb

---

definers are adjectives (both attributive and predicate structure) and appositional words and phrases." A *qualifier* is "a modifier that in some way limits or constrains the scope of the word it modifies. Common examples of qualifiers are words in the genitive and dative case." Definitions taken from the OpenText.org website, "Introduction to the Annotation Model." www.opentext.org/model/introduction.html.

[8] This expression, in each of the oblique cases, is very common in Paul. See also Rom. 8:18, 11:5; 2 Cor. 8:14; 1 Tim. 4:9; 2 Tim. 6:17; Titus 2:12.

indicates that the referent is a subclass of *time*, whose chief identifying characteristic is that it belongs to the time of *now*.

In Matt 3:7, the element in the definer position is a participle:

τίς ὑπέδειξεν ὑμῖν φυγεῖν ἀπὸ τῆς μελλούσης ὀργῆς;

Who told you to flee from *the coming wrath?*

In this example, *wrath* is also characterized as belonging to experience of an actual thing, or perhaps better, a specific instance. It is not wrath as an abstraction, but the wrath of God that will be revealed at a specific point in time and space. Since this is a future event, it is further defined by the participle as wrath that is *coming* or *about to be.*

In the New Testament, instances of the first attributive position outnumber the second by a significant majority. Using the OpenText.org Syntactically Analyzed Greek New Testament in the Logos Libronix Digital Library, it is possible to construct queries that will provide simple occurrence numbers for each book of the New Testament.[9]

The data reveals a clear preference for the first attributive structure among all the New Testament writers except John. Among the rest, Mark's usage reveals only a marginal preference for the first attributive structure, while all others prefer the first attributive by a substantial margin. In general, the New Testament writers prefer the first attributive structure by more than a 2:1 margin.[10] If the Gospel and letters of John, which may

---

[9] It must be noted that the results provided here, while essentially accurate, are not absolute due to various factors associated with this type of electronic corpus. The first qualification has to do with the accuracy of the electronic tagging. For example, in Mark 13:11, the head term τὸ πνεῦμα τὸ ἅγιον is incorrectly tagged. πνεῦμα is tagged as the definer, while ἅγιον is tagged as the head. For this reason, it is excluded from the query results. The second qualification has to do with the construction of the queries. A group such as τὸ πνεῦμα τὸ ἅγιον is typically tagged as a head term. However, when in the genitive case, the group is tagged as a qualifier. Recognition of these distinctions allows the researcher to construct appropriate queries to capture each occurence of a particular structure. However, it must be allowed that a structure may, on occasion, perform a function outside of those recognized by the researcher, which will result in an occurrence that is not captured by the query. For the present purpose, I have attempted to independently verify the numbers provided so that the potential for an over/under variable is negligible. On the positive side, the OpenText.org tagging allows the researcher to make important distinctions. For example, participles sometimes function as a definer. However, there are structures that, at a glance, may look like the second attributive structure with a participle, but upon closer examination are not so, but are actually an embedded clause.

[10] As noted, this analysis is limited to articular constructions. When anarthrous attributive structures are included, the percentages shift significantly. For example, when employing articular attributive structures, the author of Luke/Acts employs the first attributive structure 63% of the time (the fact that nineteen instances of the second attributive struc-

	1st	2nd
Matthew	69	20
Mark	24	19
Luke	35	23
Acts	57	31
Romans	33	2
1 Corinthians	47	5
2 Corinthians	28	1
Galatians	13	0
1 Thessalonians	2	1
2 Thessalonians	2	0
Philippians	5	0
Philemon	3	0
Colossians	2	2
Ephesians	12	4
1 Timothy	23	1
2 Timothy	12	1
Titus	10	1
Hebrews	21	9
James	7	3
1 Peter	18	0
2 Peter	24	1
Jude	7	0
John	37	44
1 John	2	6
2 John	0	1
3 John	0	0
Revelation	65	56
	558	231

reflect a more idiosyncratic usage, are eliminated from the count, this ratio jumps to nearly 3:1. In addition, there is evidence that speakers and writers display a preference for the second attributive structure for certain referents:

---

ture are τὸ πνεῦμα τὸ ἅγιον increases this to 72%). Likewise, Paul used the first attributive structure 91% of the time. However, when anarthrous structures, whether attributive or predicate, are taken into consideration, "the adjectival modifier follows its noun approximately 75% of the time in Luke and Mark," while preceeding it "approximately 65% of the time in Paul," Porter, *Idioms*, 290–1. The use or non-use of the article clearly plays a role in the choice of attributive structure.

τὸ πνεῦμα τὸ ἅγιον (28)
ὁ πατὴρ ὁ οὐράνιος (7)
ὁ υἱός μου ὁ ἀγαπητός (7)
τοῦ θεοῦ τοῦ ὑψίστου (3)
τὸ πνεῦμα τὸ ἀκάθαρτον (9)
τὸ πνεῦμα τὸ πονηρὰ (4)

The overall pattern of usage indicates a clear preference for the first attributive structure.

In general, markedness theorists agree that widespread distribution or frequency is a characteristic of unmarked forms. While this may, superficially, suggest that the first attributive structure is the unmarked form, we have been warned that simple numbers do not always support this conclusion. Combined with the characteristic of structural complexity, the argument is strengthened. However, it is far from conclusive. Further evidence is needed. The exceptions to this are Mark, where the number of instances is virtually equal, and the Johannine corpus, which heavily favors the second attributive structure. For the moment, we note that, for the most part, there is an overwhelming preference for the first attributive structure. This strongly suggests that it is the default, and thus unmarked, structure. In addition, we noted in chapter 2.2 that structural complexity may also be an indicator of markedness. Though perhaps only to a small degree, the second attributive structure is the more structurally complex of the two. As seen in Part 2, the article and definer in the second attributive structure function like a reduced form of a defining relative clause. It is noteworthy that this corroborates the guidelines provided by Aristotle in his *Art of Rhetoric.* According to the philosopher, the first attributive structure is "concise," while the second attributive structure is "lofty."[11] It is reasonable to conclude that the "concise" structure is the default or unmarked structure, while the "lofty" structure is the marked structure. Our observations would seem to bear this out. Based on this, it is possible that the second attributive structure was employed, at times, to indicate prominence or salience.

In standard Greek usage, the article and the head term combine to indicate that the information supplied by the head term is to be used to identify a class. By using the head term and the article to bracket a determiner, the speaker or writer indicates that a subclass is in view, whose identity is based on the information provided by the determiner. The determiner

---

[11] Aristotle, *Rhetoric*, III.6.

plays a key role in the group by further defining the head term. Bracketing the determiner draws the recipient's attention to this fact. In the second attributive structure, the article and definer function like a reduced defining relative clause, which also indicate that the referent is a subcategory of the class indicated by the head term.

2. Qualifiers and Group Structures

Whereas the unmarked position of definers is before the head, the unmarked structure for qualifiers is for the qualifier immediately to follow the head, as seen in the following examples:

Matt 2:2, ὁ τεχθεὶς βασιλεὺς τῶν Ἰουδαίων
The one born king of the Jews

Acts 1:19, τῇ ἰδίᾳ διαλέκτῳ αὐτῶν
Their own language

Acts 2:8, τῇ ἰδίᾳ διαλέκτῳ ἡμῶν
Our own language

Acts 3:10, ἐπὶ τῇ ὡραίᾳ πύλῃ τοῦ ἱεροῦ
on the beautiful gate of the temple

Rom 8:11, τὰ θνητὰ σώματα ὑμῶν
Your mortal bodies

2 Cor 4:13, τὸ αὐτὸ πνεῦμα τῆς πίστεως
The same spirit of faith

In the ordering of the group, the qualifier takes priority over other modifiers that follow the head term. Thus, the default structure is the one in which the qualifier is the element that immediately follows the head. When a speaker or writer employs a qualifier in the second attributive structure, the qualifier generally has priority over the determiner in ordering of the group. In the unmarked structure, the qualifier is the first element to immediately follow the head, followed by the determiner.

Matt 5:29, ὁ ὀφθαλμός σου ὁ δεξιὸς
Your right eye

Matt 6:14, 26, 32, ὁ πατὴρ ὑμῶν ὁ οὐράνιος
Your heavenly father

Matt 15:13; 18:35, ὁ πατὴρ μου ὁ οὐράνιος
My heavenly father

Mark 9:7, ὁ υἱός μου ὁ ἀγαπητός
My beloved son

Luke 2:7, τὸν υἱὸν αὐτῆς τὸν πρωτότοκον
Her firstborn son

Luke 6:6, ἡ χεὶρ αὐτοῦ ἡ δεξιά
His right hand

Luke 15:25, ὁ υἱὸς αὐτοῦ ὁ πρεσβύτερος
His older son

Eph 1:13, τῷ πνεύματι τῆς ἐπαγγελίας τῷ ἁγίῳ
The Holy Spirit of the promise

1 Thess 4:8, τὸ πνεῦμα αὐτοῦ τὸ ἅγιον
His Holy Spirit

2 Tim 4:18, τὴν βασιλείαν αὐτοῦ τὴν ἐπουράνιον
His heavenly kingdom

1 John 4:9, τὸν υἱὸν αὐτοῦ τὸν μονογενῆ
His one and only son

2 John 11, τοῖς ἔργοις αὐτοῦ τοῖς πονηροῖς
By his evil works

Rev 2:19, τὰ ἔργα σου τὰ ἔσχατα
Your last works

Very rarely is this structure altered. Examples are few:

Eph 4:30, τὸ πνεῦμα τὸ ἅγιον τοῦ θεοῦ
The Holy Spirit of God[12]

Rev 6:17, ἡ ἡμέρα ἡ μεγάλη τῆς ὀργῆς αὐτῶν
The great day of his wrath

Just as rarely, the qualifier is positioned at the front of the group.

---

[12] This may be explained by the overwhelming preference for the second attributive structure for *the Holy Spirit*.

John 18:10, αὐτοῦ τὸ ὠτάριον τὸ δεξιόν
His right ear

Rev 14:18, σου τὸ δρέπανον τὸ ὀξὺ
Your swift sickle

These observations demonstrate that the default or unmarked ordering of the qualifier is as the first element immediately following the head.

In certain instances of the first attributive structure, a speaker or writer will move a genitive qualifier forward so that it stands between the article and the Head. In this structure, the article and Head delimit the boundaries of the nominal group. Because this represents a reordering of the default structure, this structure is a marked form. Placing the qualifier in this position in the structure gives it greater prominence. However, this does not mean that the qualifier alone is being highlighted. As a qualifier, it is an element of the group structure. Its primary function is still that of a modifier within the group. By using the article and the head term to bracket the qualifier, the speaker or writer indicates that the limiting function of the qualifier is to be interpreted as playing a greater role in the identification of the thing that is designated by the group. The head term identifies the class. The article indicates that the class is being characterized as concrete. The qualifier, when bracketed by the article and head term, does not merely identify a sub-class. By employing this structure, the speaker or writer indicates that the information provided by the qualifier plays a more significant role as the identifying feature of the class.

Matt 5:30, εἰ ἡ δεξιά σου χεὶρ σκανδαλίζει σε

If *the right of you hand* causes you to stumble

In written translation, this may be rendered "If *your* right hand causes you to stumble." In spoken English, this element would receive greater vocalized stress. This is not merely an attempt to focus attention on the recipient by the use of the second person pronoun, as if this element alone is being highlighted. Instead, the speaker is placing greater emphasis on the fact that the hand that has been identified is the one that belongs to the recipient. In this way, the role of this element as a member of the group is recognized and maintained.

Matt 12:31, δὲ ἡ τοῦ πνεύματος βλασφημία οὐκ ἀφεθήσεται.

But *the of the Spirit blasphemy* will not be forgiven.

The default ordering of this group would have been ἡ βλασφημία τοῦ πνεύματος. As with the previous example, in spoken English, one could simply say "blasphemy of the Spirit" without differentiating between the elements. Conversely, one might say "blasphemy of the **Spirit**," where the bolded words represent greater vocalic stress. In Greek, this may be accomplished by employing a marked structure. By moving the qualifier forward and bracketing it between the article and the head, the speaker indicates to the recipients that the function the qualifier performs in identifying the thing designated by the group is to receive greater prominence.

> John 5:47, εἰ δὲ τοῖς ἐκείνου γράμμασιν οὐ πιστεύετε πῶς τοῖς ἐμοῖς ῥήμασιν πιστεύσετε;
>
> But if you do not believe *the of that one scriptures*, how will you believe *the my words?*

The demonstrative pronoun ἐκείνου directs the recipient backward into the text to *Moses*. By moving the pronoun forward and bracketing it, the speaker gives it greater prominence in the group structure: "But if you do not believe *his* writing, how will you believe *my* words?" The use of the demonstrative, rather than personal, pronoun gives further prominence to this element. It is noteworthy that, in the following clause, the marked structure τοῖς ἐμοῖς ῥήμασιν is used in favor of the default structure τοῖς ῥήμασιν μοῦ. This is a frequent occurrence in the fourth Gospel.

Below are additional examples that illustrate the use of this structure.

> Matt 13:55 οὐκ οὗτός ἐστιν ὁ τοῦ τέκτονος υἱός
> Is not this the builder's son?
>
> Rom 3:5, διὰ τῆς πίστεως ἐν τῷ αὐτοῦ αἵματι
> Through faith in his blood
>
> Rom 6:6, ὁ παλαιὸς ἡμῶν ἄνθρωπος συνεσταυρώθη
> Our old person was crucified with [him]
>
> Rom 6:12, μὴ οὖν βασιλευέτω ἡ ἁμαρτία ἐν τῷ θνητῷ ὑμῶν σώματι
> Therefore, sin must not rule in your mortal body
>
> 1 Cor 15:40, ἑτέρα μὲν ἡ τῶν ἐπουρανίων δόξα ἑτέρα δὲ ἡ τῶν ἐπιγείων
> On the one hand others have heavenly glory, but others earthly glory
>
> Heb 2:4, κατὰ τὴν αὐτοῦ θέλησιν
> According to his desire
>
> Heb 6:1, διὸ ἀφέντες τὸν τῆς ἀρχῆς τοῦ Χριστοῦ λόγον
> Therefore, leaving the elementary word of Christ

1 Pet 3:20, ἡ τοῦ θεοῦ μακροθυμία
The patience of God

1 Pet 4:14, τὸ τοῦ θεοῦ πνεῦμα
The Spirit of God

1 John 2:27, τὸ αὐτοῦ χρῖσμα
His anointing

It is noteworthy that the use of ἑαυτοῦ in this structure frequently has to do with familial relations.

Rom 8:3, τὸν ἑαυτοῦ υἱόν
His son

1 Cor 7:2, τὴν ἑαυτοῦ γυναῖκα
His wife

1 Cor 7:37, 38, τὴν ἑαυτοῦ παρθένον
His virgin

Eph 5:28, 33, τὰς ἑαυτῶν γυναῖκας
Their wives

1 Thess. 2:7, τὰ ἑαυτῆς τέκνα
Her children

In many instances, the emphasis is on something related to the individual's body or being.

Rom 16:4, τὸν ἑαυτοῦ τράχηλον
His neck

Rom. 16:18, τῇ ἑαυτῶν κοιλίᾳ
Their belly

Eph. 5:28, τὰ ἑαυτῶν σώματα
Their bodies

1 Thess. 4:4, τὸ ἑαυτοῦ σκεῦος
His body

The challenge of this particular usage is determining if this is an unmarked or marked form. In reference to familial relations, the reflexive pronoun very rarely follows the head term:

Luke 15:20, πρὸς τὸν πατέρα ἑαυτοῦ

To his father

The small sample size makes it difficult to draw a conclusion. On the one hand, it is arguable that this is the unmarked structure, since variations are so rare. On the other, the pronoun ἑαυτοῦ is less commonly used to show possession. Examples such as ὁ υἱός μοῦ or ὁ πατήρ σοῦ and other similar forms abound. Therefore, it is possible to interpret the choice of ἑαυτοῦ and its position as factors that operate in conjunction with one another to produce a marked form.

3. PREPOSITIONAL GROUPS AND GROUP STRUCTURES

As with other elements, prepositional groups typically follow the head term.

Matt 12:5, οἱ ἱερεῖς ἐν τῷ ἱερῷ
The priests in the temple

Luke 5:15, ὁ λόγος περὶ αὐτοῦ
The word concerning him

Luke 22:20, ἡ καινὴ διαθήκη ἐν τῷ αἵματί μου
The new covenant in my blood

Acts 21:16, συνῆλθον δὲ καὶ τῶν μαθητῶν ἀπὸ Καισαρείας σὺν ἡμῖν
And of the disciples from Caesarea, they also came with us

1 Cor 10:18, Βλέπετε τὸν Ἰσραὴλ κατὰ σάρκα
Consider Israel according to the flesh

2 Cor 7:7, τὸν ὑμῶν ζῆλον ὑπὲρ ἐμοῦ
Your zeal on my behalf

Eph 3:10, ταῖς ἐξουσίαις ἐν τοῖς ἐπουρανίοις
The authorities in the heavenly places

Like the elements observed above, prepositional groups may be moved to a position in front of the head term and bracketed by the article and head term. As with the previous examples, this structure places greater emphasis on the role the prepositional group plays in identifying the thing designated by the group.

Mark 4:19, αἱ μέριμναι τοῦ αἰῶνος καὶ ἡ ἀπάτη τοῦ πλούτου καὶ αἱ περὶ τὰ λοιπὰ ἐπιθυμίαι

The anxieties of the age and the deception of riches and *the about the rest desires*

By moving the prepositional phrase περὶ τὰ λοιπὰ forward and bracketing it with the article and Head, the speaker indicates to the recipients that this element plays a more substantial role in identifying the head than might otherwise have been interpreted.

Acts 8:14, ἀκούσαντες δὲ οἱ ἐν Ἱεροσολύμοις ἀπόστολοι ὅτι δέδεχται ἡ Σαμάρεια τὸν λόγον τοῦ θεοῦ ἀπέστειλαν πρὸς αὐτοὺς Πέτρον καὶ Ἰωάννην.

The in Jerusalem apostles, hearing that Samaria had received the word of God, sent Peter and John to them.

In this instance, the author places greater emphasis on the fact that the apostles are in Jerusalem. This is perhaps to make the distinction in locale more vivid to the recipients. The events related to the evangelistic work of Philip is Samaria have reached the ears of the apostles, who are far away in Jerusalem.

2 Cor 7:10, ἡ γὰρ κατὰ θεὸν λύπη … ἡ δὲ τοῦ κόσμου λύπη

For *the according to God sorrow* … but *the of the world sorrow*

Paul uses the "bracketing" structure twice in this passage. In the first instance, he brackets a prepositional group; in the second instance, a genitive word group (that is, a qualifier). It is likely that he chooses these structures to highlight the distinguishing features of each kind of *sorrow*. The class, *sorrow*, has at least two sub-classes: sorrow *according to* God, and sorrow *of the world*. By bracketing the modifiers with the article and Head, Paul indicates to the recipients that the qualities grammaticalized by the modifiers are not merely the identifying features of the sub-classes. They are made prominent so that the recipients identify these qualities as elements that play a significant role in the discourse.

Below are further examples of the use of this structure.

Acts 19:38, Δημήτριος καὶ οἱ σὺν αὐτῷ τεχνῖται
Demetrius and the craftsmen with him

Acts 23:21, τὴν ἀπὸ σοῦ ἐπαγγελίαν
The promise from you

Rom 10:6, ἡ δὲ ἐκ πίστεως δικαιοσύνη
The righteousness from faith

Rom 11:21, τῶν κατὰ φύσιν κλάδων
The branches according to nature [the natural branches]

Eph 6:5, οἱ δοῦλοι ὑπακούετε τοῖς κατὰ σάρκα κυρίοις
Servants obey the ones who are lords according to the flesh

Phil 4:21, ἀσπάζονται ὑμᾶς οἱ σὺν ἐμοὶ ἀδελφοί
The brothers with me greet you.

1 Tim 4:14, μὴ ἀμέλει τοῦ ἐν σοὶ χαρίσματος
Do not neglect the gift in you

1 Pet 1:11, τὸ ἐν αὐτοῖς πνεῦμα Χριστοῦ
The spirit of Christ in them

2 Pet 3:10, τὰ ἐν αὐτῇ ἔργα
The works in her

Jude 7, ὡς Σόδομα καὶ Γόμορρα καὶ αἱ περὶ αὐτὰς πόλεις
Like Sodom and Gomorrah and the cities around them

4. Complex Nominal Group Structures

In the examples above, we observed simple nominal group structures where the article and Head bracketed a single modifier. Sometimes, a writer or speaker will employ this same technique to produce more complex group structures where the article and Head bracket multiple elements.

Sometimes, a speaker or writer will bracket two modifiers rather than one:

2 Cor 13:3, ἐπεὶ δοκιμὴν ζητεῖτε τοῦ ἐν ἐμοὶ λαλοῦντος Χριστοῦ,

Since you seek evidence *of the in me speaking Christ,*

In this instance, the article and the head term, Χριστοῦ, bracket both a prepositional group and a definer. Since Paul is being pressured to defend his apostolic authority, he highlights the fact that Christ is *speaking in me,* which contrasts Paul and his adversaries.

A speaker or writer will sometimes incorporate even more elements into this type of group structure:

2 Cor 1:21, ὁ δὲ βεβαιῶν ἡμᾶς σὺν ὑμῖν εἰς Χριστὸν καὶ χρίσας ἡμᾶς θεός,

The establishing us in belief with you in Christ and appointing us *God,*

In the early chapters of 2 Corinthians, Paul expresses joy and relief at being reconciled with the Corinthian believers. This reconciliation is a micro-cosm of the reconciling work in which God is engaged with the world. Paul specifically, and believers in general, are co-workers in this ministry. The structure Paul employs in this instance draws greater attention to the fact that Paul and the Corinthians have already been the objects of God's work in this regard. After enduring a very stressful period of intense ten-sion and (at least perceived) animosity, Paul emphasizes their common faith and appointment.

In instances where a participle is functioning as the head term, the arti-cle and participle may be used to bracket the object(s) of the participle:

Rom 5:17, οἱ τὴν περισσείαν τῆς χάριτος καὶ τῆς δωρεᾶς τῆς δικαιωσύνης λαμβάνοντες

The ones the abundance of grace and gift of righteousness *receiving*

In a letter that emphasizes that justification is a free gift from God and not the result of works of law, Paul employs this structure to make *abundance of grace and gift of righteousness* prominent.

Occasionally, these structures become very elaborate, incorporating a large number of elements:

Rom 16:17, Παρακαλῶ δὲ ὑμᾶς, ἀδελφοί, σκοπεῖν τοὺς τὰς διχοστασίας καὶ τὰ σκάνδαλα παρὰ τὴν διδαχὴν ἣν ὑμεῖς ἐμάθετε ποιοῦντας

I encourage you, brothers, to take note of *the ones* divisions and offenses contrary to the teaching which you learned *causing*

Paul (or perhaps his scribe Tertius), employs the article and head term to bracket the dual objects of the participle, which are modified by a prepo-sitional phrase and a relative clause. In this instance, the disruptive and destructive work of certain individuals is given prominence by the use of this complex and elaborate structure.

In chapter 3, we observed that an articular participial clause in the so-called second attributive position functions as a relative clause. Occasion-ally, a speaker or writer will expand this construction, using the article and participle to bracket additional elements:

Jas 3:9, τοὺς ἀνθρώπους τοὺς καθ᾽ ὁμοίωσιν θεοῦ γεγονότας,

The people *the ones* according to the likeness of God *having become*

The author indicates to the recipients that the characteristic of being *the likeness of God* is a particularly important characteristic of these people. Therefore, he employs this structure to make this element prominent.

Nowhere in the New Testament are these types of construction used with such frequency as they are by the writer of 1 Peter. Not only does he seem to take great delight in using them often, but also in taking them to unparalleled (by New Testament standards) levels of intricacy:

1 Pet 1:3, Εὐλογητὸς ὁ θεὸς καὶ πατὴρ τοῦ κυρίου ἡμῶν Ἰησοῦ Χριστοῦ, ὁ κατὰ τὸ πολὺ αὐτοῦ ἔλεος ἀναγεννήσας ἡμᾶς εἰς ἐλπίδα ζῶσαν

Blessed be the God and father of our lord Jesus Christ, *the one who* according to *the* much of him *mercy begot* us into a living hope

εὐλογητὸς	S ὁ θεὸς καὶ πατὴρ τοῦ κυρίου ἡμῶν Ἰησοῦ Χριστοῦ				
	1Pet.c1_4	**P** ὁ **A** κατὰ τὸ πολὺ αὐτοῦ ἔλεος ἀναγεννήσας		**C** ἡμᾶς	**A** εἰς ἐλπίδα 1Pet.c1_5	**P** ζῶσαν

The writer is not content with a single bracket, but also incorporates a sub-group bracket into the main group.

ὁ κατὰ τὸ πολὺ αὐτοῦ ἔλεος ἀναγεννήσας

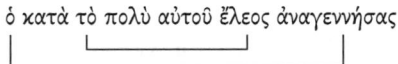

The article and head term of the participial group are used to bracket a prepositional group, delimiting the boundaries of the larger group. However, within the prepositional group is another group. The article and the head term of this sub-group are used to bracket a definer and a qualifier, delimiting the boundaries of the sub-group. The writer employs this same structure again in 1:10:

περὶ ἧς σωτηρίας ἐξεζήτησαν καὶ ἐξηραύνησαν προφῆται οἱ περὶ τῆς εἰς ὑμᾶς χάριτος προφητεύσαντες

concerning which salvation, prophets *who* concerning *the* in you *grace prophesied* diligently sought and inquired

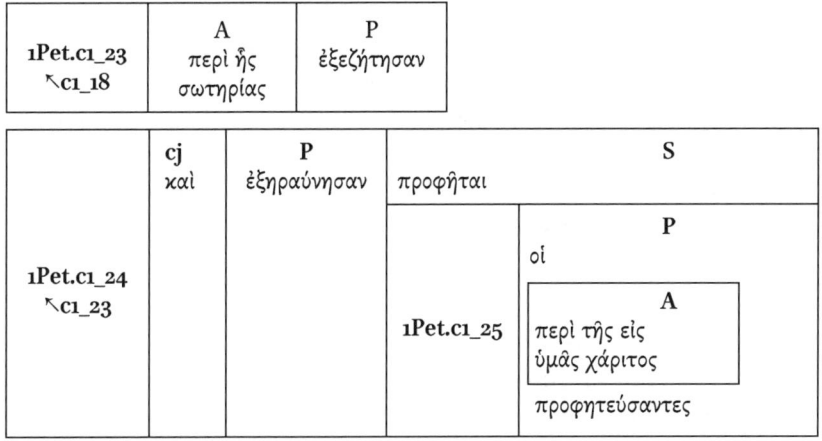

1Pet.c1_23 ⌐c1_18	A περὶ ἧς σωτηρίας	P ἐξεζήτησαν	

1Pet.c1_24 ⌐c1_23	cj καί	P ἐξηραύνησαν	S

In this instance, the structure functions as a relative clause. However, the general construction is the same as that of the previous example. The only difference is that, in the sub-group, the article and head bracket another prepositional group.

> 1 Pet 1:14, ὡς τέκνα ὑπακοῆς μὴ συσχηματιζόμενοι ταῖς πρότερον ἐν τῇ ἀγνοίᾳ ὑμῶν ἐπιθυμίαις

> As obedient children not conforming to the former in the ignorance of you *desires*

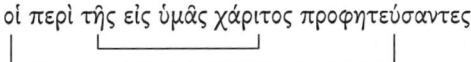

Though not as elaborate as the previous examples, this instance illustrates the writer's continued use of this structure.

> 1 Pet 5:1, ὁ καὶ τῆς μελλούσης ἀποκαλύπτεσθαι δόξης κοινωνός

> And *the of the* about to be revealed *glory partner.*

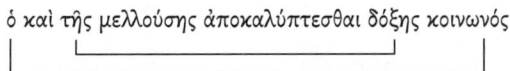

Recognizing these structures is only the first analytical step, which is the domain of the textual metafunction. As already demonstrated, the next step is to determine why the speaker or writer has chosen to structure the information in this manner. By doing so, the interpreter will be able to determine what elements of the discourse the recipients are to take special note of. This is the domain of the ideational metafunction. Finally, the interpreter must ask how the speaker or writer is using these structures to indicate his or her attitude toward both the information and the recipients, which is the domain of the interpersonal metafunction.

5. Conclusion

While the article functions primarily as a modifier within a nominal group, when so employed it may also be used as an element for creating extended and elaborate group structures. In certain instances, this may be motivated by a desire to delimit the boundaries of the group structure, which may in turn be used to produce prominence or indicate salience. It must be emphasized the article's role as a modifier takes precedence. It cannot be employed as a structural element if it is not first present as a modifier.

CHAPTER ELEVEN

CONCLUSION

The goals of this present work may be simply stated as two-fold: to clarify what the Greek article does not do, and to describe what it does do. Regarding the former, it was my intention to demonstrate conclusively that diachronic association with the historical demonstrative pronoun results in a misunderstanding of the article's function. To this end, I have demonstrated that the article is employed in a wide variety of structures that fill the same slot and performed the same or similar function as structures that employ the relative pronoun. Thus, it is more accurate to categorically associate the article with the relative pronoun. Correspondingly, I have also demonstrated that association with the English definite article as a method of describing the function of the Greek article has created more problems than it solves. The functions of the two articles are far more disparate than previously recognized.[1] Whereas the English definite article indicates to the recipient that he or she already possesses the information necessary to identify the referent, the Greek article indicates that the speaker or writer is providing the information necessary for identifying the referent. Thus, while the English definite article assumes information that both the speaker and recipient share in common, the Greek article orients this information to the speaker. In other words, the Greek article is not demonstrative in force.

With regard to what the Greek article does do, the results are also two-fold. First, the function of the Greek article must be understood in terms of subjective *characterization*. Such characterization is subjective because, as stated above, the information necessary for identification is oriented to the speaker, which he or she provides to the recipients. When used as a modifier, the speaker or writer employs the article to characterize the head term as *concrete*, as belonging to experience of an actual person or thing, or a specific instance. This does not mean that the head term corresponds to an actual person or thing in a definite sense, but that the head term is characterized as *such a person or thing*. If an actual person or thing is in

---

[1] See above, chapter 6.1, 180, fn 4.

view, other discourse features will indicate this. In this regard, the function of the article is best understood as analogous to the relative clause, which either may be used to further define an element in the discourse or may stand alone as the subject or object of a clause. In both instance, the relative pronoun indicates the speaker is providing information that the recipient is to use for the purpose of identification. The Greek article is employed in structures that function in the same way.

Second, the characterization produced by the article performs a function at the discourse level. This may be understood in terms of *figure* and *ground.* Elements that are modified by the article are understood to be *figures* in the discourse, and thus are generally more *salient.* Conversely, anarthrous elements, specifically nouns and proper names, are part of the grounding of the discourse, and thus are generally less *salient.* This is especially helpful in understanding the use of the Greek article with proper names, the explanation of which has been historically elusive.

As a structural element in the nominal group, the article demonstrates great flexibility. Speakers and writers employ it in a variety of ways to produce both simple and complex constructions. However, use in such structures presumes the presence of the article as a modifier, which is its primary function. Both the use and non-use of the article is first and foremost a deliberate choice on the part of the speaker for the purpose of characterization. Once so employed, the speaker or writer uses it to produce a variety of group structures.

As a recommendation for future grammars, students will be well served if association with the English definite article is no longer employed as the primary method of instruction regarding the article. By simply employing the gloss *the one who* or *that which* from the beginning of their language education, a much stronger and more accurate foundational understanding of the article's function will be established.

The biblical exegete stands to benefit most from a functional approach to the Greek article. Clearly, Greek speakers employed the article (or chose not to employ it) for the purpose of *grounding* certain elements in the discourse and indicating *salience.* In general, articular elements will be more salient than anarthrous elements. Participants who are identified by articular proper nouns in narrative text are generally more prominent than those who are not so indicated. As Middleton said, the article is "the symbol of that which is uppermost in the speaker's mind."[2] By applying

---

[2] Middleton, *Doctrine,* 25. See above, chapter 1.6, 63.

this to the text, the exegete is able to objectively and decisively determine what is "uppermost in the speaker's mind." In the world of biblical and theological studies, there is no shortage of opinions on this matter. A functional approach provides the exegete with the tools by which the speaker or writer's own linguist choices may be used to ascertain his or her meaning. The ability to identify those elements that the writer himself indicates are most salient enables the exegete to focus his or her attention, time and energy on those elements. By doing so, the attentive exegete is able to "get to the point" without becoming overly enamoured with trivial details, or worse, conclude that the trivial details are the point. In the end, we are most concerned with what the biblical writers were "on about." By employing the article, they have indicated to us, the recipients, that which is "uppermost in their minds."

BIBLIOGRAPHY

Andrews, Edna. *Markedness Theory: The Union of Asymmetry and Semiosis in Language.* Durham: Duke University Press, 1990.

Aristotle. *Art of Rhetoric.* Translated by J.H. Freese. Cambridge: Harvard University Press, 2006.

———. *Poetics.* Translated by Stephen Halliwell. Cambridge: Harvard University Press, 1995.

———. *Prior Analytics.* Translated by Cooke Tredennick and Hugh Tredennick. Cambridge: Harvard University Press, 2002.

Bakker, Stephanie J. *The Noun Phrase in Ancient Greek: A Functional Analysis of the Order and Articulation of NP Constituents in Herodotus.* Leiden: Brill, 2009.

Barnbrook, Geoff. *Language and Computers.* Edinburgh: Edinburgh University Press, 1996.

Barnett, Paul. *The Second Epistle to the Corinthians.* NICNT. Grand Rapids: Eerdmans, 1997.

Barrett, C.K. *The First Epistle to the Corinthians.* BNTC. Repr. Peabody: Hendrickson, 1968.

Battistella, Edwin L. *Markedness: The Evaluative Superstructure of Language.* Albany: State University of New York Press, 1990.

———. *The Logic of Markedness.* Oxford: Oxford University Press, 1996.

Beasley-Murray, George R. *John.* WBC. Nashville: Thomas Nelson, 1999.

Beaugrande, Robert de. *Linguistic Theory: The Discourse of Fundamental Works.* New York: Longman, 1991.

———. *Introduction to Text Linguistics.* London: Longman, 1981.

Biber, Douglas, et al. *Corpus Linguistics: Investigating Language Structure and Use.* Cambridge: Cambridge University Press, 1998.

Black, David Alan. "The Study of New Testament Greek in the Light of Ancient and Modern Linguistics." In *Interpreting the New Testament: Essays on Methods and Issues,* edited by David Alan Black and David S. Dockery, 377–406. Nashville: Broadman & Holmann, 2001.

Black, David Alan, ed. *Linguistics and New Testament Interpretation: Essays on Discourse Analysis.* Nashville: Broadman & Holmann, 1992.

Blass, Friedrich, and Alber Debrunner. *A Greek Grammar of the New Testament and Other Early Christian Literature.* Translated by R.W. Funk. Chicago: Chicago University Press, 1961.

Bloor, Thomas, and Meriel Bloor. *The Functional Analysis of English: A Hallidayan Approach.* 2nd ed. London: Arnold, 2004.

Bolkestein, A.M., et al. *Syntax and Pragmatics in Functional Grammar.* Dordrecht: Foris, 1985.

Brooks, J.A., and C.L. Winbery. *Syntax of New Testament Greek.* Washington D.C.: University Press of America, 1979.

Brown, Gillian, and George Yule. *Discourse Analysis.* Cambridge: Cambridge University Press, 1983.

Brown, Raymond E. *The Epistles of John.* AB. New York: Doubleday, 1982.

———. *The Gospel According to John.* 2 vols. Garden City: Doubleday, 1966.

Bruce, F.F. *The Epistle to the Galatians: A Commentary on the Greek Text.* NIGTC. Grand Rapids: Eerdmans, 1982.

———. *The Gospel and Epistles of John.* Grand Rapids: Eerdmans, 1983.

Burk, Denny. *Articular Infinitives in the Greek of the New Testament: On the Exegetical Benefit of Grammatical Precision.* Sheffield: Sheffield Phoenix Press, 2006.

Buttmann, Alexander. *A Grammar of the New Testament Greek.* Translated by J.H. Thayer. Andover: W.F. Draper, 1895.

Byrne, Brendan. *Romans*. Sacra Pagina. Collegeville: The Liturgical Press, 1996.

Caragounis, Chrys C. *The Development of Greek and the New Testament: Morphology, Syntax, Phonology, and Textual Transmission*. Grand Rapids: Baker, 2006.

Carson, D.A. *The Gospel According to John*. PNTC. Grand Rapids: Eerdmans, 1991.

Christidis, A.F. *A History of Ancient Greek: From Beginnings to Late Antiquity*. Cambridge: Cambridge University Press, 2007.

Ciampa, Roy E. "Revisiting the Euphamism in 1 Corinthians 7.1." *JSNT* 31.3 (2009) 325–38.

Ciampa, Roy E., and Brian S. Rosner. *The First Letter to the Corinthians*. PNTC. Grand Rapids: Eerdmans, 2010.

Collins, Adela Yarbro. *Mark*. Hermeneia. Minneapolis: Fortress, 2007.

Colwell, E.C. "A Definite Rule for the Use of the Article in the Greek New Testament." *JBL* 52.1 (1933) 12–21.

Cotterell, Peter, and Max Turner. *Linguistics and Biblical Interpretation*. Downers Grove: InterVarsity, 1989.

Culy, Martin M. *I, II, III John: A Handbook on the Greek Text*. BHGNT. Waco: Baylor, 2004.

Dana, H.E., and J.R. Mantey. *A Manual Grammar of the Greek New Testament*. Toronto: Macmillan, 1927.

Darby, J.N. *On the Greek Article*. London: G. Morrish, n.d.

Davids, Peter H. *The Epistle of James: A Commentary on the Greek Text*. NIGTC. Grand Rapids: Eerdmans, 1982.

Davies, W.D., and Dale C. Allison. *A Critical and Exegetical Commentary on the Gospel According to Matthew*. 3 vols. ICC. Edinburgh: T&T Clark, 1988.

Deissmann, Adolf. *Biblical Studies*. Repr. Peabody: Hendrickson, 1988.

———. *Light from the Ancient East*. Repr. Peabody: Hendrickson, 1995.

DeJonge, Casper C. *Between Grammar and Rhetoric: Dionysius of Halicarnassus on Language, Linguistics and Literature*. Boston: Brill, 2008.

Dik, Simon C. *Functional Grammar*. Amsterdam: North-Holland, 1978.

———. *Studies in Functional Grammar*. London: Academic Press, 1980.

Dionysius of Hallicarnassus. *On Literary Composition*. Translated by W. Rhys Roberts. New York: Garland, 1987.

Drumwright, Huber L. Jr. *An Introduction to New Testament Greek*. Nashville: Broadman, 1980.

Dunn, James D.G. *Romans*. 2 vols. WBC 38. Dallas: Word, 1988.

Eakin, Frank. "The Greek Article in First and Second Century Papyri." *The American Journal of Philology* 37.3 (1916) 333–40.

Eckman, Fred R., et al., eds. *Markedness*. New York: Plenum, 1986.

Ellingworth, Paul. *The Epistle to the Hebrews*. NIGTC. Grand Rapids: Eerdmans, 1993.

———. "Translating (Ho) Christos." *BT* 59.3 (2008) 145–51.

Evans, Craig A. *Mark 8:27–16:20*. WBC 34b. Nashville: Word, 2001.

Evans, Vyvyan. *A Glossary of Cognitive Linguistics*. Salt Lake City: The University of Utah Press, 2007.

Evans, Vyvyan, and Melanie Green. *Cognitive Linguistics: An Introduction*. Edinburgh: Edinburgh University Press, 2006.

Fawcett, Robin P. *A Theory of Syntax for Systemic Functional Linguistics*. Philadelphia: John Benjamins, 2000.

Fee, Gordon D. *Paul's Letter to the Philippians*. NICNT. Grand Rapids: Eerdmans, 1995.

———. "The Use of the Definite Article with Personal Names in the Gospel of John." *NTS* 17.2 (1971) 168–83.

Ferguson, Everett. *Backgrounds of Early Christianity*. Grand Rapids: Eerdmans, 1993.

Firth, J.R. *Papers in Linguistics, 1934–1951*. London: Oxford University Press, 1957.

———. *The Tongues of Men and Speech*. London: Oxford University Press, 1964.

Fitzmyer, Joseph A. *Romans: A New Translation with Introduction and Commentary*. AB. New York: Doubleday, 1993.

France, R.T. *The Gospel of Mark: A Commentary on the Greek Text*. NIGTC. Grand Rapids: Eerdmans, 2002.

Fung, Ronald Y.K. *The Epistle to the Galatians*. NICNT. Grand Rapids: Eerdmans, 1988.
Funk, Robert W. *A Beginning-Intermediate Grammar of Hellenistic Greek*. 3 vols. Missoula: Society of Biblical Literature, 1973.
———. "The Syntax of the Greek Article: Its Importance for Critical Pauline Problems." PhD diss., Vanderbilt University, 1953.
Furnish, Victor Paul. *II Corinthians: A New Translation with Introduction and Commentary*. AB. New York: Doubleday, 1984.
Garland, David E. *1 Corinthians*. BECNT. Grand Rapids: Baker, 2003.
Givón, Talmy. *Functionalism and Grammar*. Amsterdam/Philadelphia: John Benjamins, 1995.
———. *Syntax: A Functional-Typological Introduction, Vol. 2*. Amsterdam/Philadelphia: John Benjamins, 1990.
Goodwin, William W. *A Greek Grammar*. Repr. Eugene: Wipf & Stock, 2003.
Gould, Josiah B. *The Philosophy of Chrysippus*. Albany: State University of New York Press, 1970.
Green, Joel B. "Discourse Analysis and New Testament Interpretation." In *Hearing the New Testament: Strategies for Interpretation*, edited by Joel Green, 175–96. Grand Rapids: Eerdmans, 1995.
———. *The Gospel of Luke*. NICNT. Grand Rapids: Eerdmans, 1997.
Guelich, Robert A. *Mark 1–8:26*. WBC 34a. Nashville: Word, 1989.
Hagner, Donald A. *Matthew 1–13*. WBC 33a. Nashville: Word, 1993.
———. *Matthew 14–28*. WBC 33b. Nashville: Word, 1995.
Halliday, M.A.K. *An Introduction to Functional Grammar*. London: Arnold, 2004.
Halliday, M.A.K., and Raqaiya Hasan. *Cohesion in English*. New York: Longman, 1976.
———. *Language, Context and Text*. Oxford: Oxford University Press, 1989.
Harris, Murray J. *The Second Epistle to the Corinthians*. NIGTC. Grand Rapids: Eerdmans, 2005.
Haspelmath, Martin. "Against Markedness (and what to replace it with)." *Journal of Linguistics* 42.1 (2006) 258–70.
Heimerdinger, Jenny, and Stephen Levinsohn. "The Use of the Definite Article before Names of People in the Greek Text of Acts with Particular Reference to Codex Bazae." *FN* 5.9 (1992) 15–44.
Hoey, Michael. *Patterns of Lexis in Text*. Oxford: Oxford University Press, 1991.
Horrocks, Geoffrey C. *Generative Grammar*. London: Longman, 1987.
———. *Greek: A History of the Language and its Speakers*. New York: Longman, 1997.
Jannaris, A.N. *An Historical Greek Grammar: Chiefly of the Attic Dialect*. London: Macmillan, 1897.
Jelf, William Edward. *A Grammar of the Greek Language, Chiefly from the German of Raphael Kühner*. 2 Vols. Oxford: John Henry Parker, 1851.
Jewett, Robert. *Romans*. Hermeneia. Minneapolis: Fortress, 2007.
Keener, Craig S. *A Commentary on the Gospel of Matthew*. Grand Rapids: Eerdmans, 1999.
———. *Matthew*. IVPNTC. Downers Grove: InterVarsity, 1997.
———. *The Gospel of John: A Commentary*. 2 vols. Peabody: Hendrickson, 2003.
Kennedy, Graeme. *An Introduction to Corpus Linguistics*. New York: Addison Wesley Longman, 1998.
Knight, George W. *The Pastoral Epistles*. NIGTC. Grand Rapids: Eerdmans, 1992.
Kress, G.R., ed. *Halliday: System and Function in Language*. London: Oxford University Press, 1976.
Kruse, Colin G. *The Letters of John*. PNTC. Grand Rapids: Eerdmans, 2000.
Kühner, Raphael, and Friedrich Blass. *Grammatik der Griechischen Sprache*. 2 vols. Hannover: Verlag Hahnsche Buchhandlung, 1978.
Lane, William L. *Hebrews*. 2 vols. WBC 47. Nashville: Word, 1991.
Lee, David. *Cognitive Linguistics: An Introduction*. Oxford: Oxford University Press, 2001.
Levinsohn, Stephen. "Anarthrous References to the Holy Spirit: Another Factor." *BT* 44.1 (1993) 138–44.

Liddell, H.G., and R. Scott. *Greek-English Lexicon with a Revised Supplement.* Oxford: Clarendon Press, 1996.

Lightfoot, J.B. *St. Paul's Epistle to the Philippians.* Repr. Lynn: Hendrickson, 1981.

———. *The Epistle of St. Paul to the Galatians.* Repr. Lynn: Hendrickson, 1981.

Louw, Johannes P. *Semantics of New Testament Greek.* Philadelphia: Fortress, 1982.

Luschnig, C.A.E. *An Introduction to Ancient Greek.* 2nd ed. Indianapolis: Hackett, 2007.

Luz, Ulrich. *Matthew.* 3 vols. Hermeneia. Minneapolis: Fortress, 2007.

Lyons, John. *Introduction to Theoretical Linguistics.* Cambridge: Cambridge University Press, 1968.

———. *Language and Linguistics: An Introduction.* Cambridge: Cambridge University Press, 1981.

Machen, J. Gresham. *New Testament Greek for Beginners.* New York: Macmillan, 1928.

Manolessou, Io. "The Evolution of the Demonstrative System in Greek." *Journal of Greek Linguistics* 2 (2001) 119–48.

Marcus, Joel. *Mark 1–8.* New York: Doubleday, 2000.

Marshall, I. Howard. *The Epistles of John.* NICNT. Grand Rapids: Eerdmans, 1978.

———. *The Gospel of Luke: A Commentary on the Greek Text.* NIGTC. Grand Rapids: Eerdmans, 1978.

Martin, J.R., and David Rose. *Working with Discourse: Meaning Beyond the Clause.* 2nd ed. New York: Continuum, 2007.

McEnery, Tony, and Andrew Wilson. *Corpus Linguistics.* 2nd ed. Edinburgh: Edinburgh University Press, 2001.

Middleton, Thomas Fanshaw. *The Doctrine of the Greek Article.* Repr. Eugene: Wipf & Stock, 2005.

Moo, Douglas J. *The Epistle to the Romans.* NICNT. Grand Rapids: Eerdmans, 1996.

Moravcsik, E., and J. Wirth. "Markedness: An Overview." In *Markedness*, edited by Fred. R. Eckman, et al. 1–11. New York: Plenum, 1986.

Morris, Leon. *The Epistle to the Romans.* PNTC. Grand Rapids: Eerdmans, 1988.

Moule, C.F.D. *Idiom Book of New Testament Greek.* Cambridge: Cambridge University Press, 1953.

Moulton, James Hope. *A Grammar of New Testament Greek.* 3rd ed. Vol. 1 *Prolegomena.* 4 vols. Edinburgh: T&T Clark, 1908.

———. *An Introduction to the Study of New Testament Greek.* London: Kelly, 1895.

Moulton, James Hope, and Wilbert Francis Howard. *A Grammar of New Testament Greek.* Vol. 2 *Accidence and Word Formation.* 4 vols. Edinburgh: T&T Clark, 1929.

Nolland, John. *The Gospel of Matthew: A Commentary on the Greek Text.* NIGTC. Grand Rapids: Eerdmans, 2005.

Nuyts, Jan. "Cognitive Linguistics and Functional Linguistics." In *The Oxford Handbook of Cognitive Linguistics*, edited by Dirk Geeraerts and Hubert Cuyckens, 543–65. Oxford: Oxford University Press, 2007.

Oakes, Michael. *Statistics for Corpus Linguistics.* Edinburgh: Edinburgh University Press, 1998.

O'Brien, Peter T. *The Epistle to the Philippians.* NIGTC. Grand Rapids: Eerdmans, 1991.

———. *The Letter to the Ephesians.* PNTC. Grand Rapids: Eerdmans, 1999.

———. *The Letter to the Hebrews.* PNTC. Grand Rapids: Eerdmans, 2010.

Palmer, L.R. *The Greek Language.* London: Faber & Faber, 1980.

Perry, Alfred M. "Translating the Greek Article." *JBL* 68.4 (1949) 329–34.

Porter, Stanley E. *Idioms of the Greek New Testament.* 2nd ed. Sheffield: Sheffield Academic Press, 1994.

———. Review of *Granville Sharp's Canon and Its Kin: Semantics and Significance*, by Daniel B. Wallace, *JETS* 53.4 (2010) 828–32.

———. "Studying Ancient Languages from a Modern Linguistic Perspective: Essential Terms and Terminology." *FN* 2.4 (1989) 147–72.

Porter, Stanley E., and D.A. Carson, eds. *Discourse Analysis and Other Topics in Biblical Greek.* Sheffield: Sheffield Academic Press, 1995.

——. *Discourse Analysis and the New Testament: Approaches and Results.* Sheffield: Sheffield Academic Press, 1999.

——. *Linguistics and the New Testament: Critical Junctures.* Sheffield: Sheffield Academic Press, 1999.

Porter, Stanley E., and Matthew Brook O'Donnell. "Conjunctions, Clines and Levels of Discourse." *FN* 20 (2007) 3–14.

Porter, Stanley E., and Matthew Brook O'Donnell, eds. *The Linguist as Pedagogue: Trends in the Teaching of Linguistic Analysis of the Greek New Testament,* Sheffield: Sheffield Phoenix Press, 2009.

Porter, Stanley E., et al. *Fundamentals of New Testament Greek.* Grand Rapids: Eerdmans, 2010.

Reed, Jeffery T. *A Discourse Analysis of Philippians: Method and Rhetoric in the Debate over Literary Integrity.* Sheffield: Sheffield Academic Press, 1997.

——. "Identifying Theme in the New Testament: Insights from Discourse Analysis." In *Discourse Analysis and Other Topics in Biblical Greek,* edited by Stanley E. Porter and D.A. Carson, 75–101. Sheffield: Sheffield Academic Press, 1995.

Robertson, A.T. *A Grammar of the Greek New Testament in Light of Historical Research.* Nashville: Broadman, 1934.

Robinson, Thomas A. *Mastering New Testament Greek: Essential Tools for Students.* Peabody: Hendrickson, 2007.

Rosen, Haiim B. "Early Greek Grammar and Thought in Heraclitus: The Emergence of the Article." *Israel Academy of Sciences and Humanities* 7.2 (1988) 21–62.

Runge, Steven E. *Discourse Grammar of the Greek New Testament.* Peabody: Hendrickson, 2010.

Sansone, David. "Toward a New Doctrine of the Article in Greek: Some Observations of the Definite Article in Plato." *Classical Philology* 88.3 (1993) 191–205.

Schreiner, Thomas. *Romans.* BECNT. Grand Rapids: Baker, 1998.

Schiffrin, Deborah, et al., eds. *The Handbook of Discourse Analysis.* Malden: Blackwell, 2001.

Schwyzer, Eduard. *Griechische Grammatik.* 2 vols. Munich: C.H. Beck, 1950.

Sharp, Granville. *Remarks on the Uses of the Definitive Article in the Greek of the New Testament.* Repr. Roswell: The Original Word, 1995.

Silva, Moisés. *Biblical Words and Their Meanings: An Introduction to Lexical Semantics.* Grand Rapids: Zondervan, 1994.

Sinclair, John. *Trust the Text: Language, Corpus and Discourse.* London: Routledge, 2004.

Smalley, Stephen S. *1, 2, 3 John.* WBC 51. Waco: Word, 1984.

Smith, Jay E. "Slogans in 1 Corinthians." *Bibliotheca Sacra* 167.665 (2010) 68–88.

Smyth, Herbert Weir. *Greek Grammar.* Edited by Gordon M. Messing. Cambridge: Harvard University Press, 1956.

Spielmann, Kent. "Participant Reference and Definite Article in John." *Journal of Translation and Text Linguistics* 7.1 (1995) 45–85.

Stubbs, Michael. *Discourse Analysis: The Sociolinguistic Study of Natural Language.* Oxford: B. Blackwell, 1983.

Summers, Ray. *Essentials of New Testament Greek.* Nashville: Broadman, 1950.

Swartz, Steve. "The Holy Spirit: Person and Power. The Greek Article and Pneuma." *BT* 44.1 (1993) 124–38.

Taylor, John. *What is the Power of the Greek Article and How May it be Expressed in the English Version of the New Testament?* London: Taylor and Walton, 1842.

Teeple, H.M. "The Greek Article with Personal Names in the Synoptic Gospels." *NTS* 19.3 (1973) 302–17.

Thiselton, Anthony C. *The First Epistle to the Corinthians.* NIGTC. Grand Rapids: Eerdmans, 2000.

Thompson, Geoff. *Introducing Functional Grammar.* 2nd ed. London: Arnold, 2004.

Tibbs, Clint. "The Holy Spirit and A Holy Spirit: Some Observations and a Proposal." *BT* 61.3 (2010) 152–63.

———. "PNEUMA as "Spirit World" in Translation in the New Testament," *BT* 62.3 (2011) 172–84.

Turner, David L. *Matthew.* BECNT. Grand Rapids: Baker, 2008.

Turner, Max. "Modern Linguistics and the New Testament." In *Hearing the New Testament: Strategies for Interpretation,* edited by Joel Green, 146–74. Grand Rapids: Eerdmans, 1995.

Turner, Nigel. *A Grammar of New Testament Greek.* Vol. 3 *Syntax.* 4 vols. Edinburgh: T&T Clark, 1963.

———. *A Grammar of New Testament Greek.* Vol. 4 *Style.* 4 vols. Edinburgh: T&T Clark, 1976.

Wallace, Daniel B. *Granville Sharp's Canon and Its Kin: Semantics and Significance.* New York: Peter Lang, 2009.

———. *Greek Grammar: Beyond the Basics.* 2nd ed. Grand Rapids: Zondervan, 1996.

Wallace, Stephen. "Figure and Ground: The Interrelationships of Linguistic Categories." in *Tense-Aspect: Between Semantics and Pragmatics,* edited by P. Hopper, 201–23. Amsterdam: John Benjamins, 1982.

Wenham, J.W. *The Essentials of New Testament Greek.* Cambridge: Cambridge University Press, 1965.

Westcott, B.F. *The Epistle to the Hebrews.* Repr. Grand Rapids: Eerdmans, 1973.

———. *The Epistles of St. John.* Repr. Grand Rapids: Eerdmans, 1966.

———. *The Gospel According to John.* Repr. Grand Rapids: Eerdmans, 1971.

Westfall, Cynthia Long. "The Analysis of Prominence in Hellenistic Greek." In *The Linguist as Pedagogue: Trends in the Teaching of Linguistic Analysis of the Greek New Testament,* edited by Stanley E. Porter and Matthew Brook O'Donnell, 75–94. Sheffield: Sheffield Univeristy Press, 2009.

Winer, George Benedict, and Gottlieb Lünemann. *A Grammar of the Idioim of the New Testament.* 7th ed. Edited by J.H. Thayer. Translated by Edward Masson. Andover: W.F. Draper, 1874.

Wuest, Kenneth S. "The Greek Article in New Testament Interpretation." *Bibliotheca Sacra* 118 (1961) 27–34.

Zerwick, Maximilian. *Biblical Greek Illustrated by Examples.* Rome: Pontifical Biblical Institute, 1963.

INDEX OF ANCIENT AUTHORS

INDEX OF MODERN AUTHORS

SCRIPTURE INDEX